A Brave New Series

GLOBAL ISSUES
IN A CHANGING WORLD

This new series of short, accessible think-pieces deals with leading global issues of relevance to humanity today. Intended for the enquiring reader and social activists in the North and the South, as well as students, the books explain what is at stake and question conventional ideas and policies. Drawn from many different parts of the world, the series' authors pay particular attention to the needs and interests of ordinary people, whether living in the rich industrial or the developing countries. They all share a common objective – to help stimulate new thinking and social action in the opening years of the new century.

Global Issues in a Changing World is a joint initiative by Zed Books in collaboration with a number of partner publishers and non-governmental organizations around the world. By working together, we intend to maximize the relevance and availability of the books published in the series.

Participating NGOs

Both ENDS, Amsterdam
Catholic Institute for International Relations, London
Corner House, Sturminster Newton
Council on International and Public Affairs, New York
Dag Hammarskjöld Foundation, Uppsala
Development GAP, Washington DC
Focus on the Global South, Bangkok
Inter Pares, Ottawa
Public Interest Research Centre, Delhi
Third World Network, Penang
Third World Network–Africa, Accra
World Development Movement, London

About this Series

Communities in the South are facing great difficulties in coping with global trends. I hope this brave new series will throw much needed light on the issues ahead and help us choose the right options.

Martin Khor, Director, Third World Network, Penang

There is no more important campaign than our struggle to bring the global economy under democratic control. But the issues are fearsomely complex. This Global Issues Series is a valuable resource for the committed campaigner and the educated citizen.

Barry Coates, Director, World Development Movement (WDM)

Zed Books has long provided an inspiring list about the issues that touch and change people's lives. The *Global Issues* series is another dimension of Zed's fine record, allowing access to a range of subjects and authors that, to my knowledge, very few publishers have tried. I strongly recommend these new, powerful titles and this exciting series.

John Pilger, author

We are all part of a generation that actually has the means to eliminate extreme poverty world-wide. Our task is to harness the forces of globalization for the benefit of working people, their families and their communities – that is our collective duty. The Global Issues series makes a powerful contribution to the global campaign for justice, sustainable and equitable development, and peaceful progress.

Glenys Kinnock MEP

About this Book

Little has been written on aid other than the usual uncritical reports of donor agencies. In this important book David Sogge suggests the principles that should govern a very different pattern of globalization, one based on democracy and equal relations between Third World and donor countries – a far cry indeed from the present situation.

Samir Amin, writer

Highly critical of the way foreign aid has worked in practice, this ambitious book also outlines some core principles which could lead to aid making a positive difference for poor people.

Roger Riddell, author of Foreign Aid Reconsidered

Give and Take should be *the* primer on the aid industry. David Sogge makes clear why aid, in its present incarnation, will never help the poor.

Joe Hanlon, author of Mozambique: Who Calls the Shots?

David Sogge takes us up and down the 'aid chain' and through the chequered history of foreign assistance. Impressively researched and reasoned, *Give and Take* leaves no doubt that calls for greater aid are pure folly until today's 'market fundamentalism' and other donor agendas are rejected and systems of accountability to the poor we claim to assist are established.

Doug Hellinger, Executive Director, The Development GAP

About the Author

David Sogge works as a self-employed analyst in the aid industry. He holds degrees from Harvard, Princeton and the Institute of Social Studies. Since 1970 he has held staff positions in American, Canadian and Dutch private aid agencies and has carried out many dozens of evaluation and policy development assignments for multilateral, bilateral and private aid agencies and for policy activist organizations. Among his publications are a book about Angola, articles about foreign aid, an edited book on aid and the civil sector in Mozambique, and the edited volume *Compassion and Calculation: The Business of Private Foreign Aid* (Pluto Press, London, 1996). He is a Fellow of the Transnational Institute, Amsterdam.

Give and Take: What's the Matter with Foreign Aid?

DAVID SOGGE

University Press Ltd
DHAKA

White Lotus Co. Ltd
BANGKOK

Fernwood Publishing Ltd
NOVA SCOTIA

Books for Change
BANGALORE

David Philip
CAPE TOWN

Zed Books
LONDON · NEW YORK

Give and Take: What's the Matter with Foreign Aid? was first published in 2002 by

In Bangladesh: The University Press Ltd, Red Crescent Building, 114 Motijheel C/A, PO Box 2611, Dhaka 1000

In Burma, Cambodia, Laos, Thailand and Vietnam: White Lotus Co. Ltd, GPO Box 1141, Bangkok 10501, Thailand

In Canada: Fernwood Publishing Ltd, PO Box 9409, Station A, Halifax, Nova Scotia, Canada B3K 5S3

In India: Books for Change, 139 Richmond Road, Bangalore 560 025

In Southern Africa: David Philip Publishers (Pty Ltd), 208 Werdmuller Centre, Claremont 7735, South Africa

In the rest of the world: Zed Books Ltd, 7 Cynthia Street, London N1 9JF, UK and Room 400, 175 Fifth Avenue, New York, NY 10010, USA.

Distributed in the USA exclusively by Palgrave, a division of St Martin's Press, LLC, 175 Fifth Avenue, New York, NY 10010

Cover designed by Andrew Corbett
Designed and set in Monotype Bembo and VAG Rounded by Ewan Smith, London
Printed and bound in the United Kingdom by Cox & Wyman, Reading

A catalogue record for this book is available from the British Library
US CIP data is available from the Library of Congress
Canadian CIP data is available from the National Library of Canada

ISBN 1 55266 084 2 pb (Canada)
ISBN 81 87380 68 3 pb (India)
ISBN 0 86486 591 0 pb (Southern Africa)
ISBN 1 84277 068 3 hb (Zed Books)
ISBN 1 84277 069 1 pb (Zed Books)

Contents

Tables, Figures and Boxes

Tables

Figures

Boxes

Abbreviations and Acronyms

CPIA	Country Policy and Institutional Assessment
DAC	Development Assistance Committee (OECD)
DfID	Department for International Development
ECA	export credit agency
ECLA	Economic Commission for Latin America (UN)
ECOSOC	Economic and Social Council (UN)
GDP	gross domestic product
HIPC	heavily indebted poor country
ICRC	International Committee of the Red Cross
IFAD	International Fund for Agricultural Development
IFI	international financial institution
IIA	investment insurance agency
ILO	International Labour Organization
IMF	International Monetary Fund
NIEO	New International Economic Order
OA	official aid
ODA	official development assistance
OECD	Organisation for Economic Co-operation and Development
PRSP	Poverty Reduction Strategy Paper
QUANGO	quasi-autonomous non-governmental organization
UNCTAD	United Nations Conference on Trade and Development
UNDP	United Nations Development Programme
UNICEF	United Nations Children's Fund
UNRISD	UN Research Institute for Social Development
USAID	US Agency for International Development
WIDER	World Institute for Development Economics Research
WTO	World Trade Organization

Foreword and Acknowledgements

'Follow the money!' That advice, from a tipster code-named Deep Throat, helped news reporters in the early 1970s expose corrupted links of power in Washington DC going right to the top. For anyone wishing to understand power in North–South relations, that shrewd tip can't be bettered. The following pages may have none of the whodunnit drama of exposé journalism, but they do extend to Washington DC, corruption, power and, of course, money.

This book is meant chiefly for inquiring general readers as an introduction to some issues of foreign aid. It was written at a desk in Amsterdam, The Netherlands, from March through October 2001, on the basis of routine visits to libraries, including the virtual library of the Internet. It draws on the writer's own professional work close to foreign aid and its natural habitats: agency head offices and sub-offices, consulting groups, academic kibitzers, grantees and 'target groups' at the end of aid chains. However, the book could make only indirect use of that professional experience. That is because most of the writer's contracts with aid agencies forbid disclosure of information about them and the outcomes of their work. With a couple of exceptions, therefore, only material in open circulation has been cited.

The book had to be selective in other respects. Where there was a choice of ways to illuminate issues, the views of well-informed figures within or friendly to the aid system were selected instead of the views of critical outsiders. That selection bias may help readers get a sense of the rumblings of dissent in and around the foreign aid industry. There, attitudes might be summed up in the remark of the American anti-Cold War cartoon strip character Pogo: 'We have met the enemy, and he is us.'

Thanks are due to Robert Molteno, Director of Zed Books, for having proposed the creation of this book, and for his counsel about its shape and content. No Deep Throats provided spicy anecdotes or data, but colleagues and friends sparked ideas, suggested further references and spotted errors. Particular thanks are due to Kees Biekart, Wim Bossema and John Saxby for their comments, to the Centre for Development Studies of the University of Natal, South Africa, for financial support, and to Florrie de Pater for no dull moments.

PROLOGUE
A Tale of Two Foreign Aid Initiatives

Western Europe 1948–52

After the Second World War, much of Western Europe was in ruins. Tens of millions of people were uprooted and a hundred million were hungry. Transport, industries and whole cities were crippled. Needing a prosperous Europe, and fearing the electoral popularity of left-wing parties there, the US government launched its first major foreign aid initiative: the Economic Recovery Program, as proposed by Secretary of State George Marshall. Over four years, US$13.3 billion (about $87.5 billion in 1997 dollars) went to 16 countries, accounting for an average of about 10 per cent of their recorded gross domestic product (GDP) in this period.

Marshall aid operated under recipient-friendly terms. It was left to the *Europeans* to:

- decide who got what amounts of aid;
- monitor spending together with the Americans;
- repay the money in national currencies, then to decide jointly with the Americans how to invest the resulting counterpart funds;
- manage their foreign exchange and trade policy, including the raising of high barriers to imports, such as against US tobacco and manufactured goods; and
- design and follow the aid as a *plan*, inspired by Keynesian thinking, as a means of saving capitalism by regulating it; there was no room for free-market fundamentalism and certainly no room for rule by gangsters.[1]

In its recovery, Europe did not depend on this aid alone. Indeed, most investment came from internal sources. The USA *gave* a lot, on friendly terms; those billions were equivalent to more than four per cent of American GDP. At the same time, the USA quietly *took* a lot: after the war, wealthy Europeans had stashed away billions in US banks – equivalent, perhaps, to the aid flowing in the opposite direction. Yet there is no question that the Marshall Plan boosted recovery, especially in Austria, the Netherlands, Ireland, France, Norway and Italy. It was a big foreign aid success story never equalled before – or since.

Eastern Europe and the Ex-Soviet Union 1990 to Today

In the late 1980s, before the collapse of state socialism, indices of living standards in Russia and most of Eastern Europe were roughly those of Ireland or Portugal.[2] These societies had many shortcomings, but they were not inert. Their economies were relatively efficient at converting modest per capita output into adequate levels of. well-being and security. When the political collapse came, economic and social institutions and norms were weakened, but remained intact.

Then the aid industry arrived. Western donors and lenders were in a triumphant mood. They had a vision and a universal doctrine: Market Fundamentalism. 'Spread the truth,' said Lawrence Summers, then senior economist at the World Bank, 'the laws of economics are like the laws of engineering, one set of laws works everywhere.' With power, money and missionary zeal, the commanding heights of the aid system took charge: the US Treasury, IMF, World Bank and USAID. There was little room for recipient control, except by colluding local technocrats and shadowy figures in 'business'. There was no room at all for meaningful public accountability.[3]

From 1990 through 1999 net official assistance to Eastern Europe and the ex-Soviet Union totalled US$44 billion,[4] equivalent thus to about half the Marshall aid, and spread over a much larger population. Much of this money never entered the targeted lands, being absorbed by Western consulting firms and others. For the aim was less to revive these economies than to demolish the state socialist set-up. The aid system's programme was rapid and radical: shock therapy. Governments had to end price controls, slash public spending, raise real interest rates, sell off public assets and de-regulate capital flows. For Russia, that last measure helped speed the outflow of hundreds of billion dollars – some of it aid money – to offshore financial circuits promoted and protected by the West.[5]

The result was massive poverty and upward redistribution of income and wealth. Winners included gangster-entrepreneurs and foreign private investors. Losers were many tens of millions of common citizens and wage-earners, many of whom simply stopped receiving wages. In most places the economy and the society were rapidly disorganized and criminalized. Republics in the Caucasus, Central Asia and the Balkans were pushed into civil war.

Washington and other capitals promoted these changes by covering them with a fog of aid-speak. Inspired and led by market evangelists such as Summers, who later became US treasury secretary and is now president of Harvard University, the aid industry's 'star-struck transitologists' perfected the discourse:

They gave the name of 'banks' to money-laundering outfits. They described as 'entrepreneurs' schemers who enriched themselves at public expense by exploiting political contacts. They referred to formerly state-owned enterprises that still depended on massive budgetary subsidies as 'privatised'. They depicted the civil war among oligarchs to seize the country's natural-resource wealth as a 'rocky path' to a free-market system. They persisted in applying the 'free market' label to a system thick with monopolies where creditors and competitors alike were routinely murdered by hit-men. They gave the name of 'monetarism' to a policy that resulted in the proliferation of barter transactions and the virtual demonetisation of the economy. Focusing exclusively on the growth of the stock exchange index, they christened the world's worst economy as 'the best performing emerging market'. They used the word 'capitalism' to denote a system without stable property rights or other conditions for encouraging investment and in which fraudulent bankruptcy is considered a normal business practice. And they never stopped calling by the name of 'reform' a scam to loot the country's wealth and impoverish the vast majority of its citizens.[6]

That impoverishment beggars the imagination. World Bank data provide some idea of its scale: in 1987 the number of destitute people in Eastern Europe and the ex-Soviet Union was about one million; by 1998 it was 24 million; in addition, 30 million had fallen into the close-to-destitution category of those with incomes between $1 and $2 per day.[7] Hunger and political tension swept into four Central Asian republics. In the Kyrgyz Republic, the most intensively 'reformed' of the four, 12 per cent of the population had been classified as poor in 1987–88; after seven years of free-market therapy, fully 88 per cent had fallen into poverty.[8] Countries such as Poland, Hungary and Estonia have since recovered a little from the blow, but like the rest, they emerged as split-level societies, with a few winners and many losers. In Russia and the Ukraine, indices of living standards and income inequality in 1998 resembled those of Panama or Mexico. In the twentieth century, this was an economic disaster without precedent in peacetime.

Was the aid industry to blame? Mainstream observers, such as those given prominence in *The Economist*, assert that neither the top of the aid system nor its fundamentalist orthodoxy should be held to account for this catastrophe. The cause, they say, was an inevitable result of the system's collapse, and unfortunate meddling by the communist old guard. Yet Nobel Prize economist Joseph Stiglitz, a senior policy-maker in Washington throughout the period, tells a different story about the reasons for failure of 'reform'. For him there is no doubt about the culpability of the aid institutions and their doctrine:

> One variation on this theme is to blame the failure of the shock therapy reforms on corruption and rent-seeking at every turn, without recognizing any role of the institutional blitzkrieg in destroying but not replacing the old social norms – and thus in removing the last restraints against society-threatening levels of corruption. This is like using a flame-thrower to burn off an old coat of house paint, and then lamenting that you couldn't finish the new paint job because the house burned down.[9]

Nearly fifty years separate these two cases, yet the greater gulf between them is not temporal but ideological. The first was based on solidarity and public control at the receiving end; it was successful, with beneficial outcomes for millions. The second was based on what might be termed Market Leninism: coercive intent and non-accountable control from the top under a fog of Orwellian propaganda; for its designers it too was successful, but with terrible outcomes for millions. Much of what appears in the following pages has risen and fallen on these ideological tides.

Notes

1. Ellwood, D. (1992) *Rebuilding Europe*, London: Longman.

2. UNDP (2000) *Human Development Report 2000*, New York: UNDP, Table 7, pp. 178–9.

3. Wedel, J. (1998) *Collision and Collusion: The Strange Case of Western Aid to Eastern Europe 1989–1998*, New York: St Martin's Press.

4. OECD tables. Web address: www.oedg.org/scripts/cde.

5. The Russian Interior Ministry estimated $230 billion. *Interfax* 11 March 1999, cited in Feffer, J. (1999) *Containment Light. U.S. Policy Toward Russia and Its Neighbors*, Foreign Policy in Focus, Washington, DC: IPS.

6. Holmes, S. (2001) 'Transitology' (review of *Failed Crusade: America and the Tragedy of Post-Communist Russia* by Steven Cohen), *London Review of Books*, 23 (8), 19 April: 32–5.

7. The term destitute refers to those living below US$1.08 per day

(1993 purchasing power) in 1998. http://www.worldbank.org/research/povmonitor/index.htm. According to Bank estimates for 1998, about 98 million people in these two regions lived on less than $2 per day.

8. Babu, S. and W. Reidhead (2000) 'Poverty, food security and nutrition in Central Asia: a case study of the Kyrgyz Republic', *Food Policy*, 25: 649.

9. Stiglitz, J. (1999) paper for the Annual Bank Conference on Development Economics, Washington, DC, cited in Martin, B. (2000) *New Leaf or Fig Leaf? The Challenge of the New Washington Consensus*, Washington: Bretton Woods Project, web address: http://www.brettonwoodsproject.org/reports/. At the end of 1999, the behest of US Treasury Secretary Summers, Joseph Stiglitz was forced to resign as senior economist at the World Bank.

ONE

Foreign Aid: A Problem Posing as a Solution?[1]

A token of concern, power and expertise, aid is given with a glow of satisfaction. A badge of candidate-membership in the club of modern nations, aid is received with gratitude. Givers and receivers, at least in their public utterances, applaud foreign aid as a good thing that should continue.

Yet something is the matter with foreign aid. Where it dominates, pride and ambition have given way to dependence and deference. In some aid-targeted places, public management and services have decayed or collapsed, poverty and inequality have worsened, and insecurity prevails. The paradoxes can be grotesque. Since 1990, the foreign aid industry has presided over societies toppling into criminal disorder and violence. There were so many helping hands in Rwanda, yet those hands helped position that country at the edge of the abyss of genocide – only to disclaim any responsibility in the aftermath.[2]

Exempt from punishment if things go wrong, aid planners have returned again and again from their drawing-boards with new, improved, fail-safe strategies involving yet another flight into the future. Today, however, some proposals have begun to sound worthwhile. In the late 1990s, half a century after aid began, aid industry leaders let it be known that their chief mission is, after all, to help improve the lives of poor people.

For the OECD club of rich countries and for the World Bank, the official purposes of aid at the beginning of the twenty-first century may be stated as basically three:

- reducing material poverty, chiefly through economic growth, but also through provision of public infrastructure and basic social services;
- promoting good governance, chiefly in effective, honest and democratically accountable institutions to manage the economy and the legal order, but also in promotion of civil and political rights; and
- reversing negative environmental trends.

If seriously pursued, such aims would shift aid on to promising new paths. For as enforced by its most powerful institutions up to now, many aid policies have not favoured emancipatory politics or economics. Except for a brief period in the mid-1970s, anti-poverty measures and human rights never enjoyed real support at the top of the aid system.

It is true, and possibly significant, that in a few cases (Korea, Botswana, Honduras) aid has been associated with poverty reduction, improved social services and competent public institutions. Yet in other places (Cuba, China, Kerala state in India) Western aid was irrelevant or of only minor importance in building competent public sectors and in lifting millions out of poverty.[3]

In a much larger number of countries, aid volumes correlate with erratic and slow advances towards such goals, and even reversals. Some of yesterday's major aid recipients – Congo-Kinshasa, Guiné-Bissau, Haiti, Liberia, Sierra Leone, Somalia – are today's collapsed states. Worryingly, the link between aid and bad politics goes further than mere anecdote. Research noted later in this book suggests that the greater a country's dependence on aid, the worse the quality of its public institutions. The evidence has grown: on many occasions, foreign aid has been a problem posing as a solution.

Such a conclusion sounds unfair. Many would argue that aid itself is blameless, but has failed to work well because it was hijacked for selfish political and commercial purposes. It has favoured the wrong countries, the wrong leaders and the wrong sectors, and has been badly supervised and accounted for besides. Proposals about aid then come down to: reform it, but especially give more of it. Such arguments sound beneficent, but are they? They would carry more weight if it could be shown, consistently and clearly, that foreign aid in its reformed versions is achieving anti-poverty, good governance results. But that is not (yet) the case.

A greater unfairness arises from the kind of attention aid gets. Posed as a remedy to the enormous, old, complex problems of poverty, growth and governance, foreign aid faces expectations it cannot reasonably meet. It is simply overburdened with too much hope and hype. Aid thus becomes a fall guy and a distraction. While its advances and setbacks get attention, other forces are meantime at work: unfair trade, brain drain, capital flight, lowered public revenues, technological change, warlord/druglord wars, and other dynamics seemingly beyond public control. These help erase the modest gains achieved with aid. Aid has sometimes helped to camouflage such trends, and to drive them.

This warped structure of attention has begun losing some of its distortions. Policy-makers now say they wish to harmonize aid policy with other policies to make them cohere. European governments have promised to bring North–South policies on foreign trade, human rights, military support and aid into align-ment. Aid's powers to remedy poverty and misgovernment are now confidently broadcast, drowning out older claims about its powers to boost output. The IMF no longer uses the detested term structural adjustment[4] about its standard austerity recipe: the term today is 'poverty reduction and growth'.

Lions don't lie down with lambs. Are we supposed to believe that a similar wonder is at hand? Aid system actors have frequently re-defined their job descriptions and fled into the future. Are today's transformations any different? Whatever the case, aid now faces new expectations, and tougher, more complex standards by which it may be judged.

Charity market advertising may keep romanticizing it, but

foreign aid no longer sits tall on a white horse. It is but one (lightweight) potential contributor to solutions among other (heavyweight) instruments. Yet it cannot yet be written off as an outdated sideshow in the repertoire of geopolitics. For in the last half of the twentieth century, aid's leading institutions, the IMF, World Bank and the Bank's surrogates, the regional development banks – referred to here as international financial institutions or IFIs – have been assigned strategic roles. Their power is far out of proportion to the funds they manage. Why that should be so, and what lessons that may have, are topics addressed in this book.

This book is written in the belief that pressure pays. Recent moves towards realism and pro-poor policies are the result of years of probing and criticism. Some pressures came from courageous truth-tellers within the aid industry. But its leadership would never have moved without the patient but assertive argument by sceptical aid-watchers among academics and journalists, by people at the receiving end, and especially by policy activists South and North on the fronts of environment, human rights, gender equity, trade, capital flows and peace. That is, the aid system can be made to change – but only if publicly shamed, prodded and cajoled into doing so. Some within the industry agree with the critics and welcome the pressure. In the balance is whether this pressure can nudge things beyond the modest shifts of emphasis towards funda-mental changes in the wider rules governing relations between rich and poor.

Many Tasks, Many Friends, Many Guises

- Aid is help.
- Aid reflects altruism.
- Aid flows from rich to poor.
- Aid reduces poverty.
- Aid is intended to reduce poverty.

These are among claims made for aid. They are also its shibboleths, the catch-phrases that distinguish believers from doubters. Indeed, they are utterances of belief, not fact. At best they are half-truths.

For at least three decades, research has exposed them as seriously misleading, if not wholly false. The exposés stand out in book titles: *The Myth of Aid, Aid as Imperialism, Aid as Obstacle, Deadly Aid, Giving is Taking, Lords of Poverty, Famine Crimes, The Road to Hell: The Ravaging Effects of Foreign Aid and International Charity, Masters of Illusion, Lethal Aid,* and *Aiding Violence: The Development Enterprise in Rwanda.*[5]

Are these merely outbursts of reactionary cranks and social Darwinists? Hardly. They are reasoned and carefully documented studies whose authors want a fairer world, and public measures to achieve it. They start from an optimistic view that genuine help is a good and necessary thing. Critics of aid on the right, on the other hand, start from pessimistic assumptions. They worry about public claims on private accumulation, free-riders and other drags on the forward motion of market systems. Yet on certain matters, such as the dangerous liaisons between aid and dictatorship,[6] a few critics on the libertarian right hold outspoken views echoing those on the left.

Optimism about the importance of genuine assistance is likewise a starting-point of this book, though it has been tempered by the findings in the writings just noted. Given the appalling outcomes of the official aid system's two-decade infatuation with many ideas from the political right, there are good reasons to avoid its starting-points, though its conclusions about the powers of big aid institutions merit attention.

Since the 1970s aid has come under fire from both ends of the political spectrum. The charge sheet includes Afghanistan, Angola, Liberia, Congo-Kinshasa, Somalia and South Vietnam, where US aid kept venal and violent clients on life-support systems. Also shaping public opinion has been a succession of aid scandals such as the British aid-for-arms deals with Malaysia and Indonesia, exposed in 1994; the outrageous graft in Italian aid that came to a head in 1996;[7] and revelations in 1998 that between a fifth and a third of the World Bank's $30 billion aid to Indonesia

had – with the apparent knowledge of the Bank – disappeared
into the ruling dynasty's pockets. Add to these the regular trickle
of stories about failed projects, waste, exaggerated agency claims
and plush lifestyles[8] and the loss of faith on the part of the Western
public is not so surprising. The surprise comes in the fact that,
despite waning belief that aid makes any lasting difference, most
Northern citizens still feel bound to give it. In past times, policy
elites favoured aid more than taxpaying publics. Today it's the
other way around: although they are worried by the scandals,
most people continue to feel an obligation to give, while policy
elites show deepening disenchantment with aid.[9]

The established aid system is under pressure. Official aid budgets
did suffer cuts after 1993, but aid was not the only sector to
tighten its belt in that period. Since 1999, overall aid spending has
rebounded somewhat. Like a hero in a folktale, it overcomes
adversity in pursuit of its noble mission. Little penetrates its
armour, and little adheres to its non-stick surface.

This is extraordinary. It seems hardly in keeping with the
temper of the times. For on the domestic front in Northern
countries, social services and protection for disadvantaged people
have been pushed far down political agendas, especially in the
Anglo-Saxon countries. Right-wing think-tanks and politicians
advocate minimal public responsibility for the poor. They warn
that unless cities, provinces and nations cut their welfare burdens,
they will end up losers in the global competition to attract mobile
investors. On the plane of global policy, Northern political elites
talk about the poor in muted, ritual tones; they raise their
voices slightly when mounting small wars or disparaging anti-
globalization protests. But despite this cool official climate, the
aid industry has shown great powers of adaptation, protective
colouration and survival. The heroic quest continues.

Is this a case of hope triumphing over experience, or is something else going on? Aid has meant different things to different
people. Down through the decades, constituent parts of the aid
system have operated in ways that make it resemble:

- a financial services industry, promoting exports and loans on easy terms, and quietly insuring creditors against bad debts;
- a technical services industry, improving know-how and infrastructure;
- a 'feel-good' and image industry that can relieve guilt and subtly pander to the satisfactions of parental/paternal authority;
- a political toolshed stocked with carrots and sticks to train and discipline clients; and
- a knowledge and ideology industry, setting policy agendas and shaping norms and aspirations.

Each aid-giving nation displays its own mix of these and other roles. Yet, as many have repeatedly observed, official aid is ultimately just another instrument to project power beyond national borders, a tool of foreign policy. Foreign aid has traditionally been the domain of policy elites and certain outwardly oriented business groups. Aid issues may be matters of national prestige, but they rarely excite passions or win votes. Hence aid's balloon-like tendency to float above the sweaty business of politics, and to escape public attention.

To overcome such political isolation, aid institutions have enlisted many allies, from farmers to bankers, transporters to church people, academics to media moguls. Aid's colours span the spectrum from socialist red to liberal blue. Rationales gravitate towards the political middle – the purple zone where red and blue meet, and where bipartisan or consensus politics rule in back rooms. Its multiple roles have served a wide range of political, military, financial, commercial and psychological interests – often at the same time. These interest coalitions help account for aid's remarkable ability to survive, but also for its ability to accumulate and decorate itself with many goals and purposes. Hence in public comment on aid the frequent allusions to Santa Claus and Christmas trees.

Yet most foreign aid is not about beneficence, but about power. The metaphor of the chain, the standard hierarchy of the aid system, conveys this. This book's fourth and fifth chapters describe aid's structure in terms of a chain. Standard writings focus on the financial and material cargo flowing towards end-points. Of special interest in this book are non-material flows: the attention-structuring, problem-defining, role-assigning flow of ideas – the cults that go with the cargo. Aid has been one of the ways in which powerful institutions encode their doctrines and impose them on the less powerful. The seventh chapter considers how money talks.

Command over ideas is often more decisive than the mere transfer of resources. That helps explain why elites keep backing aid institutions despite the lack of good evidence that aid regularly achieves its advertised objectives and despite mounting evidence that aid can help make things worse. The eighth chapter discusses some of these outcomes.

The expanded reproduction of the aid industry itself, involving political, business and non-profit allies, has been an important outcome. But support and collusion are by no means the only responses. Resistance to the arrogance, coercion and self-interest of the aid system has grown, especially since the 1980s. Among officials at the receiving end this resistance has been covert and subtle. In the streets and assembly halls in the South and the North, activists from labour, human rights, environment, debt and indigenous peoples' organizations have mobilized overt and vocal resistance. Once dismissed as silly idealists with no grasp of economics and policy sciences, this movement's knowledge-based members have marshalled facts and arguments with increasing effect.

Some aid institutions in the UN system, and a few private aid agencies, are actively in sympathy with this movement's ideals. At the commanding heights of the aid system, its criticisms have begun to get a respectful hearing. Indeed, the IFIs now take an anti-poverty, pro-democracy line adapted from their critics. Their message is becoming one of 'Don't fight us. Join us.' They insinuate that it is the critics who lack accountability, transparency and compassion for the poor.

This book draws on those conflicts and debates. They make the aid system one of the more accessible arenas of world politics. It is a forum where political and economic scenarios are proposed and new rules hammered out. Here and there some actors in the aid system are helping create the spaces where alternative ideas can emerge to shift rules in emancipatory directions.

Main Themes

In aid's early decades, policy talk was about gaps and shortfalls in poor countries' finance. Today many more gaps claim attention, including some in aid theory and practice itself. This short introductory book must limit itself to only a few areas where crucial gaps or tensions are found.

The serious ones are about power – who gets what, when, how, and on whose terms. Conventional aid bodies have done pretty well at enhancing their own powers. Indeed, they form a puissant constellation of banks, agencies and foundations – some of which enjoy financial and ideological power with global reach. Yet, apart from some exceptional episodes, they have failed to enhance the powers of ordinary citizens, least of all the poor, to obtain the decent living standards they are entitled to. On the contrary, aid has often frustrated their claims. It encourages rulers to pay more attention to powerful outsiders, including donors and lenders. Aid can thus hinder a vital public give-and-take between states and citizens, the political anchoring for emancipatory development.

This book looks at the gaps between emancipatory potential – the growth of capabilities to achieve social, economic and political rights – and the crippling practices actually observed. It traces emancipatory and democratic deficits to the ways in which money and ideas are deployed down through chains of power. It considers current steps towards reform, and norms that might be useful in improving them or finding alternatives to them.

One assumption this book does not make: that aid yields 'development'. This link is commonly seen as natural and self-evident. Simplified, one of the syllogisms runs as follows. Development results from economic growth. Economic growth results from investment. Aid is an investment. Development results from aid. That kind of reasoning risks projecting fact from theory. A closer look reveals big discrepancies. Research results presented in the eighth chapter show that since 1980, as aid doctrines and coercive practice have intensified in Africa, rates of recorded growth have turned negative and rates of progress in well-being have declined.

Can foreign aid make people poorer? Perhaps, but the point here is that aid and development are different, and not necessarily compatible things. Big, old, complex things like growth and development should be distinguished from the relatively small and new things in the aid system. This book does not enter the important debate about the concept of development. It sees the relation between today's foreign aid and development as much more problematic and complex than the presumed link between, say, hospitals and health, or between television news and well-informed publics.

Context

The modern aid system was born midway through the twentieth century. It is now middle-aged. During its lifetime, centuries-old processes making the world a single place began to speed up. Many have seen this globalizing trend as a good thing. Foreign aid would, it was assumed, help ensure a happy ending, that is, everyone's living standards converging upwards. But trends towards convergence, chiefly in East Asia, have today been overtaken by divergence. In much of the planet, the happy ending is not happening. Polarized development, often shadowed by violence, is a hallmark of the era of foreign aid.

Local rulers and their merchant and servitor classes have long been supported by surpluses derived both at home and from linkages abroad. Recently, elites have begun drawing their chief sources of wealth, status and cultural cues from external sources. The era of foreign aid coincides with the growth of a cosmopolitan 'North' in the 'South'.

Meanwhile, in North America and Europe, shifting balances in world markets, setbacks to the power of organized labour, increasing austerity in state social protection, and the flow of millions of people seeking livelihoods in richer areas are helping to generate stratified, dead-end and precarious lives lower on social ladders, where women end up shouldering most burdens. In 1998 a high-ranking US official said that 'a child born in New York today stands a smaller chance of living to five or learning to read than a child born in Shanghai'.[10] There is a large and growing 'South' in the 'North'.

If Northern trends, which one sociologist has termed 'the Brazilianization of the West',[11] are just becoming detectable, analogous trends in the real Brazils and Bosnias of this world have assumed huge, unmistakable proportions. Sociologists and economists speak no longer of social marginalization, but of exclusion.[12] In analysing the roots of civil wars and migration, the social critic Hans Magnus Enzensberger offers this analysis:

> State-organized crime continues to be widespread. The overarching, anonymous world market, however, appears ever more clearly as the instance which condemns increasingly large sections of mankind to superfluousness. It does so not through political persecution, by command of the Führer or party resolution, but spontaneously, by its own logic, so that more and more people fall out of it. The result is no less murderous, but the guilty are even less likely to be brought to book than before.[13]

In a word, today's market system produces a split-level world. In it, many face futures of poverty and humiliation. In certain settings it easily becomes an incubator of angry and desperate young people for whom recruitment into sects, neofascist gangs and suicide commando cells is a short and easy step. For the purposes of this book, the following aspects are worth noting.

MONEY: SUPRA-TERRITORIAL AND DE-REGULATED   For most
of the twentieth century, leading Western and especially US elites
have pursued a major goal: freedom for capital. The last two
decades of the twentieth century saw major advances in deregulation. Its beneficiaries have been Northern bankers, asset managers,
their stockholders and their close associates (as close as a few
steps through revolving doors) in government and international
agencies. They form a potent circuit of global firms and individuals
with oracular powers as The Markets. Their achievement of new
liberties not only coincided with a boom in foreign aid, but also
took place under the conscious auspices of the IMF, the US
Treasury and others at the top of the aid pyramid.[14]

Over-accumulation, concentrated in financial centres, has sent
financial surpluses cascading into markets for currencies, stocks
and bonds. Speculation has pushed aside productive investment.
Short-term gain has pushed aside long-term balance. Trade wars
have intensified. Surplus goods have cascaded into lower-income
markets in barely disguised dumping. The effects are now beginning to register: 'Global capital markets have acted as gigantic
engines of inequality, transferring wealth from the weak to the
strong, from debtors to creditors, wage earners and taxpayers to
the holders of paper claims, from productive to financial activity.'[15]

The Markets have helped de-legitimize and crowd out progressive state action. In much of the USA, in New Zealand and
the Canadian province of Ontario their influence has weakened
public measures to protect the poor and excluded. Their influence
in lower-income lands is more serious. For Irma Adelman, a
distinguished mainstream analyst of economic change and public
policy, the implications for democratic control and for foreign
aid are deeply worrying:

> [F]inancial globalisation imposes severe fundamental constraints
> on the policy levers which governments can exercise in their
> management of the domestic economy, thereby creating a crisis
> of the state. The new international environment thus has major

implications for the future role of the state and the future potential for foreign assistance. In view of the critical importance of governments to economic development, the current loss of autonomy imposed by the institutions of the current global financial system is scary.[16]

MONEY-POWER'S CREED Preparing the ground for the rise of money-power was the revival of older ideologies into a new creed, neoliberalism – or in the term used approvingly by the IMF, market fundamentalism.[17] The Thatcher and Reagan administrations of the 1980s used this doctrine to roll back Keynesian policies prevailing from the 1930s through the 1960s. Those policies justified state intervention such as job schemes to boost demand and controls over prices and wages. As applied via the foreign aid system, market fundamentalism crystallized in the 'Washington Consensus'.[18] It aimed to de-legitimize and shrink public powers over firms and capital flows.

ONE OR SEVERAL CAPITALISMS? The fundamentalist counter-revolution exposes differences, and a struggle, between two kinds of market systems: stock market capitalism, favoured in the Anglo-Saxon countries of the USA and Britain (with Canada, Australia and New Zealand swept along by the force of this current) versus the welfare capitalism of Western Europe and Japan. The latter are under pressure to reform, that is, to embrace Anglo-Saxon capitalism.[19] Under this doctrine, the interests of waged employees, local communities, the collective sector and the environment have come to be subordinated to one main purpose: shareholder value. At stake in this rivalry is nothing less than public choices about the good life. Are social protection and social cohesion to be seen as rights, and therefore as obligations to be met through public action? Or can there be no strong rights and obligations given that market forces determine life chances? This contest has direct bearing on the principles guiding foreign aid.

DOMESTICATED STATES   Downsizing the state was part of the advertised theory. But when in high political office, market fundamentalists have shown no hesitation in using strong, centralized authority to preserve the value of currencies, maintain high real interest rates, and insure big investors against loss. That was of special importance where public and private creditors faced non-repayment of debt accumulated in what is today termed emerging markets, that is, low-income countries. The implicit principle is: privatize accumulation, socialize risk.

DOMESTICATED CIVIL SOCIETIES   Market fundamentalism also favours state measures to curb 'troublesome' parts of civil society, notably trade unions. Rising inequality is a direct result. Comparative research shows that better distributions of income are due chiefly to one factor: the strength of organized labour.[20] Otherwise, market fundamentalism's forward march has coincided with civil society growth in de-politicized directions. Financial surpluses, ideas, and increased spare time for voluntary effort have combined to drive countless initiatives. For governments seeking to shed collective sector tasks, this offers advantages: they can enlist non-profits under terms such as faith-based initiatives and public–private partnerships to provide education, health, social work and other caring services. This trend is manifested in the several thousand private aid agencies based in Northern countries and many tens of thousands of non-profits in the South and East. Most of this growth has occurred under the auspices of foreign aid.

DISARRAY AND RESISTANCE   On the fronts of politics, social movements have emerged in civil society across a broad spectrum of impulses, from good to bad to ugly. Some of these movements are bent on exclusion, being driven by religious fundamentalism, ethnic bigotry, xenophobia and racism. The deregulation of financial flows and the arms trade have been a great boon to the violent and criminal ones. Others pursue broadly emancipatory purposes including environmental sanity, an end to discrimination against women and minorities, and a better deal for the poor and middle classes generally. Both fundamentalist and emancipatory movements have shown they can exert leverage. They often start at local levels, usually in cities, and build up in political blocs that mainstream politicians can't ignore. More common, certainly outside Latin America, are the atomized struggles of poor people to make gains incrementally, through what one sociologist terms 'quiet encroachment'.[21] Defence of these small, slowly and informally acquired gains can drive organized resistance, and constitutes what an African observer, writing about her continent, has termed 'collective insubordination'.[22]

§

Posing as a solution, foreign aid has become a problem as it is harnessed to market rules and doctrine in a world rapidly becoming one place. It has been cast in diverse and even contradictory roles in dramas of power and accumulation. In them, other actors with far less noble motives have played far more powerful roles. The following pages consider how it has been used as a supporting actor masquerading as the star.

Notes

1. This phrase crops up repeatedly in serious discussions of foreign aid, such as Korten, D. (1991) 'International assistance: a problem posing as a solution', in R. Krishnam, J. M. Harris and N. R. Goodwin (eds) *A Survey of Ecological Economics*, Washington, DC: Island Press.

2. Uvin, P. (1998) *Aiding Violence, the Development Enterprise in Rwanda*, West Hartford, CT: Kumarian Press.

3. See Ranis, G. and F. Stewart (2000) 'Strategies for success in human development', *Journal of Human Development*, 1 (1): 49–69. In May 2001, World Bank President James Wolfensohn said: 'Cuba has done a great job on education and health … and it does not embarrass me to admit it.'

4. Structural adjustment refers to a set of policy measures along lines of the 'Washington Consensus' (see note 18 below) that the World Bank, the International Monetary Fund (IMF) and other donor agencies such as USAID required of most recipient governments as a condition of aid.

5. Goulet, D. and M. Hudson (eds) (1970) *The Myth of Aid*, Maryknoll, NY: Orbis; Hayter, T. (1971) *Aid as Imperialism*, Harmondsworth: Penguin; Lappé, F. M. and others (1980) *Aid as Obstacle: Twenty Questions about our Foreign Aid and the Hungry*, San Francisco: Institute for Food and Development Policy; Erler, B. (1985) *Tödliche Hilfe: Bericht von meiner letzten Diensreise im Sachen Entwicklungshilfe*, Freiburg: Dreisam Verlag; Hoebink, P. (1988) *Geven is Nemen: De Nederlandse ontwikkelingshulp aan Tanzania en Sri Lanka*, Nijmegen: Stichting Derde Wereld Publikaties; Hancock, G. (1989) *Lords of Poverty*, London: Macmillan; de Waal, A. (1997) *Famine Crimes: Politics and the Disaster Relief Industry in Africa*, Oxford: James Currey; Maren, M. (1997) *The Road to Hell: The Ravaging Effects of Foreign Aid and International Charity*, New York: The Free Press; Caufield, C. (1996) *Masters of Illusion. The World Bank and the Poverty of Nations*, New York: Henry Holt; Rugumamu, S. (1997) *Lethal Aid: The Illusion of Socialism and Self-Reliance in Tanzania*, Trenton, NJ: Africa World Press; Uvin, P. (1998) *Aiding Violence: The Development Enterprise in Rwanda*, West Hartford, CT: Kumarian Press

6. Boone, P. (1995) *Politics and the Effectiveness of Foreign Aid*, Working Paper, W5308, Cambridge, MA: National Bureau of Economic Research web address: http://papers.nber.org/papers/W5308.

7. See Lancaster, C. (1999) *Aid to Africa: So Much to Do, So Little Done*, Chicago, IL: University of Chicago Press, pp. 160–4.

8. Such things are catalogued with great verve in the books by Hancock (1989), Caufield (1996) and Maren (1997); see note 5 above. From Southern observers, telling snapshots appear both in journalistic accounts, such as Sainath, P. (1996) *Everybody Loves a Good Drought: Stories from India's Poorest Districts*, London: Penguin Books India, and in novels, such as Farah, N. (1999) *Gifts*, New York: Arcade.

9. van de Walle, N. (1999) 'Aid's crisis of legitimacy: current proposals and future prospects', *African Affairs* (98): 337–52.

10. US Deputy Secretary of the Treasury Lawrence Summers, *Remarks to Committee for Economic Development* in Chicago, 20 May 1998 (press release), Washington, DC: US Treasury Department.

11. Beck, U. (2000) *Brave New World of Work*, Cambridge: Polity Press.

12. de Haan, A. and S. Maxwell (eds) (1998) *IDS Bulletin*, special issue on Poverty and Social Exclusion, 29 (1).

13. Enzensberger, H. M. (1994) *Civil Wars*, New York: The New Press, p. 116.

14. Pauly, L. (1997) *Who Elected the Bankers? Surveillance and Control in the World Economy*, Ithaca, NY and London: Cornell University Press. This shift

of power has not been apparent to everyone, even those in high office, who should know better. Early in his tenure as US president, an astonished Bill Clinton remarked to his aides: 'You mean to tell me that the success of the program and my reelection hinges on the Federal Reserve and a bunch of fucking bond traders?', Woodward, B. (1994) *The Agenda*, New York: Simon & Schuster.

15. Polanyi-Levitt, K. (2000) 'The Great Transformation from the 1920s to the 1990s' in K. Polanyi-Levitt and K. McRobbie (eds), *Karl Polanyi in Vienna: The Contemporary Significance of the Great Transformation*, Montreal: Black Rose Books.

16. Adelman, I. (2000) 'The role of government in economic development', in F. Tarp (ed.), *Foreign Aid and Development: Lessons Learnt and Directions for the Future*, London: Routledge, p. 75.

17. IMF (2000) *World Economic Outlook October 2000*, Washington, DC: International Monetary Fund.

18. The economist John Williamson coined the term 'Washington Consensus' in a 1989 article. It refers to a set of policy ideas that crystallized in the 1980s in the US Treasury, Federal Reserve, IMF and World Bank, favouring outward-oriented trade and investment policies, low inflation, balanced budgets, lowered exchange rates, privatization, deregulation (especially of the banking system) and strict protection of private property. For a backward glance, see Williamson, J. (1999) *What Should the Bank Think About the Washington Consensus?*, Washington, DC: Institute for International Economics, web address: http://www.iie.com/papers/williamson0799.htm.

19. Dore, R. (2000) *Stock Market Capitalism: Welfare Capitalism. Japan and Germany versus the Anglo-Saxons*, Oxford: Oxford University Press.

20. Rueda, D. and J. Pontusson (2000) 'Wage inequality and varieties of capitalism', *World Politics* (52): 350–83.

21. Bayat, A. (2000) 'From "dangerous classes" to "quiet rebels". Politics of the urban subaltern in the global South', *International Sociology*, 15 (3): 533–57.

22. Monga, C. (1996) *The Anthropology of Anger: Civil Society and Democracy in Africa*, Boulder, CO: Lynne Rienner.

TWO
Who is Aiding Whom?

The Sahel countries had record harvests both of non-food crops like cotton and of food crops during the big famine of the 1970s. The ships bringing relief from Europe were sent back loaded with food produced for European consumers.[1]

Foreign aid is full of ambiguities and double bottoms. It does not fit neatly into any one of the three ways people are said to go about their material transactions: coercion, exchange and gift-giving.[2] Being tied with geo-politics, trade and banking, foreign aid can't be classified as purely gift-giving. Giving and getting have shadow sides, where even in daily life they can mask exchange or coercion. Across cultures, people have been wary of gifts. In some Western and non-Western languages, words for 'gift' share the same root as words for 'poison'.[3]

Aid is routinely portrayed as high-minded beneficence. But a little probing around an aid deal will usually expose a lively intermingling of high and low intentions. The bigger the stakes, the greasier the fingerprints of commerce, geo-politics and ideological crusading. Newcomers to the foreign aid business embody this. Public figures in industries as diverse as oil prospecting, media networks, computer software and popular entertainment want to be donors. Not only do they hand over cash, they also study the subject, swap ideas with the experts and busy themselves in the details of aid provision. The New Rich, like those with Old Money whose privately endowed foundations were among fore-runners to the modern aid system, have learned that 'noble expenditure' is among the best means of self-defence in the court of public opinion.[4] As long as some rich people and firms can portray their kind as beneficent, the day of reckoning with normal progressive taxation can be postponed for ever. The gratifications of giving are many, including a better bottom line.

The case of taxes and their avoidance recalls the fact that beyond coercion, exchange and gift-giving there is a fourth type of transaction, that based on obligation. Progressive taxation is a main example. It is self-imposed, and accepted by huge majorities as both fair and a good idea. It makes possible the provision of public goods and the combat of public bads. Still other kinds of public policy are based on obligation. Think of health insurance companies' duties (in some welfare states) to provide insurance cover to persons regardless of risk. Yet foreign aid is only rarely grounded in obligation. The duties of the International Committee of the Red Cross and the UN High Commissioner for Refugees are established in law and practice, but elsewhere in the aid system, no one is a duty-bearer.

GIVING AND TAKING: INSEPARABLE TWINS Aid has deep and tangled roots in the history of Western expansion. Needing a respectable rationale for imperial rule in Africa and Asia, British ideologists came up with the notion of a Dual Mandate. One face of the mandate was trusteeship: Britain had paternal obligations toward its subject peoples; it had to take decisions on their behalf, protect them and guide them. The other face was accumulation: the colonial power had to develop the colonies' economies for profit and insert them into the world system run by the West. The unspoken rationale of the aid regime strikingly resembles the Dual Mandate.

Guiding the USA was a vision of an open frontier.[5] France pursued a *mission civilisatrice*. Detectable in these and other colonial ideologies were two drives: giving and taking. To legitimize those two purposes – trusteeship for others and accumulation for one's self – colonial powers elaborated doctrines of modernization and development. To manage the territories politically, they imposed systems of indirect rule via local potentates. In the end, however, colonialism was too costly. The trustee and mercantile rationales could not be sustained, at least under one imperial flag.

As people in the South asserted rights to speak for themselves and manage their own affairs and resources, Western powers had to drop their talk about civilizing missions and mandates towards 'backward' areas. Former overseas dominions were repackaged as exclusive clubs: America's Good Neighbours in Latin America, Britain's Commonwealth, France's *francophonie*, Europe's ex-colonies assembled as the Lomé group, and Japan's flock of 'flying geese' in Asia.[6] Northern officials collaborated with the new ex-colonial leaders, cultivating them through elite networks. Some African rulers took their vacations, had their suits made, and sent their children for schooling in Europe.

Behind rhetoric about self-determination, the US and European powers have used aid to compete with one another through their colonial and neo-colonial systems.[7] Trade and investment wars have gone on in the name of a super-project of social engineering called 'development'.[8]

The Players

The aid system has played with a fixed cast, but has also seen givers and receivers come and go. Major trends and episodes may be summarized as follows.

AT THE PROVIDER END   The USA has held commanding positions, first as the major bilateral donor, but also the driving force behind the IFIs. Japan's aid effort has grown dramatically: in the 1990s it became the biggest spender in absolute terms. Figure 2.1 shows the relative importance of main aid providers from 1960 to 2000.

For the Soviet Union and its Eastern European allies the role of aid donor ended around 1990, whereupon, broken up and broken down, they became net aid recipients. The period 1973–

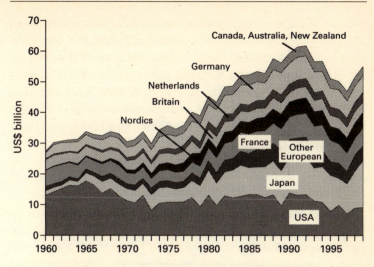

Figure 2.1 Net ODA in billions of US dollars of 1999

92 saw a number of oil-producing countries (chiefly Saudi Arabia and the Gulf States) appear for a while as heavyweight donors. Peaking at $9.6 billion in 1980, their grants and loans went chiefly to Asian and African countries with large Islamic populations. Much of the money went into projects in transport and energy; theirs was an aid programme for Islam and for the oil industry.

Foreign aid comprises many kinds of flows. This book's chief focus is on foreign aid as used by officials (most of the time) in the strict sense of flows from official sources under soft or 'concessional' terms, chiefly for purposes of economic development and welfare. Resources for political or military purposes are thus, in principle, excluded. When directed towards low-income countries of Asia, Africa and Latin America it is termed 'official development assistance' (ODA); when directed towards Eastern Europe, the ex-Soviet Union or other 'countries in transition' it carries the less condescending label 'official aid' (OA). In this book, OA is included in ODA unless otherwise noted.

Since the early 1980s bilateral or country-to-country aid has accounted for about two-thirds of total ODA. About one-third of net ODA has flowed from multilateral bodies: the IFIs, European Union channels and the United Nations agencies. Multilateral aid has helped shield donors from the political risks of acting alone where recipient sovereignty is breached, namely in attaching macro-economic and political conditionality to aid. It has also helped in special cases such as South Africa and Namibia, where donors together helped pull the plug on apartheid.

AT THE RECEIVING END   Recipient countries form a mixed group. Former colonial or current neo-colonial relationships strongly determine who gets what from whom. This appears in informal spheres of influence: the USA in the Middle East and Latin America, Australia in Papua New Guinea and Fiji. Appendix A provides a snapshot of top recipients of 14 major donors at the

---

Box 2.1 Inflated figures

Official aid figures involve statistical gimmickry. There are at least two reasons radically to discount official data.

First, donors have artificially inflated spending figures by including items not strictly ODA: administrative overheads (officially 5.4 per cent of ODA in 1999), imputed costs of people from low-income countries studying in the North, costs of assisting asylum-seekers in the North, and the repayment of old debts by the issuing of new loans. Donors thus ignore definitional rules they themselves agreed to in the Development Assistance Committee (DAC) of the OECD. The economist and aid specialist Kunibert Raffer concludes that: 'if ODA had been measured strictly according to the DAC's own criteria, the total of DAC aid would have been roughly $20 billion lower in 1994 than official data claim'.[9]

Second, development banks are also recipients. They receive replenishments from donor countries, and they receive

end of the 1980s and the end of the 1990s. Geography, colonial history and culture are decisive for France, Britain and Portugal, countries whose aid goes chiefly to their ex-colonies. Historical ties show up in Germany's aid to Turkey. For over a decade the same populous countries have been among the top four recipients of total bilateral ODA: Indonesia, China, India and Egypt.

The poorest countries have never been the highest priority; they account for less than one-third of total ODA. More important have been those in the 'other low-income' category such as Indonesia, China, Côte d'Ivoire, India and Pakistan, and 'lower-middle-income' category, such as Egypt, Jordan, Guatemala, Bolivia and the ex-Yugoslavian states. Table 2.1 presents net ODA disbursements in the 1990s across six categories.

Poverty may be a main justification for aid, but it has seldom been the main criterion for allocating it. If aid were distributed

---

loan repayments with interest. More than ever, they work to make profits.[10] Researchers have probed the grant element of official loans – much of which count as ODA – to learn just how soft or concessional their terms are compared with terms low-income borrowers face on the open market. The results are startling: official loan terms can be hard, sometimes harder than those of the open market. Indeed, for ten countries the grant equivalent of official loans was consistently *negative*. That is, while appearing to provide soft loans to Argentina, Brazil, Colombia, Korea, Mexico, Peru, Romania, Russia, Uruguay and Turkey, the multilateral banks were, at no risk to themselves, taking in billions in above-market-rate profits. Poor borrowers have been providing money on concessional terms to aid system lenders. By re-calculating the real grant equivalent of about forty thousand official loans made in the period 1975–95 the researchers conclude that 'since 1985 net ODA considerably overstates aid flows – by as much as 25–30 per cent in recent years'.[11]

according to a simple head count of poor people, then China, India and other South and East Asian countries would have received most of it. But in the 1990s they received only about one-third of ODA. Other factors, such as size of a country's population, count. For a given poverty rate, smaller countries tend to receive more aid. Imperial scrambles for territories and preferences for island and enclave nations have biased aid's distribution.

As shown in Figures 2.2 and 2.3, both bilateral and multilateral ODA have been directed towards poorer countries, but not the poorest.

TABLE 2.1 Total net ODA disbursed over the years 1990–99 [number of countries as of 2001 shown in brackets]

Country category as set by United Nations	Billions of US$ of 1998	% of total
Least developed countries [49]	144.1	32
Other low-income (1998 GNP < $760 per capita) [23]	131.8	29
Lower-middle-income countries and territories (1998 GNP $761–$3030 per capita) [46]	142.6	31
Upper-middle-income countries and territories (1998 GNP $3031–$9360 per capita) [32]	17.5	4
High-income countries and territories (1998 GNP > $9360 per capita) [2]	8.1	2
Central and Eastern European Countries and New Independent States of the former Soviet Union [12]	9.8	2

Source: OECD online database 2001.

Who's Really Aiding Whom?

Aid's public image is one of Western beneficence and non-Western beggary. Apart from a parade of stories told to make benefactors feel good about their aid, there is rarely a hint that the North gets

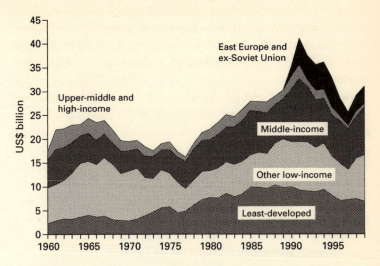

Figure 2.2 Destinations of DAC donors' net bilateral ODA in US dollars of 1999

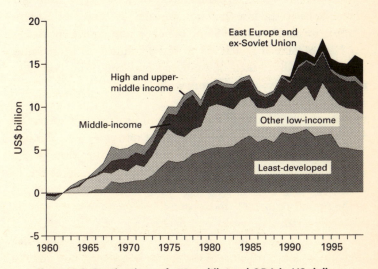

Figure 2.3 Destinations of net multilateral ODA in US dollars of 1999

something in return. On the contrary, the usual insinuation is of unproductive and ungrateful welfare queens living high on Northern generosity. That is an illusion. Foreign aid is a sideshow. Real benefits, and real costs, appear in quite different and larger flows and blockages.

Between richer and poorer countries, gains and losses can be estimated in various ways. Official flows in funds, goods and people can be compiled with some accuracy. But the global growth of unregistered transactions – in illicit goods, tax evasion, remittances – blow large holes in the data. Lack of information is in part a result of deliberate deregulation of capital, and the rewarding of old practices of bank secrecy, tax paradises and fictitious bookkeeping.

Table 2.2 shows only recorded transactions. In the case of worker remittances, actual values are far larger. In the case of tiny Somaliland, for example, they total about half a billion dollars annually.[12] Personal transfers surpass all official and non-governmental aid. In 1998, officially recorded remittances from the Netherlands to 42 low-income countries (exclusive of Eastern Europe) totalled about US$ one billion, a sum equivalent to 115 per cent of official Dutch aid to those countries.[13] Most value, however, is redistributed upwards and outwards, from poorer to richer. These flows take the following forms.

BRAIN DRAIN Richer places gain from professionals migrating from the South, many of them trained at university level through aid-funded bursary programmes. The UN estimates that African professionals departing for work abroad numbered about 27,000 in the 15 years up to 1975, 60,000 from 1985 to 1990, and 200,000 in the period 1990–99.[14] Today an estimated one in three African university graduates works outside Africa.[15] Asia has suffered a 'haemorrhaging of talent', particularly to the USA, where 'stay rates for advanced students in the engineering disciplines and the sciences can be higher than 75 per cent for students from particular countries'.[16]

TABLE 2.2 Some major flows in 2000 (in US$ billions)

	East Asia	Europe and Central Asia	Latin America and Caribbean	Middle East and North Africa	Southern Asia	Sub-Saharan Africa
Net transfers, foreign debt	-33	-5	-47	-11	1	-6
Foreign direct investment net	58	29	76	5	3	7
Portfolio equity flows	29	6	10	1	2	1
Profits on foreign direct investment	-17	-3	-22	-2	-1	-5
Aid grants excl. technical assistance	3	8	3	3	3	10
Workers' registered remittances	2	6	15	12	18	2

Source: World Bank (2001) *Global Development Finance 2001.*
(Negative signs indicate outward flows, mainly to the North.)

CAPITAL FLIGHT   Northern financial circuits gain from Southern capital, whether looted or legitimately saved. To escape regulation and taxation, well-connected firms and persons use many scams including mis-invoicing of imports and exports and suitcases of cash to stash wealth abroad. Tax havens help account for the difference between the $85 billion poor countries should receive in taxes from foreign corporations and the $50 billion they actually receive.[17]

> [B]y the end of 1990 the cumulative total of flight capital from developing countries was approximately $700 billion, equivalent to more than half the size of the external debt of developing countries. In effect, roughly half of the foreign borrowing by developing countries was transformed into an outward movement of private capital by citizens of the indebted countries.[18]

Figure 2.4 indicates the importance of capital flight in some selected African countries. Researchers have speculated that the impact 'of a return of such (relatively) huge investment flows would clearly be massive'.[19]

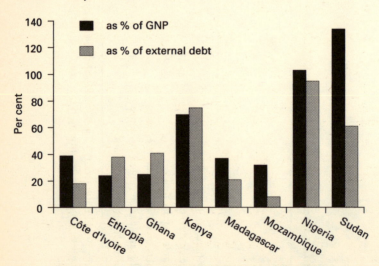

Figure 2.4 Importance of capital flight for eight African countries, 1991

NORTHERN TRADE BARRIERS Northern business interests gain from excluding imports from the South. 'Each year developing countries lose about $700 billion as a result of trade barriers in rich countries: for every $1 provided by the rich world in aid and debt relief, poor countries lost $14 because of trade barriers'.[20]

LOSSES DUE TO NORTHERN DUMPING Northern interests gain from crushing Southern competition. Crop and livestock agriculture have been especially hard hit. 'In some African countries where it costs $74 to produce 100 kilos of maize, the local market price fell to $21 due to subsidized Northern exports.'[21] In 1986, Haiti was largely self-sufficient in rice, a staple food for its people. Forced by donors and lenders to drop trade restrictions, the country was flooded with rice from the USA, where farmers are subsidized. 'By 1996, Haiti was importing 196,000 tons of foreign rice at the cost of $100 million a year. Haitian rice production became negligible. Once the dependence on foreign rice was complete, import prices began to rise, leaving Haiti's population, particularly the urban poor, completely at the whim of rising world grain prices.'[22]

REPAYMENT OF DEBT Debt repayment from poor to rich far exceeds aid. In 2000, lower-income countries paid to their creditors, net of what they received in new long-term loans, $101.6 billion — more than three times what they received in aid grants in that year. In 1999 the imbalance had been even greater: lower-income countries had paid to creditors almost five times more than what they received in aid grants.[23]

From 1992 to 2000, debt repayments as a share of poor country earnings from their exports and services changed as follows. Repayment of loan principal rose from 14 to 19 per cent; repayment of interest on loans rose from 8 to 10 per cent. All together in 1999, debt repayments (interest + principal) consumed 28 per cent of the earnings of lower-income countries.[24]

UNFAVOURABLE TRENDS IN TERMS OF TRADE Trade losses

swamp aid flows. The purchasing power of most Southern exports has fallen steadily throughout the era of foreign aid. 'Right through the 1980s, commodity prices fell on average by 5 per cent annually in real terms. By 1990 they were 45 per cent below their 1980 level ... Between 1980 and 1991, the developing countries suffered an estimated cumulative loss in total export earnings in real terms of US\$290 billion, an annual average loss of US\$25 billion.'[25] 'For the nonoil African countries, excluding South Africa, the cumulated terms of trade losses [from 1970 to 1997] represent almost minus 120% of GDP, a massive and persistent drain of purchasing power.'[26] The usually optimistic World Bank estimates that the purchasing power of most commodity exports in 2010 will be lower than it was in 1997.[27] These dismal trends stand in contrast to the unremitting pressure aid providers have put on low-income countries to 'export their way out of poverty'.

§

Aid is an ambiguous, two-faced thing. There is commonly a lot less to it than meets the eye. Under its many padded layers, the business of giving camouflages its much larger and inseparable twin, taking. Neither bilateral nor multilateral aid is targeted in proportion to the poverty at the receiving end. The terms of loans from the helpers can be as hard as, if not harder than, the terms set by merchant bankers. Finally, aid flows are simply dwarfed by the flows from poor to rich.

None of the foregoing should be read as new or astonishing. Most of these processes are not the result of intentional scheming or wickedness, but merely the unreflecting pursuit of the rules of the game. Most depend on collusion within the cosmopolitan 'global North', such as between bankers and other business people in both richer and poorer countries. A story of uniquely predatory Northern actors victimizing uniquely defenceless Southern actors is a myth. Predation is worldwide, though some countries are better-positioned that others to practise it.

Notes

1. Raffer, K. (1987) *Unequal Exchange and the Evolution of the World System*, New York: St Martin's Press, p. 269.

2. Davis, N. Z. (2000) *The Gift in Sixteenth-Century France*, Madison: University of Wisconsin Press.

3. Mauss, M. (1925, 1967) *The Gift: Forms and Functions of Exchange in Archaic Societies*, New York: Norton, p. 62.

4. In its closing arguments about the social importance of wealthy individuals, *The Economist* recently pleaded: 'Don't let's be beastly to the rich' in *The New Wealth of Nations: A Survey of the New Rich* (special supplement), 16 June 2001.

5. 'Nelson Rockefeller ... tied the approach [to aid] directly to the frontier thesis: "With the closing of our own frontier," he pointed out, "there is hope that other frontiers still exist in the world"... Such testimony offers considerable support for [the] generalization that Americans viewed the frontier "not as a line to stop at, but as an *area* inviting entrance".' Williams, W. A. (1974) 'The frontier thesis and American foreign policy' in *History as a Way of Learning*, New York: New Viewpoints, pp. 155–6.

6. The term 'flying geese' refers to a proposed hierarchy of East Asian economies under Japanese leadership, replacing to some extent an earlier concept, the 'Greater East Asia Co-Prosperity Sphere'. Arase, D. (1995) *Buying Power: The Political Economy of Japan's Foreign Aid*, Boulder, CO and London: Lynne Rienner, p. 252.

7. In the late 1940s the UK created state enterprises such as the Colonial (later Commonwealth) Development Corporation to boost production in the colonies. The aim was both to overcome shortages in Britain and to fend off US economic and political domination. See Cowen, M. (1982) 'The British state and agrarian accumulation in Kenya', in M. Fransman (ed.), *Industry and Accumulation in Africa*, London: Heinemann, pp. 142–69.

8. The critique of 'development' and pursuit of 'post-development' paradigms appear in Sachs, W. (ed.) (1992) *The Development Dictionary*, London: Zed Books, and in Rist, G. (1997) *The History of Development*, London: Zed Books. For a critical look at these ideas see Nederveen Pieterse, J. (2000) 'After post-development', *Third World Quarterly*, 21(2): 175–91.

9. Raffer, K. (1997) 'Controlling donors: on reform of development assistance', *Internationale Politik und Gesellschaft* (4): 361.

10. The European Bank for Reconstruction and Development, the aid system bank with the largest single portfolio in Eastern Europe, has had to

pursue profitable investments to cover losses. See 'Europe's bank rethinks development', *The Economist*, 17 April 1999. The British aid ministry's Commonwealth Development Corporation, renamed CDC Capital Partners, abandoned agriculture in pursuit of higher returns in things such as telecoms, banks, petroleum and real estate. See 'Two fingers to the poor', *The Economist*, 16 June 2001.

11. Chang, C. and others (1998) *Measuring Aid Flows, a New Approach*, Washington, DC: World Bank, web address: http://www.worldbank.org/research/growth/abschang.htm.

12. Ahmed, I. (2000) 'Remittances and their economic impact in postwar Somaliland', *Disasters* 24 (4): 383.

13. Netherlands Ministry of Foreign Affairs (2000) *Internationale Samenwerking*, January, p. 35.

14. United Nations Department of Public Information (2000) *Africa Recovery*, July.

15. 'Why Nigerians are not returning home', *The News* (Lagos), 4 October 2000.

16. Altbach, P. and T. Davis (1999) 'Global challenge and national response: notes for an international dialogue on higher education', in P. Altbach and P. Petersen (eds), *Higher Education in the 21st Century: Global Challenge and National Response*, IIE Research Report 29, Institute of International Education, New York, p. 15.

17. Oxfam UK (2000) *Tax Havens: Releasing the Hidden Billions for Poverty Eradication*, 6/2000, Oxford: Oxfam UK, web address: http://www.oxfam.org.uk/policy/papers/taxhvn/tax.htm.

18. Griffin, K. and T. McKinley (1993) *A New Framework for Development Cooperation*, Occasional Paper 11, September, New York: UNDP, web address: www.undp.org/hdro.

19. FitzGerald, V. and A. Cobham (2000) *Capital Flight: Causes, Effects, Magnitude and Implications for Development*. Oxford: Finance and Trade Policy Research Centre, Queen Elizabeth House, p. 18. Figure 2.4 is based on this paper.

20. 'The world must rein in the wreckers who trade in misery', *Guardian Weekly*, 18–24 January 2001.

21. Raffer, K. and H. W. Singer (1996) *The Foreign Aid Business*, Cheltenham: E. Elgar, p. 33, citing *UN Human Development Report 1994*.

22. Aristide, J. B. (2000) *Eyes of the Heart: Seeking a Path for the Poor in the Age of Globalization*, Monroe, ME: Common Courage Press, pp. 11–12.

23. World Bank (2001) *Global Development Finance 2001*, Washington, DC: World Bank, p. 246.

24. IMF (2000) *World Economic Outlook October 2000*, Washington, DC: International Monetary Fund, Table 42.

25. South Centre (1999) *Financing Development: Issues for a South Agenda*, Geneva: South Centre, web address: http://www.southcentre.org/publications /financing/.

26. Gelb, A. (1999) 'Where are We Now? Reforms, Performance and Country Groups in Africa', paper for presentation to the workshop 'Can Africa Claim the 21st Century?' African Development Bank, mimeo.

27. 'A raw deal for commodities', *The Economist*, 17 April 1999, p. 96.

THREE
The Aid Regime and Power Agendas

The poor complain. They always do. But that's just idle chatter.
Our system brings rewards to all, at least to all that matter.[1]

It has been called a sector, an enterprise and an industry. As a
hierarchy of bodies whose practices converge around a set of
rules, the aid system may also be called a regime. It is a system of
power doing its work in a wider realm of international politics.
During the Cold War, the Soviet Union and its allies formed
their own modest aid regime. That collapsed around 1990, whereupon most of its members found themselves at the receiving end
of today's only major regime, that of the OECD club of rich
countries.

This chapter looks at what drives the regime, what institutions
occupy its commanding heights, what checks and balances constrain its members' powers, and what rules are supposed to guide
it. The chapter sets the stage for the following two chapters about
aid chains at upper and lower levels.

Is the aid regime one coherent thing? Some specialists have
voiced doubt on the point, arguing that Western aid was at best
an arbitrary set of practices run by each country according to its
own rules and purposes. France, for example, has frequently gone
its own way. Japan makes business the centrepiece of its aid.

More frequently at the non-conforming fringe have been a
few smaller, trade-dependent countries with robust traditions of
domestic social welfare: Norway, Sweden, Denmark, Canada and
the Netherlands. As middle-power internationalists, from the

mid-1970s to the late 1980s this so-called Like-Minded Group tried to harmonize their aid and related policies along social-democratic lines. Much earlier than others, they focused on poverty and on political and civil rights. Since 1975, all except Canada have met the UN spending norm of 0.7 per cent of GNP. This suggests that a Nordic–Dutch sub-regime of aid exists, or did exist.

Today's aid regime discourages non-conformity. Indeed it looks, talks and walks like a state-run monopoly. It is a prime candidate for break-up and for the cure it blithely prescribes for others: competition. Why such structural adjustment is unlikely may be apparent in the following pages.

Why Provide Foreign Aid?

Rarely has *one* compelling drive been pre-eminent, although victory in the Cold War was clearly the dominant purpose in the aid regime's first four decades. Assigning a *single* motivation to the aid regime would be absurd. Aid's motives are always mixed. Hence the risks of incoherence – the frustration of some aims by other aims – are always high.

The mix changes over time, and varies between donors. Small trading nations will pursue a mix of aims different from those of a continental super-power. The useful question, then, is: what motives predominate? Aid specialists have probed the matter and commonly locate motives in three clusters.

STRATEGIC SOCIO–POLITICAL MOTIVES
- *Short-term* Abroad, to reward and keep a client 'on side' politically during negotiations, wars or other crises; to defuse public protest and insurrection; to provide a base for intelligence-gathering; to influence decision-making in international fora. At home, to reward or retain loyalty of ethnic/political constituencies, to be seen to be 'doing something' during a crisis.
- *Longer-term* Abroad, to gain regular access to and loyalty of

leadership at the receiving end; to win or deepen acceptance of a doctrine or model of development; to reinforce a country's place in a larger economic, political and military system; to stabilize economic or demographic trends in a country or region in order to stem unwanted effects such as terrorism and migration; in international institutions, to set and steer economic and political agendas. At home, to consolidate political support of voter and contributor constituencies, particularly the private sector, but also those with ethnic ties to aid recipients.

MERCANTILE MOTIVES
- *Short-term* Abroad, to seize market opportunities. At home, to promote interests of a sector of business and related employment; to improve the lender/donor's balance of payments; to assure the solvency of creditor banks, public or private.
- *Longer-term* Abroad, to win, expand, protect trade and investment opportunities, including strategic access to raw materials and cheap labour; to shape and stabilize North–South economic roles and hierarchies; in international institutions, to win and stabilize adherence to economic rules. At home, to consolidate and protect economic sectors.

HUMANITARIAN AND ETHICAL MOTIVES
- *Short-term* To show concern and compassion for victims of war, upheaval and natural catastrophes;
- *Longer-term* Abroad, to demonstrate concern about poverty, human rights abuse including the human rights of women; to compensate for damages. At home, to show solidarity with a particular country or group, to claim the high moral ground.

Discussions of what motives actually drive aid frequently get clouded by talk about what *should* drive it. Debates about it can evoke public displays of doubt or pride about national character and power. Are we a generous people? Are we pulling our weight in the world? A study of how Dutch, Belgian and British politicians talked about their nations' foreign aid roles in the period

1975–90 reveals much about national self-regard. Dutch rhetoric shows a self-image of 'The Activist': aid should be used to advance social justice, development and stability. Belgian politicians, by contrast, talked about their country's interests in terms of 'The Merchant': aid should benefit the domestic and international market. In British parliamentary debates, the dominant role conception was that of a 'Power Broker': aid should support friendly governments and advance British power and influence.[2]

Greater solidarity at home can mean greater beneficence abroad. Strong political commitments to domestic welfare, as in Nordic countries, are associated with strong aid performance, measured both by quantity (aid spending as a proportion of national income) and by quality (proportion of aid aimed at poverty reduction). Weak commitments to domestic welfare, as in the USA, coincide with weak aid quantity and quality.[3]

Some have argued that the Western foreign aid regime arises from ethical and humanitarian motives.[4] Certainly moral concerns influence conventional talk about aid, especially talk for the public at large. The World Bank's corporate motto since the late 1990s has been: 'Our dream is a world free of poverty.' But does donor practice match this talk? A team of researchers has probed the determinants of aid-giving behaviour, comparing US, French, Japanese and Swedish bilateral aid flows to Africa in the 1980s. They looked at how these donors distributed their aid according to recipient countries' strategic importance, economic potential for the donor, and humanitarian need. The results pour cold water on the notion that humanitarianism drives foreign aid. Ideology and the pursuit of commercial advantage are the main determinants.

Official aid is seldom a tool of altruism, even in Sweden, whose aid was long assumed to be driven by humanitarian concerns. Data suggest that Sweden acts rather more as a Merchant than an Activist, even in the 1980s, when it made important contributions to political change in southern Africa.[5] Since then, Swedish commerce and investment, including corruption-tainted sales of weapons to South Africa, have been consistent with those findings. Other researchers have reached similar conclusions: 'the direction of foreign aid is dictated by political and strategic considerations, much more than by the economic needs and policy performance of the recipients. Colonial past and political alliances are the major determinants of foreign aid.'[6]

As noted elsewhere in this book, national aid agencies have largely fallen into step behind the IMF and World Bank. Yet here and there motives are getting re-mixed. Beginning in 1997 a streak of idealism was detectable in British aid policy. Like other donors, the UK sees aid as a means to hitch low-income wagons to turbo-charged global markets. But it also accepts that aid should help civil society activists to mount pressure on decision-makers to protect citizens' rights – even where those rights are frustrated by market forces. US policy, on the other hand, shows a different trend. It has downgraded foreign aid to Africa and the Caribbean, regions targeted in its Trade and Development Act of 2000, whose theme is business, as usual. Low-income countries, as far as the USA is concerned, have to export their way out of poverty.

Motives behind aid never come in fixed and stable proportions. One observer therefore concludes: 'Perhaps the safest generalization to make is that foreign aid, when used alone or in combination with other policy instruments, has a unique ability to allow the donor to demonstrate compassion while simultaneously pursuing a variety of other objectives.'[7]

TWO NEGLECTED MOTIVES Aid usually revolves around self-interest, but two types of motivation are often overlooked: obligations to compensate for suffering and damage, and imperatives to respond to common problems of a region or the globe.

Compensation From the late 1940s to 1981, Japan made grants totalling $1.9 billion to 13 Asian countries; commercial gain was part of its mix of motives, but the formal purpose was to compensate those countries for losses in the Second World War and during Japan's prior colonial exploitation.[8] Through treaties and commissions, the USA instigated and enforced Japanese reparations. In so doing it applied a double standard, since elsewhere Western powers have 'always insisted aid must not and cannot be seen as a form or compensation or reparation for damages inflicted by colonialism'.[9] In the 1970s, for example, Southern advocates of a New International Economic Order found no Western sympathy for their proposal to create judicial means to take ex-colonizers to court for 'development damage'. Today, countries hurt because of policies imposed by the World Bank and IMF have no means of legal redress.

Common interest Deadly microbes, criminal mafias, radioactivity and greenhouse gases easily spill across borders. Migrants in search of a better life are now entering richer areas at faster rates. Global risks are increasing and vocal publics are demanding protection and guarantees of compensation. Such trends are concentrating the minds of politicians and policy-makers. Up until recently, complacent in their fortress nations, they paid little attention to approaches built around global and mutual interests. Today, among some policy elites and activist groups, an understanding is slowly crystallizing that lands both rich and poor face a common fate, whether they exist together in a region such as the Mediterranean basin, or together in a single Planet Earth. Where common interest is a point of departure, joint and reciprocal initiatives can be a fairly short step. Hence recent talk about global public goods[10] and warnings, in the wake of the suicide attacks in September 2001, that prosperous countries should prepare for significant transfers from rich to poor. That, however, would mean largely junking today's arrangements and moving towards genuine redistribution – something wholly different from today's aid system.

Why Seek and Accept Aid?

Leaders of countries struggling out of the ruins of war may think they have a good case to get help from abroad. But having a good case is not enough. In Moscow on 22 February 1918, facing a desperate situation, the Bolshevik Central Committee met to consider requesting aid from the USA and European powers. Lenin cast the crucial vote in favour. But the Russians' appeal for help came to nothing.[11]

Asking for aid can be risky and humiliating. Leaders may first have to settle internal disagreements. The aid-seeker has to qualify as deserving and compliant, on terms set by powerful outsiders. Desperate circumstances and a fervent wish to modernize – as with regimes in Cambodia, Angola, Nicaragua, Egypt and other countries that the West has chosen to boycott at certain times – won't make you eligible for aid if donors don't like your politics.

During the era of East–West competition there was more room for manoeuvre at the receiving end. Donors and lenders didn't set many conditions for their clients and friends. They tolerated local industrialization and rarely mentioned human rights. In some Southern countries, elites pursued assertive forms of nation-building in which a guiding principle was self-reliance. In newly independent Tanzania, the leadership's 1967 development manifesto, the *Arusha Declaration*, urged caution about foreign aid:

> Even if it were possible to get enough money for our needs from external sources, is this what we really want? ... Gifts which increase, or act as a catalyst to, our own efforts are valuable. But gifts which could have the effect of weakening or distorting our own efforts should not be accepted until we have asked ourselves a number of questions.[12]

Negotiating aid from both East and West was a way to assert sovereignty and non-alignment. Nehru, Nasser, Sukarno and other giants of twentieth-century nationalism had visions of modernization and self-determination. For them, aid was a way to pursue *political* projects serving *national* purposes. Today such motives may look merely quaint, even backward, for from Albania to Zambia, aid-seekers are supposed to present their lands as *economies* serving *international* purposes.

In calculating advantages and disadvantages, elites turn to aid where other options look worse. Governments usually prefer to tax exports in order to gain revenues they can use as they wish. For aid revenues go mainly to projects, where donors and lenders are in charge. From Guinea in the 1960s to Botswana and Eritrea in the 1990s, African leaders have sometimes spurned aid because it would compromise their autonomy.

The stakes can be high where elites and their constituencies have come to depend on aid for their personal and political survival. Soliciting aid can then reach the depths of cynicism. In Somalia in the 1980s and Eastern Zaire in the 1990s, authorities and warlords used people as human bait, herding tens of thousands into camps as proof of humanitarian need. Rulers have routinely sought aid to feed their systems of patronage, to retain loyalty among security forces and other crucial blocs in government and among allies in trade, industry, the media and even agriculture.

Post-colonial rulers have shown great skill at turning their dependence on aid into an instrument of power, including power over donors.[13] During the Cold War some could threaten to ally themselves with the Soviet Union against Western powers. Figures such as Zaire's Mobutu exploited Franco-American rivalries. Sudanese leaders courted ties with 'rogue states' such as Libya to worry the US State Department so that its officials would over-rule US Treasury Department and IMF demands that Sudan first repay its debts. Leaders of countries with diamonds, oil and other sub-soil riches could disguise mineral deals as aid deals, secure in the knowledge that their colluding Western political figures could be blackmailed. Strongmen on the other side of the East–West fence have also turned aid to their advantage: in the 1970s the Rumanian dictator Nicolae Ceauçescu got billions from the World

Bank in a cunning game to wriggle free of his patron, the Soviet Union.

Playing the aid game can help rulers gain room to manoeuvre towards outsiders. But it can also help them disengage from citizens. Extracting revenues from the public is a demanding and even dangerous job. Rulers must negotiate with citizens and businesses about taxes they pay and the public services they get in return. Leaders must also show how they spent the money. This is the essence of downward accountability and citizen-state reciprocity – in a word, give and take. Aid, on the other hand, can release politicians from such bothersome duties.

Today, extracting aid requires subtle bargaining with donors and lenders. Aid-seekers have to learn 'the politics of the mirror'. 'This consists essentially in addressing the foreign "other" – in this case potential aid donors – in the language that is most congenial, and crucially, most easily reinforces the belief that they (outsiders) understand what [the recipient] needs.'[14] Such behaviour renders the aid encounter closed, manipulated and unaccountable. Yet, with some exceptions, aid providers prefer to make their deals behind closed doors, out of range of inquisitive parliamentarians, reporters and policy activists.

Market Power and Aid Power: Sharing the Same Address

The world's power elite – bankers, fund managers, media magnates, captains of industry, political leaders, military chieftains – may give little more than a passing thought to the aid system. While useful as a means to be seen to be doing something about poverty and crises, foreign aid in their terms is largely a harmless sideshow. Yet that is not to say that key aid institutions are unimportant. On the contrary. Aid monies and most of their destinations may be of piffling importance alongside the big stakes in trade wars and military balances, but aid is the home and *raison d'être* for institutions of major significance for those elites.

These elites are found within global networks, the most important being in Washington, DC and New York. According to a senior member of a major political research institute, the planet's truly powerful may number no more than five thousand people.[15] Members of this elite circuit shuttle between for-profit, public and non-profit sectors. The media give ample and respectful attention to their ideas, portraying them as non-partisan and non-ideological. At the centre of this microcosm are leaderships of ministries of finance and central banks, in regular liaison with those managing financial markets. Foreign policy elites, whether in official positions or in think-tanks, complement and at times engage in polite disputes with their counterparts in the financial world.

Here we arrive at a paradox bordering on an absurdity: global institutions promoting retreat of the state and free-market fundamentalism – policies not usually associated with balanced growth, environmental sanity, protection from shocks and poverty reduction – constitute the control rooms of the aid system, with fresh mandates to promote economic growth, better environments, stability and rising living standards of the poor.

The IFIs have been assigned two big political tasks. First they are supposed to promote 'development', a deeply political matter that aid managers prefer to treat in soothingly technical terms. Second, they do their work chiefly by telling governments how to run their affairs. In lower-income countries they exercise intrusive political authority, although their statutes explicitly forbid it. Their power has been summarized as follows:

[T]he IMF is actually the most powerful of these actors, and together with the World Bank – with which it normally acts in concert – probably the most powerful, unchecked institution of any kind in the world. This is because the Fund sits at the head of a creditors' cartel. Because of an informal arrangement among creditors, a country that is not approved by the IMF will not be eligible for most World Bank lending, credit from other multilateral institutions (e.g. the Inter-American Development Bank), loans and aid from developed country governments, and very often private credit as well. This gives the IMF the power to decide the most important macroeconomic policies for dozens of countries, often with disastrous results.[16]

Observers have for decades criticized these institutions' appropriation of power. Once dismissed as left-wing carping, such critical views have begun reaching the mainstream. For example, the head of the University of Toronto's Center for International Studies, a reputed economist and former investment banker, has posed the issue in a book, *Who Elected the Bankers?*[17] In it, he reveals the IMF's essentially political functions. As powers over economic policy shifted from national governments to global financial interests, the IMF and World Bank have successfully buffered the winners against the anger of the losers. Political leaders can shrug off unpleasantness by claiming: 'Our hands are tied. The IMF made us do it.'

Respect for national sovereignty, and the principle of non-interference in politics may appear in the statutes of the IFIs, but those became dead letters long ago. Such pretences were openly abandoned in the case of Eastern Europe. In 1991, the top of the aid system set up the European Bank for Reconstruction and Development with a political mandate, namely to demolish the existing system and remodel Eastern Europe along Western lines.

The following paragraphs sketch some institutions at the top of the aid regime, and the limits to their public accountability. They form a nested hierarchy of authority. Those below mask and buffer the power of those above.

CENTRAL BANKS Parliaments may still hold formal powers to appoint central bank chiefs, but the bankers' autonomy from democratic politics is now an article of faith. Fighting inflation, necessary to meet financiers' demands for positive real interest rates, is their main job. The importance of that task has grown in step with central bank powers over national and transnational economies.[18] At the same time, moneyed interests (some of whom wield enormous influence over the security and economies of lower-income countries) have made sure that their billions may move freely and secretly in and out of offshore banks beyond the reach of any banking regulator or tax authority. As these unpoliced flows are crucial to destabilizing drug and civil war economies in recent decades, and to political Islam, serious dilemmas now face political classes sworn to protect free capital flows.

FINANCE MINISTRIES Ministries of finance enforce doctrine, and wield bureaucratic power besides. They make key appointments at the top of the aid system, such as the executive directors at the World Bank. The US Treasury Department, whose officials are in daily contact with the IMF and World Bank, is the kingpin. It acts also as an aid agency itself, providing technical assistance for bankers and business people in nearly thirty countries. It possesses a multi-billion-dollar fund, beyond parliamentary oversight, to bail out states and private firms in crises, such as Mexico, Indonesia and Russia in the 1990s. At the receiving end, the aid system has reorganized governance by catapulting finance ministry and central bank officials into positions of great authority and status. Their powers now extend well beyond the fine-tuning of interest rates and banking rules. Most adhere to fundamentalist economic models and norms – the result of decades of indoctrination.

INTERNATIONAL MONETARY FUND AND WORLD BANK Set up for different tasks, these multilateral banks have expanded their powers, with resulting 'mission creep'. The IMF assumed its present role in the aid regime in the 1970s, after the USA changed the rules of the post-war international financial system.[19] Designed like joint stock companies, the Bank and the IMF are formally owned by their 183 state shareholders. The IMF prefers to be seen as a world revolving fund belonging to its member states.[20] In fact, it is a powerful bank with policing and ideological powers, owned and run by rich creditor countries. The greater the shareholding, the greater the voting power. Formal voting is rare, as norms of consensus, discretion and camouflage rule. Real power to set agendas and steer policy rests with senior staff, making the board's role that of a rubber stamp. In sum, the IMF is not very representative, transparent nor accountable. Yet it regularly acts as lawmaker, judge and sheriff when it comes to the openness and public legitimacy of borrowing countries' governance.

The World Bank's 20-member full-time Board of Executive Directors sets policy and approves funding. Here too, votes are weighted by the value of each country's financial participation. Western executive directors report mainly to their home ministries of finance, not to their bilateral aid authority. Where finance ministers are held to public account about their representatives at the Bank and the Fund, the possibility of democratic oversight exists.

The USA enjoys supremacy over the IFIs.[21] All the Bank's presidents have been US citizens approved by the US Treasury. They are chosen for their establishment backgrounds and abilities to get things done in the Washington–New York elite networks. Many shadow powers are on Wall Street, where the World Bank raises most of its funds, and leverages yet more money in special consortia. It pays strict attention to the wishes of private investment banks such as Goldman, Sachs and private credit rating agencies like Standard & Poor's and Moody's. These rating agencies base their judgements not on Bank effectiveness in aid, least of all in poverty reduction, but rather on Western government readiness to guarantee Bank solvency. Fear that these private surveillance firms might raise doubts among bond traders is a major reason the IFIs enjoy virtual guarantees against failure. Governments cover bad loans no matter what. Risks are socialized to taxpayers in the North and especially to poor country residents, including those not yet born.

They have multinational staffs and pepper their public utterances with terms such as partnership and ownership. The principle of foreign aid run by the community of nations may be a good one, but the multilateralism of these banks is fraudulent. They are effectively owned and run by Western finance ministries, chiefly that of the USA. The conservative MIT economist Rudiger Dorbusch summed it up neatly: 'The IMF is a toy of the United States to pursue its economic policy off-shore.'[22] The aid system could not ask for an institutional home with more financial and ideological clout. But it is not the clout of the poor, whom they are supposed to serve.

FOREIGN MINISTRIES Powers over aid flows have never been very transparent, being tangled up with the management of diplomatic, cultural and security objectives. 'Of all terrains of political decision-making, foreign affairs is the one in which the government is least accountable, the opposition least effective, public opinion most ignorant, and secrecy most intense – the ideal situation for ministers.'[23] Bilateral aid institutions are commonly subordinate to foreign affairs ministries, if not swallowed up within them.

On bureaucratic battlefields, however, foreign policy mandarins have been ceding ground to finance ministers and central bankers. In July 2001, in the afterglow of a diplomatic triumph, European foreign ministries had to reel back aid pledges to ex-Yugoslavia in the face of EU finance ministers' insistence that Yugoslavia first repay old debts.[24] Low in the pecking order and squeezed among larger bureaucratic blocs, national aid institutions find themselves poorly protected against competing forces.

OECD (ORGANISATION FOR ECONOMIC CO-OPERATION AND DEVELOPMENT) During the Cold War, Western governments signed a treaty to set up this body, headquartered in Paris. Its chief purposes have been to shape policy consensus and Northern relations with Southern countries. It is not a bank or aid agency but a well-funded and highly influential think-tank. Its discreet but formidable presence led one critic to term it the 'Political Committee at the heart of the "Politburo" of the International of ultraliberalism'.[25] For *The Economist*, on the other hand, the OECD 'does sterling work as a talk shop and data-collection point' but is otherwise 'underemployed.'[26]

Coordination and burden-sharing of foreign aid were concerns from an early hour. On a US initiative in 1960, the OECD created a donor club, the Development Assistance Committee (DAC). It ratifies rules and key concepts, such as ODA, thus setting the basis for its chief political tasks, shaping official perspectives on aid.

Washington's grip is strong. For its first 39 years, the DAC was chaired exclusively by US foreign policy and aid officials. Links to the IMF and World Bank are routine. While not swallowing everything from Washington, most OECD staff relay the rules and discourse of market fundamentalism, occasionally putting them in terms of European liberalism. Although the DAC admitted Mexico in 1994 as an observer, low-income countries have no formal powers. Debates and progressive voices are heard within the OECD. The hammering-out of the aid system's current anti-poverty goals took place under its auspices.[27] But it remains a powerful pulpit for reigning orthodoxies.

It regularly preaches to governments in the South and East about transparency, autonomy from powerful interest groups, and other marks of good governance. Yet these are not among the hallmarks of the OECD's own governance. In the mid-1990s, for example, preparation of the abortive Multilateral Agreement on Investment (a 'magna carta for multinationals') took place under OECD auspices – largely in secret.

PARLIAMENTARY FUNDING AUTHORITIES Aid system officials may enjoy wide powers to determine who gets funds for what purposes and on what terms. But at the same time they have to account to elected officials. Parliaments hold crucial powers over purse strings. Their committees on foreign affairs or international institutions can therefore act as important sentinels. Budget approval rounds are key moments. The US Congress has been especially vigilant about the IFIs and United Nations aid agencies.

If something displeases its members or protected industries, Congress withholds funds or micro-manages loan approvals.

Most parliamentarians pay little concerted attention to North–South issues. But in the late 1990s, economic and political crises, and street protests in Seattle, Washington DC, Genoa and elsewhere have helped awaken at least some elected officials to these issues' importance, and to the top of the aid regime in particular. In March 2000 a bipartisan committee in the US Congress called for curbs on powers of the IFIs.[28] The French parliament's Finance Committee in 2000 endorsed a report critical of the World Bank. Meanwhile a non-official group, Parliamentarians against Poverty, took shape and called for democratization at the top of the aid system, including a parliamentary assembly to control the IFIs.

BILATERAL ORGANIZATIONS National donors have always preferred country-to-country aid. Bilateral institutions began emerging in the 1950s and 1960s, although in the cases of Britain, France and Belgium they were merely re-tooled versions of bureaucracies that had managed colonial affairs. Having an aid agency is a matter of self-respect for every industrial nation; Ireland established its aid agency in 1974 and the Republic of Korea created a cooperation fund in 1987.

Aid is often the object of unfriendly intra-mural football. Finance ministries get into the game because of their automatic links to the IFIs. Funding authorities meanwhile may supervise an array of complementary agencies that package aid in special ways such as loans, export credits or technical assistance or that manage aid for special purposes such as environmental protection and science. Bilateral aid agencies may also be flanked (and rivalled) by other ministries, especially those managing foreign trade and the armed forces, who may mount their own aid efforts. Official bodies with aid-giving tasks continue to multiply, checked from time to time by shake-ups and consolidations under one authority.

In the face of this proliferation, the question arises: where are the democratic checks and balances? Mainstream media tend to ignore foreign aid until stories about bailout-from-bankruptcy or humanitarian rescue appear. Their accounts of aid tend towards sensation, denouncing cathedrals-in-the-desert projects or leakage of funds. For official *independent* oversight there are generally only two kinds of bodies: budget auditing branches and parliamentary committees, supported by official and party research groups. The US General Accounting Office, for example, has carried out important economic audits of USAID, exposing its relationships with private business.[29] Occasionally official and quango[30] aid agencies face special taskforces and panels, often set up to reset priorities or settle disputes among competing bureaucratic blocs. But such efforts are often under-staffed and carry few powers. Effective accountability over foreign aid, verified by strong official bodies with independent insight into aid practice, is more the exception than the rule. Hence the vital importance of independent watchdogs.

Self-regulation – public disclosure according to rules and norms set by the industry itself – is the way many businesses and non-profits prefer to account for themselves. So too for bilateral aid. Since 1996 the DAC has carried out annual assessments of members' aid programmes; these peer review exercises yield limited, carefully worded reports within the bounds of prevailing aid talk and practice.[31] New methods of deeper-going public accountability such as social audits and independently verified assessments of corporate ethics may be advancing in the business sector and some civil society bodies, but they have yet to appear in the mainstream aid industry.

Outside government, the aid industry faces a host of lobbying interests. These can range from agribusiness and free-trade think-tanks to environmental NGOs and debt campaigners. Business groups and non-profits keep a close eye on aid budget lines, as these can represent opportunities for contracts. As many of those lobbying about aid are themselves beneficiaries of it, they naturally ask for more of it rather than press for its overhaul. Exceptions include the critical monitoring of official aid by such groups as British Overseas NGOs for Development (BOND). In the 1990s, new activist research groups such as the Bretton Woods Project and the Bank Information Center reinforced older organizations such as the Washington-based Development GAP (Group for Alternative Policies) as watchdogs.

Much outside influence has been routinized and domesticated. Almost every European government maintains an advisory council on foreign aid. These are usually composed of people from the academic, non-profit and business sectors, and specialized research institutes.[32] In 1999 the French government created a sixty-member High Council for International Cooperation composed of independent figures with public standing. This move reflected concerns to clean up French aid's image and to anchor it outside the closed circuits of the policy mandarins.

Agency directors agree that public anchoring and pro-aid lobbying are important. But they tend to grumble about what public politics lays on them: the special budget lines, and lengthening lists of issues and criteria ranging from environmental safeguards to private sector promotion to human rights. Some agency chiefs see such directives as hindrances. They argue that greater autonomy for their kind means greater aid effectiveness. Such arguments may be valid, but only in cases where a host of other conditions – competence, experience, clear objectives, valid systems for learning and long-term commitments – are met. Unfortunately, that is rarely the case. Delegation of powers to aid managers close to field realities may improve performance, but can just as easily encourge the pursuit of personal hobbies, non-transparency and diminished learning incentives.[33]

In some places, such as the Nordic countries and Britain, political bargaining has led to reasonably good public oversight without putting agencies in strait-jackets. Such cases suggest that bilateral agencies can be more transparent and responsive than the multilateral banks, export credit providers and private aid agencies.

UNITED NATIONS Created in large part to address economic, social, cultural and humanitarian problems, the UN is nominally subject to democratic rules. Its Charter assigns tasks for defining policies about development to the Economic and Social Council (ECOSOC), which then coordinates actions of UN specialized agencies to implement policies. The General Assembly elects member states to the Council's 54 seats for terms of three years; it operates on a one-state, one-vote basis. In these terms it should be the world's supreme democratic forum to steer the aid system.

But as things stand, the UN is merely a fourth pillar behind the IMF, World Bank and World Trade Organization. That fourth-rate status stems from the fact that 'the very nature of the United Nations (reflected in its real, if unofficial structure hidden beneath the ever-so-democratic flow-chart façade) as well as the primary *raison d'être* of its founders, had far more to do with maintaining the power of the World War II victors than with extending democracy, whether political or economic, across the globe'.[34] Those powers made sure that ECOSOC never became the main forum to define global aid policy.

UN agencies have entered the aid system with formal mandates. Historically these have lacked strong political, juridical and financial backing. Two kinds of optimism led much UN aid towards dead ends.

First, an optimism about technical and scientific expertise led to organizational cultures centred on professional knowledge and its problem-solving powers: health issues are best left to medical specialists, agricultural progress to crop and livestock experts, and so on. This helped build UN specialized agencies' standing and know-how, often of high calibre, but also drained development of its politics. For decades, questions of power, equitable access to services, livelihoods, security and civil freedoms stayed off the agenda. Confining the agenda to technical matters was the path of least resistance, as it didn't upset anyone North or South and favoured business and their technical products. Around the logic of sectoral specialization there grew up a fragmented structure of competing elite agencies, some of them run as personal fiefdoms rather than as publicly accountable bodies in a global civil service.

The second point of optimism was that Southern majorities in UN decision-making would make agencies more responsive to Southern concerns. There were hopes that aid would be democratized, being managed both for and by the poor countries. But lacking control over funding, Southern voting majorities have counted for little. Whether in setting agendas or appointing people to key positions, Southerners, particularly if voicing dissenting views, have faced exclusion. The leadership and management of key agencies has been disproportionately in the hands of citizens from North Atlantic countries.

Contrary to hopes of greater responsiveness, the proliferation of UN agencies (38 of them as of 2001, plus a large number of special UN funds) and competition among them have frustrated open, democratic practice. 'Round Table Conferences', organized by the UN in about 35 very low-income countries since 1970, may have encouraged donors to coordinate and to listen to recipient governments. But where UN agencies have asserted their authority and technical know-how about crises and development problems, political leaders in affected countries have tended to shrug off responsibilities that should properly be theirs. As discussed in later chapters, the aid system, illustrated in the UN but certainly not confined to it, has helped displace responsibility upwards and outwards, to international levels where there are no sanctions for failing to respond – as demonstrated shockingly in Africa's crises in the 1990s.

Rules of the Game

A regime can be defined as a set of 'implicit or explicit principles, norms and rules and decision-making procedures around which actors' expectations converge'.[35] Knowledge of rules can help predict behaviour. Some key rules guiding the aid regime are summarized below in six clusters, based on a useful overview composed in the early 1980s by the political economist Robert Wood.[36] Gaps between rules and practices have always existed, but since the 1980s, aid agency behaviour as disciplined from Washington has converged about the following principles, norms and rules.

NEGOTIATION   Aid is provided at the discretion of the donor/lender. There is no right or entitlement to aid. The donor's choice and definition of a problem, issue or population has precedence. Donors/lenders set the channels and procedures.

AID IN RELATION TO OTHER FLOWS   Aid should not compete with for-profit actors, who can effectively veto aid to certain sectors such as mining or manufacturing. Aid should thus contribute to general conditions of production and exchange, such as public works and education, and to macro-economic conditions. Donors may legitimately allocate or withhold aid in order to promote or discourage trade flows and investment capital. There are few barriers to lending; for example, loans repayable in foreign currency for activities that do not require or generate foreign currency are legitimate.

RELATIONS AMONG OFFICIAL DONORS   Aid donors/lenders should not compete with one another. Donors should not break ranks with the IMF and World Bank on policy. Promotion of rival economic paradigms is unwelcome. Mercantile competition disguised as aid, such as soft export credits, should be restrained.

RELATIONS BETWEEN OFFICIAL DONORS AND CIVIL SOCIETY   Selected civil society organizations (CSOs) in donor and recipient countries may be considered legitimate actors in aid, or discussants about aid. Terms of interaction with CSOs may be negotiated, but the donor/lender has the last word. CSOs whom donors consider legitimate are welcome to express criticism via routine channels such as lobbying; CSOs seen as non-legitimate or who mount criticism via non-routine channels of protest are unwelcome and will be ignored or firmly rebuffed.

CONDITIONALITY Conditionality[37] is a legitimate form of interference in the internal affairs of sovereign states. Donors/lenders have rights to prescribe policies, and recipient governments must promise to adhere to what is prescribed. The principle of promise (*ex-ante* conditionality) is today being supplemented by the principle of performance (*ex-post* conditionality), that is, recipients must demonstrate that they have actually applied the required policies. Norms to promote an outward economic orientation and market fundamentalism are today being supplemented by norms of poverty alleviation and good governance as defined and measured by donors. Until the mid-1990s, conditionalities were imposed from above, through non-transparent procedures; today they are supposed to be formulated through public consultation and 'owned' by recipients. Escape clause: a major donor may, at its discretion, informally drop insistence on actual observance of these norms where its other priorities, such as its strategic political or military interests, come first.

AID AND DEBT Continued eligibility for aid depends on meeting debt repayments to the important creditors, namely the IMF and World Bank. Default and formal bankruptcy status is forbidden and non-negotiable.[38] Roll-over or relief of debt is subject to prevailing conditionalities. Clubs of donors/lenders, sometimes including private creditors, manage debt refinancing.

§

This chapter has cast a cursory look at the commanding heights of the aid system, the motivations, institutions and rules which drive it, and some of the checks and balances that should make it publicly accountable but usually fail to do so. The regime operates and reproduces itself in extended hierarchies or aid chains, the motif of the following two chapters.

Notes

1. G. A. Helleiner, cited in Strange, S. (1998) 'The new world of debt', *New Left Review*, 230: 109.

2. Breuning, M. (1994) 'Why give foreign aid? Decision maker perceptions of the benefits to the donor state', *Acta Politica* (2): 121–44.

3. Noël, A. and J.-P. Thérien (1995) 'From domestic to international justice: the welfare state and foreign aid', *International Organization*, 49(3): 523–53.

4. See for example Lumsdaine, D. (1993) *Moral Vision in International Politics: The Foreign Aid Regime*, Princeton, NJ: Princeton University Press.

5. Schraeder, P. and others (1998) 'Clarifying the foreign aid puzzle. A comparison of American, Japanese, French and Swedish aid flows', *World Politics* (50): 294–323

6. Alesina, A. and D. Dollar (1998) *Who Gives Foreign Aid to Whom and Why?*, Working Paper, Cambridge, MA: National Bureau of Economic Research, web address: http://papers.nber.org/papers/W6612.

7. Arase, D. (1995) *Buying Power: The Political Economy of Japan's Foreign Aid*, Boulder, CO and London: Lynne Rienner, p. 13.

8. Ibid., pp. 28–9.

9. Raffer, K. and H. W. Singer (1996) *The Foreign Aid Business*, Cheltenham: E. Elgar, p. 108.

10. Kaul, I. (2000) 'Biens publics globaux, un concept révolutionnaire', *Monde Diplomatique*, June.

11. The USA rejected the Bolshevik appeal, thereby also ignoring the wishes of the French. It began arming a 'contra' army against the new Soviet state, backed by US troops in Siberia. The episode illustrates the age-old cynicism behind some 'humanitarian' interventions. The US secretary of state under President Woodrow Wilson proposed setting up a Commission for relief aid for Russia, as part of a strategy of armed counter-revolution. He wrote: 'Armed intervention to protect the humanitarian work done by the Commission would be much preferable to armed intervention before this work had begun.' Williams, W. A. (1974) 'American intervention in Russia 1917–1920', in *History as a Way of Learning*, New York: New Viewpoints, p. 94.

12. Cited in Rist, G. (1997) *The History of Development*, London: Zed Books, p. 128.

13. See Chabal, P. and J.-P. Daloz (1999) *Africa Works: Disorder as Political Instrument*, Oxford: James Currey.

14. Ibid., p. 117.

15. Toinet, M. F. (1995) 'Aux Etats-Unis, les croisés du libre-échange', *Le Monde Diplomatique*, February. (Marie-France Toinet of the National Foundation of Political Sciences, Paris.)

16. Weisbrot, M. (2000) *One Year After Seattle: Globalization Revisited*, Washington, DC: Center for Economic and Policy Research, web address: http://www.cepr.net/.

17. Pauly, L. W. (1997) *Who Elected the Bankers? Surveillance and Control in the World Economy*, Ithaca, NY and London: Cornell University Press.

18. Maxfield, S. (1997) *Gatekeepers of Growth: The International Political Economy of Central Banking in Developing Countries*, Princeton, NJ: Princeton University Press.

19. Precipitating this crisis was an 'underdeveloped' country, Vietnam, whose leadership insisted that it, not France or the United States, should run its own affairs. The war in Vietnam led the USA to run up a huge external payments deficit, which damaged confidence of bankers and bond traders. Refusing to adjust US priorities to the needs for financial market stability, the US Treasury in 1971 unilaterally ended the exchange-rate system at the heart of the 1944 Bretton Woods agreements. From that moment on, there developed a new role for the Bretton Woods Institutions — supervising 'development'.

20. This paragraph is based on Wood, A. (2001) *Structural Adjustment for the IMF: Options for Reforming the IMF's Governance Structure*, London: Bretton Woods Project, web address: www.brettonwoodsproject.org.

21. The USA, by far its most important shareholder at 17.56 per cent of weighted votes, has veto powers available to no other government.

22. 'World Central Bank', *Journal of Commerce*, 7 January 1999.

23. Sassoon, D. (1996) *One Hundred Years of Socialism*, London: Fontana Press, p. 177.

24. 'Brussels loses battle over aid to Yugoslavia', *Financial Times*, 17 July 2001.

25. 'L'"éminence grise" du château', *Le Monde Diplomatique*, March 1998, review of Chavranski, H. (1997) *L'OCDE au coeur des grands débats économiques*, Paris: La Documentation Française.

26. 'The talking FDI blues', *The Economist*, 14 March 1998.

27. OECD-DAC (1996) *Shaping the 21st Century: The Contribution of Development Co-operation*, Paris: OECD, web address: http://www.oecd.org/dac.

28. The so-called Meltzer report. See: http://www.econ.lsa.umich.edu/~alandear/topics/meltzer.html.

29. Berríos, R. (2000) *Contracting for Development: The Role of For-Profit Contractors in U.S. Foreign Development Assistance*, Westport, CT: Praeger.

30. Quango refers to a quasi-autonomous non-governmental organization. Commonly created by governments to carry out public tasks with public revenues, they represent a form of privatization. Statutory rules vary widely, but most quangos enjoy much independent authority. They have often been abused as means of elite political patronage and as ways to escape normal democratic oversight. In North Atlantic countries, most quangos carry out domestic tasks (managing health and school systems, broadcasting, watchdog functions, and so on), but a number carry out international tasks including foreign aid spending and knowledge-based activities related to the aid industry.

31. See OECD Online, web address: http://www.oecd.org/dev.htm.

32. Kooij, A. and R. Mevis (1994) *Cooperation of Advisory Structures for Development Cooperation Policy: A Survey in Seventeen European Countries [Summary]*, The Hague: Nationale Advies Raad web address: http://www.oneworld.org/euforic/nar/adv_syn.htm.

33. Published writings on aid management are extensive, but the invisible part of the iceberg is formed by unpublished writings (consultants' reports, internal memoranda, and so on). One classic text is Rondinelli, D. (1993) *Development Projects as Policy Experiments*, London: Routledge. On agency autonomy from domestic politics, see Lancaster, C. (1999) *Aid to Africa: So Much to Do, So Little Done*, Chicago, IL: University of Chicago Press.

34. Bennis, P. (1996) *Calling the Shots: How Washington Dominates Today's UN*, Brooklyn, NY: Olive Branch Press, pp. 46–7.

35. Krasner, S. (1982) 'Structural causes and regime consequences: regimes as intervening variables', *International Organization*, 36(2): 186, quoted in R. Wood (1986) *From Marshall Plan to Debt Crisis: Foreign Aid and Development Choices in the World Economy*, Berkeley: University of California Press, p. 96.

36. Wood, *From Marshall Plan to Debt Crisis*, pp. 94–137.

37. Conditionality refers to a stipulation or requirement agreed upon, but generally imposed by lenders or donors, under which aid is provided on condition that a recipient government takes certain policy actions. As loans are usually paid out in instalments or tranches, lenders can try to enforce compliance by the threat of withholding unpaid balances of the loan.

38. Until September 2001, when the US treasury secretary said that he favoured a bankruptcy procedure as an alternative to end IMF bail-outs. See Raffer, K. (2001) *Debt Relief for Low Income Countries: Arbitration as the Alternative to Present Unsuccessful Debt Strategies*, Helsinki: WIDER, web address: http://www.jubilee2000uk.org/analysis/articles/raffer_debtrelief_lowincome.pdf.

FOUR
Aid in Chains

The desire to help so easily becomes the desire for power.[1]

Command over leading ideas and rules of the game is, as the previous chapter notes, an important power. But much depends on how it is carried out. As in marketing or weapons systems, foreign aid relies on extended linkages to convey its ideas, money, goods and services to its targets. These devices may deliver their payloads from great heights or close to the ground, but all require organizing people in complex hierarchies. These are aid chains.[2]

Aid chains are systems of power. They consist of lines of command run from the top. They afford a lot of control, but they are not almighty. For funny things can happen to policies as they travel down aid chains. Mid-level authorities, business go-betweens, receiving-end officials and intended beneficiaries do not behave like printed circuit boards. On the contrary, they will usually interpret, negotiate, try to capture advantages, resist control and manipulate information going back up the chain. Like a digestive tract, aid chains reconstitute formal policies into 'really existing policies'. At the end of its journey down a chain, the outcome of an aid-driven plan will often look quite different from what was intended at the top.

Simplified examples appear in Figure 4.1. Most chains have at least four segments beyond the funding authority: typically first an aid agency or bank, second an operator in the public or private sectors, third a national or local authority, and fourth local collaborating bodies in the public or private sectors. At each level there are hangers-on: advisers, suppliers, media, auditors and evaluators.

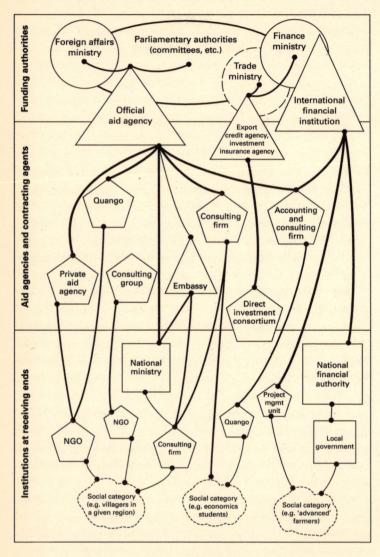

Figure 4.1 Aid chains

Theories of resource dependence help explain how aid chains work and produce tensions.[3] Organizations in a chain struggle to capture and retain resources. In so doing, they are pulled in opposite directions: they seek certainty and stability, yet they also seek to avoid external control and the vulnerability of dependence.

The metaphor of the chain speaks to top-heavy patterns of authority. Those at the top frame the questions. They also then give the answers – and not necessarily in that logical sequence. All the way down, participants have to account upwards, rarely downwards to ultimate beneficiaries. Rather than build and disperse power among citizens at the receiving end, aid chains tend to claim and gather power upwards and concentrate it at ever-higher levels. Yet if aid fails, those at lower levels commonly end up paying the bills, and getting the blame. Poverty and powerlessness may loom large in places where aid has been most intense, but those at the upper ends of aid chains are meanwhile assured of a job.

Empowerment above, disempowerment below: the tendency is clear. Where there should be functioning public systems and political give and take between rulers and citizens, there are often only skeletal institutions. Today's calls for recipient ownership, participation, transparency and good governance are certainly valid, but they are cries into what is often an echoing void.

Ownership and Initiative

Aid chains run from below are extremely rare. They crop up outside official aid systems, such as where ethnic diasporas living abroad – Albanians in New York, Palestinians in Western Europe – answer urgent appeals from home. Donors and lenders may be the owners and initiators of aid, but that is not for lack of proposals on the part of recipients. On the contrary, Southern countries have tried to set up institutions affording them some measure of control over aid. Two cases stand out.

In the 1950s, inspired by the Marshall Plan, some countries

proposed establishment of a soft-loan UN bank, the (Special) UN Fund for Economic Development. Being a UN-owned fund, recipient nations would have held strong voting powers over it. The World Bank opposed and finally killed the idea. But the Bank then dropped its earlier objections to the principle of soft loans, and occupied that higher moral ground by setting up in 1960 its own soft-loan window with a bland name, the International Development Association.

The second initiative was more successful: the International Fund for Agricultural Development (IFAD). Emerging in the mid-1970s when talk about a New International Economic Order was in the air and oil exporters' wealth was rising, it was a Southern initiative focused on lending for rural development. Managed by technocrats but with a strong sense of Southern country ownership, IFAD's governance formula departed from that preferred by donors. However, Northern donors called a strike on IFAD in the 1990s, thereby winning a new formula of governance tilted in their favour. That rescued the agency financially, but brought it into closer alignment with the top of the aid regime.[4]

Captains of the aid industry tend to rubbish ideas coming from recipients. Proposals by African governments have been unwelcome: the Lagos Plan of Action, the Final Act of Lagos, and the African Alternative Framework to Structural Adjustment Programs.[5] But even those backed by heavier political clout, such as Japanese and Malaysian proposals to set up an Asian Monetary Fund owned and run by regional governments, have likewise been vetoed in Washington. Today, industry utterances are spiked with terms like 'home-grown' and 'demand-driven'. Hollow words, going by the historical record of most official donors.

What triggers aid chains and how do they evolve? They routinely grow along paths laid down by geo-politics, culture and commerce, but they may be triggered in various ways.

CRISIS   Disaster has brought to life many aid chains. Catastrophes can seize public attention and loosen purse strings in ways that few other things can. Media officials seek dramas of distress and rescue; they find them in humanitarian stories, for which aid-providers seek publicity. Big aid chains with large public profiles are thus created. Israel's 1967 war, the collapse of the Soviet Union, and a deteriorating world environment have sparked foreign policy initiatives and aid chains with long lifespans, though of different strengths and political backing. Humanitarian aid chains develop from unlikely sources. Western military establishments, challenged to justify their budgets in the post–Cold War era, have actively worked to set them up. At another extreme is the one-man-and-a-truck NGO rolling into war-ravaged ex-Yugoslavia or Guatemala with loads of donated relief goods.

ECONOMIC CONJUNCTURES Many aid chains spring from pent-up surpluses with no place to go. Subsidized farm output is a major case in point. Food aid has mobilized the enthusiasm of farmers, seed and chemical companies, politicians, merchants, transporters, charities, and a variety of interests at the receiving end. End consumers can range from bakery training projects to public works schemes to armed forces. Food aid chains often generate yet more links, as the revenues from foodstuff sales pass to others, including agencies further up the aid chain. The bonanza of the early aid years (food aid accounted for one-third of US agricultural exports in the 1950s) helped agribusiness and the shipping industry penetrate and expand into many of the foreign markets they continue to benefit from today.

Surplus petrodollars piling up after the oil price hikes of the 1970s triggered heavy pressure on banks to sell loans. The IFIs joined the private banks in the lending frenzy. Northern hyper-consumption is another source of surpluses. Fashions change and goods become obsolete. Hence the channelling of second-hand clothing, cast-off medical supplies and refurbished tools. These too follow the axiom that over-production tends to feed aid chains that grow into commercial chains.

Stimulating the growth of aid chains over the long term are normal processes of business enterprise led by firms, organizations and consultants based in donor countries themselves. The US government makes no secret of the fact that most of its bilateral aid – about 80 per cent according to one estimate – flows back to US suppliers of goods and services. The Dutch aid ministry has for years tried to promote aid spending at the receiving end, yet about 65 per cent of its aid in 1995 was spent in the Netherlands or flowed back there.[6]

NEW IDEAS, NEW FASHIONS Like ivy on a trellis, aid chains grow on frameworks of ideas. Appendix B notes some leading fashions over five decades. Under the ideology of market fundamentalism, aid chains have shown luxuriant growth. Downsizing government, privatizing services and promoting private sector interests have added new segments and new hangers-on, as described later in this chapter. These ideas come packaged in common-sense language about administrative or market rationality. Contracting services of consultants and NGOs has been promoted as the straight and narrow path to cost reduction. Incentives, bargaining, personal choice and metaphors of commerce all enter this story.

But an interest in greater efficiency and choice does not explain why chains grow the way they do. Almost always at work are political purposes.[7] To devolve tasks to contractors is to redistribute power and to entrench new socio-economic interests, who then defend the chains and their positions in them. Privatization also enables the USA, for example, to pursue policies outside laws mandating public disclosure of information.[8] Being less subject to public oversight, privatized aid chains develop lives of their own. Aid policies may come and go, but aid chains live on.

COMPETITION As the number and variety of organizations, firms and statutory bodies involving themselves in foreign aid have grown, so too has the competition. Their struggles for growth or survival have gained intensity when crises and economic conjunctures trigger new streams of relief aid, charitable giving and new official budget lines to promote the latest aid fashion or destination. 'It can be like the Catholic and Protestant churches in Africa in the last century competing for converts,' notes an academic observer. 'They have to protect their budgets. And it is not all their fault. The European Union and individual governments, from whom they get much of their money, make the system very competitive.'[9]

SELF-REPRODUCTION Aid managers tend to see local institutions as incapable of absorbing and accounting for aid resources. Shortcomings on the recipient side have been 'seen as potentially disruptive of the donor agency's "production process", thus reinforcing the inclination among donors to grab a firmer control of the task of project design. The takeover of this task resembles the backward vertical integration of firms in the private sector. The organization expands "backwards" into the task environment and starts to "manufacture" project applications itself.'[10]

That is, chains tend to reproduce themselves. They do so, for example, when new issues crop up, exposing more gaps in local capacities. The system abhors a vacuum, so new bodies are routinely called into being to fill the gaps. From HIV/AIDS to governance to environmental management, aid activities have proliferated. Combined with a low mortality rate among aid initiatives, this high rate of birth generates a sizeable but greying bulge in the institutional population.

At this point it is useful to sketch the main institutions in the upper-middle ranges of aid chains. Their political anchoring and accountability were introduced in the preceding chapter. Some components and practices may be noted here briefly.

Multilateral Official Channels

Despite donor preference for their own, bilateral channels, multilateral aid made big strides in the 1970s as common needs among rich countries overcame their competitive urges. While OECD donors put 10 per cent of their ODA through multilateral channels in the 1960s, that share has hovered around 30 per cent since the mid-1980s. OECD countries in the 1990s disbursed their multilateral ODA in the following order of importance (with amounts given in inflation-adjusted dollars of 1998):

- The IFIs, including the World Bank group and their closely associated regional development banks for Asia, Africa, the Caribbean, Latin America, Eastern Europe, and other smaller funds together received an annual average of $7 billion or about 13 per cent of overall OECD country disbursements.
- European Union channels (the European Commission's joint programme and the separately-run European Development Fund) received an annual average of $4.6 billion or about 8.5 per cent of all OECD disbursements (for EU countries, these Europe-only channels absorbed about 16 per cent of all their aid spending).
- United Nations funds or specialized agencies (numbering close to 50 institutions) received an annual average of $4.2 billion or about 8 per cent of all OECD country disbursements.
- There are special arrangements for particular purposes. Among the best-known is the Paris Club, an informal group of 19 OECD countries constituting a joint front of official creditors to negotiate the rescheduling of debt owed by low-income nations. Since 1974 the French Treasury in Paris has served as the Club's secretariat.[11] Other examples include the Stability Pact for South Eastern Europe, a major transatlantic consortium formed in 1999 to co-ordinate economic, political and security aid in the Balkans, and the Utstein Group, formed in 1999 by aid ministers from Norway, the UK, Germany and the Netherlands for closer coordination and joint pressures on recipients to, among other things, curb corruption.

Of these, IFIs are the biggest players. They use their own accumulated revenues and raise large sums on private capital markets. All together in 1999 the multilateral banks made loans totalling $65.2 billion, of which 32 per cent went to Eastern Europe and the former Soviet Union, 31 per cent to Latin America, 28 per cent to Asia, 5 per cent to sub-Saharan Africa and 4 per cent to the Middle East.[12]

Other publicly owned development banks are increasingly active in lower-income countries. The EU's European Investment Bank, founded in 1958 chiefly to finance infrastructure in Europe, has begun making project loans (€6 billion in 2000) in Eastern Europe, North Africa and beyond.

The nominal joint management of multilateral aid chains brings advantages to donors. It helps cement international duties and policy consensus. It multiplies the impact of one's aid by combining it with others'. It can reduce risks of carrying sole responsibility if things go wrong. Other advantages claimed for multilateral aid – that it would improve transparency and quality, and reduce distorted choices based on individual donor self-interest – have yet to be realized consistently.

Multilateral aid limits opportunities for one donor country to fly its flag or to steer contracts toward its constituents. But multilateralism does hold advantages for certain countries, particularly for the well-connected. In 2000 the US treasury secretary extolled the multilateral banks for their benefits to his nation's economy, claiming that they had 'reduced tariffs in Mexico and opening up the Indian economy, which enormously benefit US producers. There are also more direct benefits for US companies: in 1998 alone, US firms received $4.8 billion from contracts arising from IFI investment and adjustment programs.'[13] That is, for every US tax dollar given to the multilateral development banks, US corporations gained about four dollars in added turnover.

When channelling their multilateral aid, OECD donors prefer the development banks above UN agencies. In the 1990s those banks received about 44 per cent of all donor disbursements to multilateral channels, whereas UN agencies got about 26 per cent of the multilateral pie. In principle, the UN's main policy-making forum for development, ECOSOC, should guide its aid. But in practice, central steering is weak. 'ECOSOC recommendations are not, however, binding on the specialised agencies. As a result, no real co-ordination occurred. ECOSOC was a post office, with in- and out-going mail both from the UN central bodies and the specialised agencies.'[14]

A practical coordinating mandate over UN agencies has fallen to the United Nations Development Programme (UNDP), set up by the General Assembly in 1965. Limited by its dependence on voluntary contributions, the UNDP's greater powers stem from its influence in policy and paradigms. In the battle of ideas inside the aid regime, the UNDP, together with the International Labour Organization (ILO), the UN Conference on Trade and Development (UNCTAD) and UN Children's Fund (UNICEF), have sometimes offered the only official dissent from the dominant ideas coming from Washington DC.

National Official Systems

Under rising pressures inside and out, national aid systems have tended to fragment. The most common schism is between the mercantile bloc, which pursues trade and investment gains for the donor's economic interests, and the development bloc, whose aims include growth, political stability or simple relief of suffering. Splits show themselves in struggles between ministries of finance and trade on the one hand, and ministries of foreign affairs on the other. Within official agencies, competing camps of 'bankers' and 'programme officers' crop up along similar lines. In recent decades, momentum has been with the business bloc.

Despite its apparent revival in the late 1990s, the anti-poverty camp in most national aid bureaucracies has had to cede ideological ground, authority and funds to new units set up for mercantile ends. The Canadian International Development Agency's Industrial Cooperation Program (CIDA INC) and the Swedish Agency for International Technical and Economic Cooperation (SWEDFUND) are examples. In the EU these publicly owned national banks are represented in a twelve-member group, the European Development Finance Institutions; together they accounted for nearly €1.7 billion in loans made in 1999, mainly in low-income countries. As the struggle for a good bottom line intensifies, tones of irony enter public debates about official aid. A recurring question is: are we supposed to do good, or merely to do well?

Even before official aid agencies appeared in the 1950s and 1960s, Northern governments had begun setting up banks and insurance companies to promote their national exports and private investment abroad. These export credit agencies (ECAs) and investment insurance agencies (IIAs) occupy a grey zone of official aid. Examples include the UK's Export Credits Guarantee Department, Canada's Export Development Corporation, Australia's Export Finance and Insurance Corporation, and a variety of US bodies including the Export–Import Bank, the US Overseas Private Investment Corporation and the Trade and Development Agency. Many Boeing passenger jets have been sold with this kind of help. The World Bank's Multilateral Investment Guarantee Agency does similar work. It too lacks transparency, rides roughshod over environmental norms and adds to social polarization. As of mid-2001 it faced a growing movement to end its public funding.[15]

Their targets are what are now termed emerging markets, where profits can be sizeable but political risk and poor infrastructure make things less attractive to private capital on its own. The business is big and lucrative: turnover for ECAs and IIAs is about $100 billion a year, dwarfing all official aid. The greater part of official debt of low-income countries is owed to ECAs. These agencies are close to the top of major aid chains. A recent study summarizes their importance as follows:

[ECAs and IIAs] are now the single largest source of taxpayer support for private sector companies seeking to off-load on to the public the financial risks of their business projects in the South and Eastern Europe. Ultimately, it is the poorest in these countries who end up paying the bill. ECA support now exceeds by far the total annual investments made by the World Bank and other multilateral development banks. With rare exceptions, the major ECAs lack mandatory environmental and development standards: in addition, they are secretive and unaccountable.[16]

These state-owned banks and insurance companies are part of every nation's arsenal in trade wars. Aid and development rhetoric helps protect them, just as camouflage netting helps protect field artillery.

Over time, Northern powers have agreed on rules of trade wars. To curb dumping and other competitive practices, they formed cartels. Under OECD auspices their representatives meet to regulate trade practices and to fix prices. One current problem is how to freshen the air where strong smells of corruption surround the deals they promote. Having long been in the shadows, export credit and investment insurance agencies are coming under public attack.[17]

One other kind of subsidy for the rich has been justified by its benefits for the poor: tax shelters. As part of its now defunct Caribbean Basin Initiative in the early 1980s, the US government revised its tax haven law, saying it would boost the economies of Barbados, Jamaica, Grenada and others specializing in offshore banking.[18] Basically a welfare scheme for footloose, often crime-linked capital, this law shelters billions of dollars a year, at no substantial benefit to equitable development in the Caribbean. Meanwhile the pay-off for other low-income countries is in fact a rip-off. Such market freedoms are a fraud, and carry obvious dangers for global security besides. Even the OECD and others in the policy mainstream are now uneasy, but they know exactly why such schemes exist. 'You ask why, if you believe there's an important role for a regulated banking system, do you allow a nonregulated banking system to continue?' former World Bank chief economist Joseph Stiglitz has said. 'The answer is, it's in the interests of some of the moneyed interests to allow this to occur. It's not an accident; it could have been shut down at any time.'[19]

BILATERAL AID AGENCIES A bilateral agency carries the donor country's flag and distributes the bulk of its aid budget.[20] Bilateral agencies once operated both as investment banks and as grant-makers. Today most make only grants or roll over debt. As agencies take on new objectives and tasks, there are signs of mission overloads. For two Swedish observers,

> An aid agency today resembles the old-fashioned department store, catering to every human need imaginable. Swedish aid, for example, has taken upon itself to assist developing countries in reducing their poverty. It shall, furthermore, work towards stimulating economic growth, a socially acceptable distribution of incomes, gender equality, protect the environment and contribute to a development of democracy and a respect for human rights.[21]

Fitted out like a Christmas tree with issues and priorities, some agencies appear to have almost decorative functions. The task overload feeds itself: as gaps between promise and performance come to light, donors and lenders reply with talk of new initiatives. By accumulating more aims and criteria, agencies find it harder to communicate on all sides without resort to deception.[22] Task overload means they have had no real focus, no touchstone of policy. In the late 1990s, there were signs of greater willingness to choose. Some bilateral agencies, such as the Danish, British and Australian, have begun moving poverty reduction to the heart of agency purposes.

SEMI-PUBLIC CONTRACTORS To cope with their many mandates, official agencies have learned to confine themselves to the wholesale end of the business. Bilateral agencies have largely stopped managing aid in detail with their own in-house staff. Instead, they prefer chains of outside organizations working under

contracts. Outsourcing has become axiomatic, lifted on an ideological tide of privatization.

Among those contracted are quasi-non-governmental organizations or quangos, public foundations, NGOs and for-profit
contracting firms. Here foreign aid differs little from practices
followed in Northern domestic realms of public welfare, culture,
education and science. An expanding Third Sector of contracted
organizations is praised as a powerhouse of civic initiative but

---

Box 4.1 Aid in Tanzania: Swedish ways, American ways

A five-year study of bilateral aid during the period 1965–95
in Tanzania reveals differences between the Swedish agency,
SIDA, and the American, USAID.[23] The study's main points
are as follows.

SIDA's approach was one of trust and long-term commitment. Swedish leaders at first held an idealized image of
Tanzania, whose post-independence leadership had a political
vision appealing to Swedish social democrats. It was Sweden's
worldwide policy to respect recipient nations' sovereignty
and to strengthen their public sectors. Aid should be recipient-
led – though with healthy doses of donor advice.

But in the mid-1980s, Sweden's domestic economy
dipped and a stronger pro-business mood emerged. African
economies, including Tanzania's, were in free-fall. Market
fundamentalism was riding high in the aid system. SIDA
stopped defending Tanzania's stand against orthodox structural
adjustment. It began to sing in 'the one-note choir of donor
voices'. Talk about recipient responsibility replaced talk about
recipient rights to chart their own course. 'SIDA's responsiveness … shifted from the recipient to the rest of the donor
community.'[24]

---

also criticized as an expedient means to privatize and thus shed public responsibilities towards the poor and excluded.

Patterns differ from country to country, but official aid has reinforced or created many thousands of institutions. As of the mid-1990s there were thought to be about 2,500 organizations of varying degrees of non-profit status, claiming to address problems of the South and East.[26] While many have accumulated tasks and resemble a department store, some are specialized. Contractors at

---

USAID's orientation was always upwards. Its Tanzania office's chief concern was accounting to Washington. By 1995, USAID's manual of administrative regulations ran to 37 volumes. The USA showed much less interest in Tanzania and provided far fewer resources than did Sweden. It showed little trust in Tanzanian capabilities. Washington dictated, Tanzania was supposed to listen.

USAID's field office enjoyed more autonomy than other donors in programme choices and spending. Its programming suffered from unstable, stop-go, *ad hoc* practices. Its rigid pro-market ideology, lack of interest in the public sector, learning disabilities and strait-jackets of rules meant low responsiveness to Tanzanian needs. Together with the World Bank and IMF, USAID used carrots and sticks to force Tanzania to undergo standard programmes of structural adjustment.

In short, by the late 1980s Swedish policy had fallen into step with the 'Washington Consensus'. Yet, the study concludes, this kind of top-down, ideologically driven 'donor coordination does not promote more effective aid'. That is because recipients have no control and feel no commitment. 'The end result is that foreign aid fails.'[25] It seems that recipient-led aid – the baby the Swedes threw out with the bathwater under pressure from Washington – was worth keeping after all.

middle levels in aid chains may be categorized according to specific task areas as follows:

Bursary management institutions　Brokerage on behalf of higher-level training institutions, especially universities, is a main task. Formal scholarship programmes gave this activity special prominence until the 1980s, when it became clear that higher education and the resulting skilled workforces can bring important benefits to Northern economies. In Britain, Australia, Canada and other countries, higher education is today a source of both prestige and foreign earnings. Like early food aid, bursary programmes helped create a lucrative market for Northern institutions. Examples include the British Council, the African–American Institute and the German Academic Exchange Service (DAAD).

Technical support and training institutions　Shorter and longer courses within existing universities, or purpose-made institutes around development disciplines, are key activities. Today, wider offerings in the South and East absorb much of the demand for specialized training, but Northern programmes aimed at specialists from lower-income countries continue. Examples are Carl-Duisberg Gesellschaft in Germany and the Royal Tropical Institute in the Netherlands.

Institutions for research and dissemination　University faculties or special units in agriculture, health and social sciences regularly get aid contracts. They train professionals from low-income countries. Some institutes receive funds and mandates to start or support projects directly. Some carry major roles in research and advice on economic policy. New issues such as conflict management have generated research–and–action NGOs and policy networks. Joint projects with Southern institutions are popular, even to the point of sharp competition among Northern university units pursuing counterparts in places like South Africa. Publishing and distance learning have grown as global communication costs have fallen. Examples include the UK's Institute of Development

Studies at the University of Sussex and the Australian Centre for International Agricultural Research.

Technical assistance institutions Following the boom of the 1960s and 1970s, many agencies that recruit and place 'volunteers' are today adjusting to reduced circumstances. Some of them have folded altogether, or have redesigned themselves for specialized tasks. Despite heavy criticism, technical assistance continues in part through quango and private aid agencies such as Denmark's MS, France's AFVP, Germany's Dienst in Ubersee, the UK's VSO, Canada's WUSC and CUSO, and the US Peace Corps.

Private aid agencies Non-profit development, relief and child sponsorship organizations took in at least $10 billion in 1998. In aggregate, about half of their income was from official sources, half from general public giving. Flows through these agencies might surpass one-quarter of total ODA, making them major players.[27] Grant-making bodies based on churches, trade unions or other social constituencies but subsidized with public funds are common in Europe. Together they form non-competing blocs accountable to aid ministries. Their closest counterparts in the USA are three statutory foundations making grants in Asia, Latin America and Africa. They, and aid bodies run by the US Democratic and Republican parties, superficially resemble German *stiftungen* run by political parties and financed with public funds. Those German party foundations, however, tend to innovate more and to exercise far more influence over aid and other foreign policy fields than do their US counterparts. Private agencies with specialized tasks in such fields as population, health or economic policy are effectively quangos bound to government through extended contracts. It's hard to distinguish some of them from for-profit contractors, described below.

Institutions to promote public awareness Official subsidies here have been controversial. Central governments of France and the USA provide next to nothing, while those of small trade-dependent countries such as the Netherlands and Sweden put millions into public education. Recipients include private aid agencies, action committees, non-profit media and other civil society bodies. These subsidies boost public commitment to foreign aid, but they may also have domesticating effects. Sharp debate and innovative criticism of foreign policy and foreign aid are heard with greater frequency in the USA and Britain – countries where public education and policy activism depend not on government subsidies but on citizens' initiative.

PRIVATE CONTRACTORS   To build a dam, audit account books or take a social survey, official aid agencies have always hired consulting firms. Among major aid contractors in the realm of information and ideas are five global companies: Anderson Worldwide, PricewaterhouseCoopers, Deloitte Touche, Ernst & Young, and KPMG. Working for both governments and corporations, they dominate markets in accountancy, management consulting and even legal advice. As authoritative private bodies with public tasks, they help promote the 'retreat of the state'.[28] In the 1990s the US government spent billions on their services to, among other things, usher capitalism into Eastern Europe and the former Soviet Union.

Technical assistance – the placement of experts – is a preferred way to influence entire public and private sectors, being a standard component of structural adjustment lending. This aid comes with a big price-tag: in the 1990s free-standing (that is, not project-based) technical assistance accounted for an average of $17 billion a year, or about 34 per cent of total net ODA. Add in the costs of technical assistance embedded in projects, plus administrative overheads, and the share of (foreign) personnel costs would approach half of total aid spending.

Procuring vehicles, tents and pumps is one thing. Managing complex social processes on behalf of poor people is another. Studies of outsourcing, for both domestic services and abroad, have questioned claims that it lowers costs and raises quality and efficiency.[29] In the USA, despite long experience in regulating private suppliers of public services, contracting welfare services tends to yield bad results.[30] Professional contractors may of course deliver expertise on particular issues in ways and at prices that no public service can match. But there is no convincing evidence of overall superiority. In balancing the interests of directors and shareholders against the interests of the poor and politically weak, firms will face obvious tensions.

This chapter has introduced the main kinds of aid agencies and how their ownership, control and tasks are affected by their place in the aid chain. Yet despite the uniformity of rules and the omnipresence of the chain, national aid systems differ from one another. Some of those differences appear in the following chapter, a continuation of this book's journey down the chain.

Notes

1. Tony Vaux (manager of emergency relief in Oxfam-UK for more than twenty years) cited in 'Stark relief', *The Guardian*, 16 May 2001.

2. For an example of the aid chain concept in use, see Fowler, A. and K. Biekart (1996) 'Do private aid agencies really make a difference?', in D. Sogge (ed.), *Compassion and Calculation: The Business of Private Foreign Aid*, London: Pluto Press, pp. 107–35.

3. For example, Pfeffer, J. and G. Salancik (1978) *The External Control of Organizations: A Resource Dependence Perspective*, New York: Harper & Row.

4. Raffer, K. and H. W. Singer (1996) *The Foreign Aid Business*, Cheltenham: E. Elgar, pp. 43–5.

5. Mkandawire, T. and C. Soludo (1999) *Our Continent, Our Future: African Perspectives on Structural Adjustment*, Trenton, NJ: Africa World Press, CODESRIA and IDRC, pp. 138–9.

6. Banekem, F. and C. Jepma (1999) 'Nederlands belang en ontwikkelingsbelang (Dutch Interest and Development Interest)' in J. Nekkers and P. Malcontent (eds), *De Geschiedenis van Vijftig Jaar Nederlandse Ontwikkelingssamenwerking (The History of Fifty Years of Dutch Development Cooperation, 1949–1999)*, The Hague: SDU Uitgevers for the Ministry of Foreign Affairs, p. 279.

7. Feigenbaum, H. and J. Henig (1994) 'The political underpinnings of privatization: a typology', *World Politics*, 42 (2): 185–208.

8. Johnson, C. (2000) *Blowback: The Costs and Consequences of American Empire*, New York: Henry Holt, p. 85.

9. 'Taking a first aid course', *Guardian Weekly*, 14 June 1998.

10. Hydén, G. (1983) *No Shortcuts to Progress: African Development Management in Perspective*, London: Heinemann, p. 178.

11. See Kaiser, J. (2001) *Debt management à la Louis XVI: A Short Promenade through the Programme and Practice of the Paris Club*, London: Jubilee Plus, web address: http://www.jubileeplus.org/analysis/articles/J_Kaiser_Paris%20Club.htm.

12. US Department of State, *Congressional Budget Justification for Foreign Operations, Fiscal Year 2001*.

13. US Treasury, news release 13 April 2000, quoting Treasury Secretary Lawrence H. Summers, cited in C. Adams (2000) 'Punishing the poor: debt, corporate subsidies and the ADB', *The Transfer of Wealth: Debt and the Making of a Global South*, Bangkok: Focus on the Global South, web address: http://www.focusweb.org.

14. De Feyter, K. (2001) *World Development Law*, Antwerp: Intersentia, p. 74.

15. Welch, C. and S. Zdeb (2001) *Risky Business: How the World Bank's Insurance Arm Fails the Poor and Harms the Environment*, Washington, DC: Friends of the Earth, web address: http://www.foe.org/international/worldbank/MIGAReport.pdf.

16. Hildyard, N. (1999) *Snouts in the Trough: Export Credit Agencies, Corporate Welfare and Policy Incoherence*, Briefing Number 14, The Corner House; web address: http://cornerhouse.icaap.org/briefings/14.html.

17. International ECA Reform Campaign website: www.eca-watch.org.

18. Library of Congress, n.d., Country Studies, Commonwealth of Caribbean Islands, http://memory.loc.gov/frd/cs/caribbean_islands/cx_appnd.html.

19. Cited in Komisar, L. (2001), 'After dirty air, dirty money', *The Nation*, 18 June, p. 16.

20. Official aid agencies rarely call all the shots about all aid chains. The US allocates its massive Economic Support Fund (ESF) – $2.3 billion in 2001 – mainly to Israel and Egypt, as well as 49 other countries or special activities from Burma to Haiti. None of these monies counts as ODA because none is for developmental or humanitarian purposes. USAID manages the ESF, but effective control is at higher levels, chiefly the Department of State.

21. Carlsson, J. and L. Wohlgemuth (2000) 'Learning in development co-operation. An introduction', in J. Carlsson and L. Wohlgemuth (eds), *Learning in Development Cooperation*, Stockholm: SIDA, p. 13.

22. Multilaterals also display this syndrome. See Wade, R. (2001) 'The World Bank as a *necessarily* unforthright organization', draft for G24 meeting, Washington, DC, 17–18 April, web address: http://ksghome.harvard.edu/~.drodrik.academic.ksg/G24Papers.htm.

23. Hyden, G. and R. Mukandala (eds) (1999), *Agencies in Foreign Aid: Comparing China, Sweden and the United States in Tanzania*, Basingstoke: Macmillan.

24. Elgström, O. (1999) 'Giving aid on the recipient's terms: the Swedish experience in Tanzania', in Hyden and Mukandala, *Agencies in Foreign Aid*, pp. 134 and 151.

25. Hyden, G. (1999) 'Foreign aid agencies, 1965–95: a comparative assessment', in Hyden and Mukandala, *Agencies in Foreign Aid*, p. 231.

26. Chabbott, C. (1999) 'Development INGOs', in J. Boli and G. Thomas (eds), *Constructing World Culture: International Nongovernmental Organizations Since 1875*, Palo Alto, CA: Stanford University Press.

27. Development Initiatives (2000) *Global Development Assistance: The Role of Non-Governmental Organisations and Other Charity Flows. Background Note on Section 4.1, DfID White Paper on Development*, Evercreech: Development Initiatives.

28. Strange, S. (1996) *The Retreat of the State: The Diffusion of Power in the World Economy*, Cambridge: Cambridge University Press, pp. 135–46. See also Simms, A. (2001) *The Five Brothers*, London: New Economics Foundation.

29. See studies cited in Berríos, R. (2000) *Contracting for Development: The Role of For-Profit Contractors in US Foreign Development Assistance*, Westport, CT: Praeger.

30. Rotker, K. (2001) 'Corporate welfare for welfare corporations', *Dollars & Sense*, January–February.

FIVE
Towards the Receiving End

When the dog was told that there was food for everyone at the wedding feast, he replied, 'We'll check that out at the ground level!' (popular saying, Niger)

This book's trip down the chain of aid began at the top, where the big ideas and rules are approved, in the safe hands of bankers and senior officials. One step further down, agencies and their contracted sub-agents translate those ideas and rules into budget lines, action and inaction. The preceding two chapters looked at those upper ends of the chain. This chapter continues the trip with the focus still on power – how aid chains build and retain it, and with what effects.

At lower levels, new segments and hangers-on appear. However, appearances can deceive. Aid can deliver bridges, vaccines and training services, but at the same time it can decimate, demoralize and corrupt a nation's corps of civil servants, teachers and health professionals. Recipients overtly welcome aid, but at the same time conceal their resistance to its rules.

At the receiving end are found political classes, public authorities, enterprises and public service systems and private contractors. At far ends of chains may be found actors in civil society. Fissures and hierarchies, often mirroring uneven development, are common here. Where foreign aid is a major source of jobs and the social wage of health and education services, and where debt repayment puts prior claims on revenues, the importance of aid chains to politics – who gets, what, when, and how – cannot be overestimated.

Chain Reactions

Aid chains do more than deliver. They also help gather information and transmit it back up the chain. Resources down, information up: that is the essence of the circuit. For some, images and stories drive a kind of humanitarian commerce. Highly successful charities depend on transmitting human interest material to those who pay to feel an inner glow of satisfaction by, for example, sponsoring a child in a faraway land. At best only half their revenues reach the end of their aid chains, the rest being absorbed in packaging, advertising, and administering their feel-good product.

Information is also the basis of accountability. In most aid chains, participants account upwards, towards funding authorities: their reports on wells dug in the recipient land, and pumps purchased in the donor land, may be crucial to negotiating next year's budget. How valid is the information? Unfortunately for both effective management and accountability, it can hide more than it reveals. Those whose livelihoods and careers depend on continued funding defend themselves by filtering and colouring information going up the chain. So begin dissembling games to keep the bosses and visiting delegations happy, the empty project façades 'for the English to see'.

Aid is supposed to foster self-reliance and thus put itself out of a job. Yet when talk turns to exit strategies, the tone is rarely one of pride and cheer. Among the development banks, agencies, project units, companies, non-profits and consultants, dependence on aid has grown. These make up aid's hardcore political constitu-ency: coalitions with incentives to keep things rolling, keep things quiet (if not secret), keep united fronts in the face of criticism and keep postponing their farewells. Many at the receiving end also hold stakes in the status quo. A Swedish observer concludes pessimistically: 'After several decades of building institutions dependent on donor financing, neither the donor nor the recipient seems to be able to envision institutions which can be financially sustained by domestic resources.'[1]

If aid dependence at the upper ends of aid chains was a sub-theme of prior chapters, this chapter's sub-text is aid dependence at lower ends. Aid dependence often matches its intensity – as indicated by aid's share of recorded GNP. The table in Appendix C presents data on 117 countries over three decades. An aid share of 10 per cent of GNP is considered very high. Where such rates persist over more than a decade, one can speak of severe aid dependence.

High aid intensity is not necessarily a bad thing over limited periods. The economies of Botswana, Taiwan and Korea were once highly geared to aid. But after its importance tapered off, competent and self-reliant states were left behind. Since the 1970s, aid intensity has declined in a few countries such as Yemen and Egypt, but in many more it has risen. Aid dependency is a matter of duration. Of 29 countries in which aid represented 10 per cent or more of recorded output in the 1990s, 17 had shown similarly high rates of aid intensity in the 1980s.

PROLIFERATION PRESSURES AND THE GARBAGE CAN   Recipients are blamed for failing to call the shots and to manage aid well. Such accusations sound valid at first, until it is recalled that aid was never theirs to control in the first place. They stand at the end of a cascade of decisions from above. Today a rising chorus of voices calls for demand-driven aid and recipient ownership. Yet many continue in their supply-driven, donor-owned ways. They justify their refusal to give up control by the passivity, incompetence and corruption they often see around them at the receiving end. Yet how did such problems arise in the first place? In many cases the aid system itself is not without blame.

At the receiving end, the multitude of aid-driven activities frustrates government efforts to govern. Officials often do not know with any accuracy who is doing what, with whom and under what terms. Aid flows in with no central oversight. It thus often lacks coherence. Country surveys of aid reveal an abundance of projects across levels, sectors and territories, but many activities escape those surveys. In broad lines, there is a double distortion: official data commonly overstate the value of flows reaching the end of aid chains, and understate the numbers of projects and the chains that bind them.

The problem in Africa is worsening. A recent study concludes that in the early 1980s Malawi was struggling 'under the burden of trying to manage 188 projects funded by 50 different agencies. Yet Kenya had 2000 donor-funded projects in 1996 and Tanzania in 1997 had 1800, while war-torn Mozambique was trying to keep track of 405 health projects funded by different donors.'[2]

Only a few aid-supported governments have managed to orchestrate aid and make it fit national priorities. They had bargaining powers because they preserved their state apparatus and showed self-confidence in the face of donor arrogance. Botswana succeeded, according to a former senior World Bank official, because it 'sent the IMF packing'.[3]

If aid chains have one law of motion, it is: Move the Money. The prosperity of aid institutions and the careers of people who run them depend on making funds flow. Cycles are short and tempos are rapid. Disbursement pressure was first diagnosed in the 1970s.[4] Since then it has been regularly deplored, though rarely by senior aid officials, whose job it is to ask for *more* money for their agencies. Aid managers are normally rewarded for spending or lending large amounts in limited periods of time. Their pursuit of 'partners' and activities will be relentless and competitive. They will hunt down places that can be targeted as 'under-borrowed'. Their usual attitude is, 'a bad project is better than none at all'.[5]

These pressures and attitudes distort views of problems and of local capacities. The result can be bloated, bankrupting initiatives. A seasoned development economist was thus moved to write a book about aid in Africa:

> Many have commented on how damaging this 'fund channeling effect' is to the quality of the projects that are funded ... If there was one single factor behind my determination to write this book

it is personal experience of the way project proposals are rated as good or bad solely by their size ... Last, but far from least, there is the way project staff become overwhelmed by demands not merely to spend the money originally allocated but to expand and take up more and more new activities, in order to use extra funds that donors have been unable to dispose of as they had originally planned. Through the developing world there are good little projects, kidnapped by aid and inflated into bad large projects by the pressure to expand at a pace far beyond any reasonable expectation.[6]

Over-funding favours leakage and sloppy management. A close observer of the issue writes: 'Competing for relatively small markets forces donors to ignore warning signs of lack of capacity, quality or integrity among recipients. Donors have no incentive to look for proof of corruption when they are themselves force-feeding the beneficiaries, who may receive large grants on the basis of mediocre or negative track records.'[7] Confronted with such charges, aid managers may cry murdered innocence. Yet the evidence of their complicity is mounting. A review of 30 years of aid-driven agricultural policy in Africa concludes that:

> all evidence suggests that the huge burst of agricultural spending in Africa of the mid-1970s, had a largely negative effect through contributing enormously to the decline in efficiency and honesty of the parastatal agencies through which it was channeled. That is, much of the inefficiency, which neo-liberals see as just an automatic consequence of 'state-control', was actually the result of ... large and poorly-controlled aid inflows during that period.[8]

Such pressures help promote the 'garbage can model'. This is a chaotic and wasteful cycle of policy-making first identified in public sectors of rich countries,[9] but widely observed where foreign aid is at work. It goes roughly like this: someone with a solution goes out in search of problems; problems are identified not in their own terms, but rather in terms of the ready-made solution; programmes are then drawn up with little time for research and testing, a lot of money up front, and little attention to how benefits will be sustained after the agency withdraws.

Solutions can thus generate other, often bigger, problems. But these become apparent only after those responsible for the first steps have moved on, and probably up, in their careers. Others are left to sort out the mess. Their solutions in turn create further problems, which then pass to others, and so on. Aid system incentives to keep the cycle turning over are strong; incentives to learn, to do things thoroughly and to stop this perverse cycle are weak. Under other names, the garbage can has long been known to aid specialists. A book about crippled or comatose aid initiatives, *Project Rehabilitation in Developing Countries*,[10] testifies to its widespread recurrence.

THE BIG BYPASS   A strong odour of the garbage can hangs over efforts to bypass national authority at the receiving end. Getting around bureaucratic blocs is of course not always a bad thing. In the early 1950s the USA insisted on bypassing vested interests in Taiwan and Korea in order to redistribute assets. In the end the strategy improved public authority, and thus the environment for growth. (See box 6.1.) Since then, however, the aid system has tended to squeeze recipient public sectors with austerity, segment them with projects, and bypass them with special task units. The results can be crippling.

Aid agencies, and expatriate managers and technicians representing them, set up and run these special units. Local professionals and other staff hired away from their country's civil service also work in them. With better staff, more money and autonomy, these aid units form privileged enclaves tasked with controlling resources and demonstrating results.

Project implementation units have seen widespread use. In Nigeria the World Bank used them to manage agricultural projects. Having more resources than the normal public sector, these units formed *de facto* a parallel Ministry of Agriculture. But after a few years everyone faced austerity and downsizing. The resulting departmental conflicts, demoralization and institutional damage left the Nigerian public sector, and Nigerian agriculture, weaker than before.[11]

'Integrated rural development' had disintegrating effects, as the recent history of Sierra Leone suggests:

> [D]onors often 'carved up' the territory of African countries, dividing it into a number of area projects, each managed by a different donor, with different objectives, equipment, extension agents and programs. In Sierra Leone, for example, the World Bank managed the Eastern Integrated Agricultural Development Project, while the Germans had the Bo Rural Development Project, and the EC funded the Northern Integrated Agricultural Development Project, etc. In most of these cases, the underfunded Ministry of Agriculture watched from the sidelines.[12]

In the 1980s, Nordic donors created MONAP, the Mozambique-Nordic Agricultural Programme. A central management unit absorbed about one-quarter of this $192 million, twelve-year effort, on which dozens of other costly aid chains depended. As in Nigeria, it constituted a parallel rural development authority.[13]

The aid system did not bring on instability and decline in rural Nigeria, Sierra Leone and Mozambique. But where aid deliberately bypassed national systems, it helped marginalize, fragment and de-legitimize national authority. In those cases, the aid system at best did nothing to block the political forces that ripped those countries' social fabric. At worst, it helped set the stage for those forces.

Despite this dubious record, special units remain the preferred means of managing aid. '[A] recent OECD and UNDP study of the aid system in Mali showed that between 1985 and 1995, the majority of donors used project implementation units rather than working through the regular bureaucracy; some donors, including USAID, the World Bank, and Germany (GTZ) used them for *all* of their projects in Mali.'[14]

Donors and lenders like special project chains because they enhance their control and lower the risk of delay, leakage to corruption, and big discrepancies between original design and end results. A professor of business administration with years of aid management experience has concluded: 'This model is in many ways the ultimate expression of a lack of trust in the recipient's ability, in combination with a lack of faith in the long-term possibility of improving capacity in the recipient's public sector.'[15]

Though diagnosed decades ago, the syndrome continues: special organizations create islands or enclaves that end up serving neither the public good nor, in the long run, the aid system itself. A rural sociologist with 20 years' experience of aid efforts summed it up in the early 1980s as follows: 'The paradox we see repeated in program after program is that in order to meet ambitious production goals new projects exclude themselves from the very organizational frameworks they are claiming to influence.'[16]

PRIVATIZATION AND DECENTRALIZATION Marginalizing national authority has gone hand in hand with downsizing and privatizing public sector management. Aid-driven pressures to decentralize have spread like a fever, creating yet more entry points for aid. Mozambique's 1997 local government law, for example, expressly permits municipal authorities to knock on donor doors. In Tanzania and Uganda, state functions are shifting to scores of quangos, firms and lower levels of government.[17]

Shifting power to democratic city governments can be a very good thing. In countries such as Brazil, South Africa and the Philippines, citizens have shown they can mobilize and voice their interests to make devolved power work for them. City politics, and negotiations around public services, can sometimes create spaces for democratic practice. In them, donors and their agents no longer face up the chain of aid but face downwards to end users.

Where citizens can defend their interests as payers of taxes and service charges, positive scenarios are possible. But that is not necessarily what the top of the aid system has in mind. For the IFIs want central governments to repay their foreign debts above almost everything else. That often means curbing and downloading spending responsibilities to lower-level authorities or private service providers. Privatization of water and other public services is also a priority because large Northern-based corporations see profitable opportunities there. To these ends, the IFIs have worked hard to insulate central treasuries from public claims. It is increasingly clear that their 'enthusiasm for decentralization derives more from adjustment requirements to relieve national public deficits and manage the debt crisis than it does from broader democratic goals'.[18]

CONTRACTORS LOWER DOWN AID CHAINS Having largely pulled out of field operations, official agencies' tasks today centre on supervising short-term contractors: for-profit and non-profit bodies, quangos, and even local government bodies forced to compete with the rest. According to market doctrine, the best possible services will be delivered at the lowest possible price thanks to competition among these contractors.

In practice, however, delivery often falls short of what market ideology promises. Many services are monopolies, and thus vulnerable to abuse. Regulation to protect the public interest is weak or non-existent. Consumers of services are unorganized and uninformed.[19] Goods and services gravitate towards those who can pay; the poor get the short end.

In such situations, informal processes crowd out formal rules, know-who overwhelms know-how. Donors find the tables turned on them as local elites learn to play the game. In Kenya, for example, those elites made sure that their women's NGO became the privileged channel for aid to women's activities.[20] In Mali, government officials played on divisions and spending pressures within USAID to favour certain local road-building enterprises.[21] If they act shrewdly, local elites can thus wield important influence lower down aid chains.

In the 1980s, Northern private aid agencies, their Southern branch offices and local NGOs gained prominence and status. This is readily apparent to informed observers in the South, such as the Indian journalist P. Sainath: 'Development theology holds that NGOs stand outside the establishment. They present a credible alternative to it. The majority of NGOs are, alas, deeply integrated with the establishment, with government and with the agenda of their funding bodies.'[22]

Agencies prefer to control chains right down to their presumed end points. They thus seek NGOs as go-betweens with local people. Where such segments are missing, donors may simply create them. Typical is the case of Marangsingh, a small poor village in Nepal, described in a donor magazine article. Having noted foreign agencies' success in bypassing central authorities, the article continues enthusiastically:

> Perhaps the most convincing indicator of success for Marangsingh's nearly-completed irrigation system is the Farmers Irrigation Association, which was created according to the requirements of Danida and the ILO as a prerequisite for their support. Recognizing that a strong, active local organization is essential for sustainability, the donors stipulated that they would only work through such organizations, and they recruited a social organizer... from a local NGO to help set one up.[23]

Building aid chains down to the grassroots is an old practice. In the 1950s in India, the Ford Foundation and the US government promoted 'community development', along with micro-enterprise, to crowd out left-wing political movements.[24] In the 1970s and 1980s, the practice reappeared on a bigger scale as 'integrated rural development'. These approaches failed not only because they tried to impose new power structures answerable to donors, but also because they opened the door to local opportunists answerable only to themselves.

In the face of aid system demand, both local elites and anti-poverty activists become enthusiastic organizers of a suitable supply. Politicians and officials create their own organizational chains in the form of cooperatives, development associations and new settlements. Aid has revived and recast older organizational forms, such as the social foundations or *yayasans* of Indonesia or the hometown associations of Africa. These may reflect genuine civic spirit, but in the hands of aid-supported elites they can camouflage political patronage networks and tax dodging.[25] From Liberia to Laos, opportunistic local organizations have sprung up in their thousands.

'Participation' is supposed to enhance the power of those at the receiving end. In practice, participation can amount to little more than swinging a shovel and following somebody else's plan. Control, not self-determination, is often the purpose. This aspect of aid chains is detectable in a UNDP project in The Gambia:

> Although the project plan for GAM/94/001 was supposed to be a 'grassroots' project based on 'identified needs' its design focused on implementation and monitoring of a preconceived set of eight outputs and 32 activities in 20 pre-selected villages. One result was to encourage project managers to focus on producing the specific products for which they would be held accountable rather than on the processes and partnerships that would be needed to sustain these products once the project funding stopped.[26]

Nevertheless, some organizations and local authorities are genuinely responsive to local priorities, committed and downwardly accountable. Politically astute and ethically motivated aid agencies have sometimes enabled them to emerge. Human rights movements in Latin America and relief programmes for Eritrea and Central America have demonstrated the possibilities. Such approaches stand out because they tend to succeed where others fail. The evidence is overwhelming: initiatives designed and driven from the outset by indigenous actors are at lower risk of failure than aid-driven initiatives, whose rates of failure are notoriously high.[27]

But where aid intensity and pressures to spend are high, the authenticity of local initiatives will tend to be low. Non-profits are either organized by donor agencies themselves, or spring up as entrepreneurial ventures to meet donor specifications. Organizations that were once member-driven have been converted into contracting social enterprises driven by competition for the donor dollar. USAID and the World Bank pioneered public service contracting of non-profits in Latin America, and the practice has spread elsewhere. Yet despite these seductive pressures, downward accountability and transparency in aid-supported popular organizations still function.[28] There are, in short, hopeful signs that aid chains do not inevitably put end users in shackles.

Consequences

Let us take stock of the previous two-and-a-half chapters. By noting some effects of aid chain dynamics, and emerging alternatives, this chapter sets the stage for the coming two chapters on the respective role of politics and ideas.

This journey down chains of aid has drawn attention to their growing numbers and the types of participants in them. Among the driving imperatives are: pursuits of economic and political aims that may or may not be coherent; drives to enter new territories with fashionable new product lines, in order to compete in markets for charitable giving and official aid contracts; incentives for new aid market entrants such as universities, city councils or oil companies; pressures to move big amounts of money in limited periods of time; pressures to control resources down to end points, using purpose-made organizations; and the perverse syndrome of the garbage can: solutions-that-beget-problems-requiring-solutions-that-beget-more-problems.

Keeping the focus on core participants, it is useful to sketch some of the effects of aid chains, in three overlapping clusters: learning effects, economic effects and political effects.

LEARNING EFFECTS   Case studies point to a scarcity of good learners at upper and middle reaches of aid chains.[29] This is not surprising. Big hierarchies based on command, control, secrecy and technocratic optimism are notoriously bad environments for learning how to learn. Know-it-all attitudes and the notion that 'there is no alternative' have made things worse by sweeping ideas from the table as forbidden and beyond discussion.

Learning disabilities have been detected in many aid agencies, including the World Bank. Such defects are contagious. Disabilities high on aid chains get passed right down the line. For example, a mediocre and largely unsuccessful model of rural extension had been approved far up the line, mainly in Washington, DC, yet aid workers struggling with its failure at ground level lacked power to tackle the upstream source of the problem.[30] At the receiving end, the following problematic effects show up again and again:

- Waves of multiple and often incoherent purposes cascade over recipients; they come rarely as choices, as on a menu, but rather as prescriptions imposed by powerful outsiders who have done all the thinking on the recipient's behalf; initiatives thus lack anchoring in national policy elites, let alone local popular wishes.
- Satisfying upper-level needs for information sets the direction, pace and content of learning; short-run needs for data about money, operations and immediate outputs combine to discourage learning about long-term purposes and knock-on effects; staff turnover drains the 'institutional memory'; where those at upper levels face pressures to tell stories with happy endings to their funding authorities, then discordant voices and accounts of failure will be ignored or punished; there will be no embracing error as a means of learning.[31]
- Lower on aid chains, recipients dependent on aid will tend to prettify or conceal information about its effects, supplying only that information that matches outlooks and prejudices of those with powers to cut off flows of resources;

- Standardized solutions promoted down the chain predispose actors to ignore local contexts, close off alternatives and under-cut recipient self-confidence and respect for local views and problem-solving capacities.[32]
- Incentives usually reward spending and action rather than inquiry, reflection and debate; aid managers are generally un-willing to spend money and time on testing and learning as these are slow, yield results that cannot be photographed, and are thus written off as non-essential.[33]

The garbage can shields policy-makers from punishment. In 1935, one of the godfathers of market fundamentalism, Ludwig von Mises, argued that socialist planning was a bad thing because planners 'could never improve upon capitalism because they would just "play" a market game without being disciplined for their mistakes. The same doubts apply to Washington-based bureaucrats "playing" at running national economies with their attention focused on career advancement in the institutions back in the United States.'[34] Error and failure are routinely reproduced because these Market Leninists enjoy non-accountable power. As a political scientist once quipped, being powerful means you can afford not to learn.[35]

The idea that organizations should learn how to learn has inspired many positive effects. But it is also controversial. Learning is no good thing if it merely helps the powerful do a better job of coercing others and silencing dissenters. In this sense, learning disabilities at the top of aid chains may have blocked improve-ments, but at the same time afforded dissenters useful occasions to sharpen their critiques and counter-proposals.

ECONOMIC EFFECTS Aid chains not only channel resources, they absorb them. Costs of management and public relations have to be met all the way down. As new agencies enter the market, competition intensifies. Those dependent on charitable giving have to advertise to stand out from the rest. Everyone ends up spending more on marketing and less on concrete activities. In Britain, the average charity in 1992 spent 80 per cent of its funds on programming; in 1997 it spent only 67 per cent.[36]

Where many parties are linked, there come additional costs of merely transacting business: contracts to be negotiated, compliance to be monitored, tenders to be issued, and so forth. The less the basis for trust, the greater the need for legal, auditing and even security services. Money channelled through strangers bound in impersonal contracts is 'cold', and requires safeguards. That pushes up costs. All other things being equal, the greater the trust, the lower the costs along an aid chain.[37] Aid based on solidarity can be more efficient than aid based on the politics of domination.

Aid demands the time of senior officials at the receiving end. As others are also bidding for that time, its price tends to rise. Aid then becomes a pay-off to authorities for their attention and loyalty. As a former senior US aid official points out, it 'is a little like political campaign contributions: it can facilitate the access of those providing it to those receiving it'.[38]

Aid dependency can trap recipients in cycles of low efficiency and low effectiveness. The garbage can of cascading policies and the sub-industry of project rehabilitation add to costs. Recipient capacities to manage their own affairs and mobilize their own revenues are thus bled by a thousand cuts. Among the most commonly cited are:

- drain of the time of national officials, who must deal with demands for access, information, logistical help to hundreds of aid-related visitors, and participation in workshops of some-times dubious value for hosts, though of importance for prestige-seeking donors;[39]
- drain of staff from public sectors into aid agencies and their projects;
- drain of public revenues, as priority goes to debt repayment and the running costs of aid-financed investments;
- reduced tax effort and reduced revenue self-reliance;[40]

- Lost investments, and lost momentum due to stop-go, chop-and-change behaviour by donors and lenders; the more volatile the aid, the less effective it is.[41]

When such effects are combined with market fundamentalist measures to force down real wages and cut back the social wage of public services, capacities to govern will tend to worsen. In many African settings, 'more aid actually weakened the polity. The proliferation of donors with individual projects created a complex nightmare of planning, oversight, evaluation and negotiation in weak states. Donor demands overwhelmed government capacity.'[42] As early as the 1960s, observers had detected public institutions in Africa buckling under aid pressures. But only in the mid-1990s did the World Bank and others begin to rethink absorption capacity as a cluster of problems to which the aid system itself contributes.

POLITICAL EFFECTS Weakened in these ways, public sector management is often neither robust nor responsive to citizens. Where public services and protection worsen, reciprocal give and take between citizens and officials will decay. Recent political history in Africa and the republics of the former Soviet Union show this. As aid chains grow, the following patterns in political life tend to emerge.

- For rulers and insider political classes generally, lines of accountability run upwards and outwards, chiefly towards donors/lenders, but also towards those with private financial and commercial power; downward accountability to citizens becomes empty ritual; the externalization of governance is today most apparent in heavily aid-dependent countries such as Malawi and Nicaragua.
- For citizens, development choices and initiatives are in the hands of foreigners or local actors who 'do their thing' but are not accountable to public authority; this creates a 'tyranny of structurelessness' in which a lot seems to be going on, but

there is no coherence and little forward motion;[43] commitment to public services diminishes, thus further eroding national politics and state legitimacy already made fragile by mal-distribution and mal-administration.

- Where not (or no longer) enjoying access to aid, competitor political movements will face incentives to set up their own aid chains, such as from ethnic diasporas in richer countries; they may use violence to corner markets in drugs, diamonds and other contraband, making political life even more fragile.

- The state will lose powers to negotiate and enforce terms for foreign trade and investment, thereby weakening safeguards for social, political, cultural and environmental interests.

- Growing cleavages and competition among groups and agendas in civil society, as backed or opposed by donors (for example, social strata and business groups privileged by outwardly oriented policies versus labour and human rights groups); sometimes, as in the case of Kenya, these compete with other groups backed by the ruling politicians.[44]

Such outcomes are not inevitable. In recent decades, Sri Lanka reduced donor steering, while Vietnam never allowed donors to gain an upper hand in the first place. Finally, aid can have emancipatory political effects. Financial aid to activist groups and independent media has sometimes helped bring about major non-violent political change. The case of Scandinavian and other European aid for groups pursuing majority rule in southern Africa in 1970–94, and US and European aid for Serbia from 1999 to 2001, show that aid can be effective if carefully provided to emancipatory social movements.

Some Ways Out

When tribunes of the aid system announce a 'new approach' or a 'major advance', the response is often a big yawn. And rightly so; after all, a lot of yesterday's widely heralded innovations –

getting prices right, integrated development, basic needs – today sound like sales talk about dubious second-hand autos. Many today rest on a junk-heap of cast-off ideas.

Yet almost any innovation that promises to counter the worst effects of power inequalities, and to nudge the aid system towards norms of mutuality and democracy, merit attention. A few approaches now detectable outside the mainstream show some promise.

SOUTH–SOUTH AID   Pioneered by Cuba, Vietnam, China and Taiwan on a country-to-country basis and multilaterally by the UN programme of Technical Cooperation among Developing Countries and the UN Volunteers, this approach draws its strength from the closeness of fit between Southern technicians and their Southern host environments. Programmes built around the Northern Expert have been dogged by problems of socio-economic distance, cultural gaps, high costs and mediocre results.[45] Such problems do not disappear where people are recruited in lower-income countries, but they tend to be less acute. Aid chains tend to be shorter and less expensive. A few technical assistance agencies are recruiting more people from the South and East.[46] Stimulating South-South ties are regional and global political links promoted, for example, through the Group of 77 countries of the South.[47]

REGIONAL INTER-GOVERNMENTAL ACTION   The idea of neighbours jointly tackling neighbourhood problems has natural appeal. To manage shared resources in river basins, to study crop varieties and health problems, or to combat crime are all purposes attracting recipients and donors alike. Where they are responsive to people of a region, inter-state bodies can help shift authority and accountability downwards. Anchored in this way, they might provide regional public goods that are better-targeted and more sustainable than those promoted through aid chains from above and outside.[48]

The merits of regional initiatives will depend, however, on

whose interests they serve. Donors have usually welcomed regional technical and economic action where it locks peripheral economies more firmly into systems of trade and investment serving donor economies. The Southern African Development Community is a case in point. Set up in 1980 by nine African heads of state to counter apartheid South Africa, it rapidly became a platform by which aid providers mounted transport, communication, and other projects to reinforce external trade. Improving internal African markets was a sideline. A main result is the region's increased outward orientation – including its debt bondage worsened by those lender-led projects.

ACTIVIST, PROFESSIONAL, AND MUNICIPAL NETWORKING Organized in networks rather than chains, lateral flows of knowledge and ideas are spreading thanks to falling costs of telecommunication and travel. In technical realms from potatoes to pastoralism, much of this is initiated by aid agencies. In other realms – mutual learning between South Africa and South Asia about organizing low-income neighbourhoods, flows of Brazilian NGO know-how to Angola, or the global campaign against privatization of drinking-water systems – activists have taken the initiative to enrich their practice and motivate one another. These networks are helping redefine the alternatives, build recipient self-confidence and consolidate social movements. In the face of this competition, the World Bank is scrambling to reassert its intellectual authority, as discussed in Chapter 7.

The role of non-professionals has been a fresh addition, though it is largely under-reported in official aid statistics. Initiated in Europe in the early 1950s, the practice of twinning or city-linking gained momentum in North Atlantic countries in the 1970s.[49] Today thousands of local government bodies manage aid for purposes ranging from fire-fighting to city management. While many are modest and hinge on solidarity, others involve big stakes. For example, an alternative to automobile-centred urban transport has emerged since 1992 in Kunming, China, whose urban planners sought technical cooperation from counterparts from Zurich, Switzerland. That sister-city programme is one of thousands now enjoying public subsidies across Europe and Canada. In France, half of all provinces and the majority of large and mid-sized municipalities run 6,000 such initiatives in 114 countries.[50]

SECTOR-WIDE APPROACHES   In the 1970s a few donors began experimenting with aid targeted at whole sectors such as health, transport and fisheries, or to categories such as urban development, embracing many sectors within limited zones. Nordic and Dutch bilateral agencies saw it as the path to greater strategic effectiveness, improved chances of sustaining benefits, and greater control and responsibility at the receiving end.

In practice, however, IMF and World Bank supervisors override recipient control. A surfeit of 'reform', mainly promotion of market fundamentalism, has replaced a surfeit of projects. Outside control has thus increased. Yet a few have moved to shift power towards recipients. In the mid-1990s the Nordics and Dutch revived original aims to enable national governments to set anti-poverty priorities for certain sectors and negotiate funds accordingly. In principle, recipients rather than aid providers are in charge. Health and education are the main sectors tested thus far.[51]

Recipients welcome the sector-wide approach because it allows them more room for manoeuvre. But the approach faces several challenges. To be negotiated and managed well, sectoral programmes require sophisticated policy expertise; many governments, particularly those subject to decades of downsizing and brain drain, don't have this capacity.[52]

Second, to promote anti-poverty action, political leaders have to turn their policy compasses around. Some of them are accustomed to calling in the police, if not death squads, when challenged by those demanding a better deal for the poor. Elites have grown accustomed to being told that greed is good and that benefits of growth may some day trickle down to the poor. In many places, top dogs benefiting from market fundamentalist policies – the sell-off of public assets, the rise in private schools and clinics and good private housing – are not about to welcome policies benefiting bottom dogs. Unless of course the bottom dogs can bite.

A third challenge is convincing donors and lenders to let go. They will have to give up their entanglements with long aid chains and hangers-on, their wish to fly their nation's flag and to promote their professional careers through projects. Under recipient-driven aid they will have to content themselves merely with writing cheques and ensuring that accountability develops within countries, perhaps at the cost of accountability to themselves.[53]

The Like-Minded group of the Nordics and the Dutch, now joined by the UK and Ireland, intends to move further in this direction. The World Bank is also enthusiastic, but seems incapable of kicking its habits as a control freak, poor listener and poor learner.[54] The sector-wide approach may thus collapse, like so many other well-meaning aid initiatives, under the weight of centralized control. Yet, scaled up and taken to a logical end, the sector-wide approach could one day transform aid provision into something resembling the EU's Structural Funds: collective sector revenues going routinely via public channels to reduce inequalities among regions.

LOCAL FUNDS UNDER PUBLIC MANAGEMENT A small-scale variant of sector-wide, recipient-controlled aid is the local development fund. With it local authorities invest in infrastructure and services at county or district levels while at the same time enabling citizens to learn what it's like to plan and control public choices. In the 1990s the UN Capital Development Fund adopted this approach, thus moving beyond the crowded and problematic field of micro-finance. In 1997 the Danish agency Ibis began developing it in northern Mozambique, an area of low literacy and no history whatsoever in democratic planning. Today these agencies and their local collaborators can point to promising results in improved public decision-making and improved public goods.[55]

The approaches hold promise because they keep important choices in the public realm and hold public officials accountable to citizens rather than to donors. Harmful aid practices that bypass public institutions and politics, effectively casting them on a garbage heap to rot, are thereby curbed. These funds are variants of the public action approach – a topic to be revisited in the concluding chapter.

Conclusions

Much of the foregoing suggests the value of pursuing shorter chains, horizontal links among neighbours and other lower-income lands, the breaking up of aid industry monopoly practices and, above all, the closing of gaps between citizens at the receiving end and those who take aid decisions on their behalf.

To do away with the coercive, centralized, capricious, self-interested and undemocratic practices guiding aid up to now, a number of seasoned aid specialists have made creative proposals for change.[56] A common denominator is a joint funding pool. That kind of fund could be set up at regional, sub-regional or even national levels and fed by funding authorities: rich country parliaments, or, in more Utopian versions, a United Nations empowered to tax as well as to spend. Governments would draw on such funds according to plans generated by open political processes. Public watchdogs using local languages, especially in the electronic media, would follow the money from start to finish. Donor agencies' powers would shrink. The World Bank and its associates would cease to be privileged public institutions. A regulated private banking sector would fill the gap.

Such ideas may sometimes betray unchecked enthusiasm for setting up new institutions without pausing to look at potentials, case by case, of existing public bodies. Normal public social security systems, for example, are far more cost-effective than specially created social safety nets or the proliferation of charity NGOs. Public systems have been adapted and broadened for anti-poverty purposes in India and other very low-income countries.[57] Thus the potentials of the recipient-driven, sector-wide approach remain to be developed. Much depends on the adequacy of public institutions and the quality and transparency of the politics that drive them. The following chapter expands on those issues, which the aid industry has recently rediscovered.

Notes

1. Edgren, G. (2000) 'Fashions, myths and delusion: obstacles to organisational learning in aid agencies', in J. Carlsson and L. Wohlgemuth (eds), *Learning in Development Cooperation*, Stockholm: SIDA, pp. 41–68.

2. Bräutigam, D. (2000) *Aid Dependence and Governance*, 2000: 1, Stockholm: Almquist & Wiksell for the Expert Group on Development Issues, p. 25, web address: http://www.egdi.gov.se/pdf/20001pdf/2000_1.pdf.

3. Joseph Stiglitz, cited in 'IMF's four steps to damnation', *The Observer* (UK), 29 April 2001.

4. Tendler, J. (1975) *Inside Foreign Aid*, Baltimore, MD: Johns Hopkins University Press, pp. 88–90.

5. From an OECD study cited in van de Walle, N. (1996) 'The politics of aid effectiveness' in S. Ellis (ed.), *Africa Now. People, Policies and Institutions*, The Hague: DGIS (Netherlands Ministry of Foreign Affairs), p. 239.

6. Morton, J. (1994) *The Poverty of Nations: The Aid Dilemma at the Heart of Africa*, London: British Academic Press, pp. 23–4.

7. Cooksey, B. (1999) 'Do aid agencies have a comparative advantage in fighting corruption in Africa?', *9th International Anti-Corruption Conference, Durban South Africa*, Transparency International, web address: www.transparency.de/iacc.

8. Friis-Hansen, E. (2000) *Agricultural Policy in Africa after Adjustment*, CDR Policy Paper, Copenhagen: Centre for Development Research, p. 95.

9. Cohen, M. and others (1972) 'A garbage can model of organizational choice', *Administrative Science Quarterly*, 17: 1–25; John, P. (1998) *Analyzing Public Policy*, London: Pinter, pp. 174–5.

10. Kirkpatrick, C. (ed.) (1991) *Project Rehabilitation in Developing Countries*, London: Routledge.

11. Paul, S. (1990) *Institutional Development in World Bank Projects: A Cross-Sectoral Review*, Working Paper 392, Washington, DC: World Bank Country Economics Department, p. 40.

12. Bräutigam, *Aid Dependence and Governance*, p. 39.

13. Adam, Y. (1991) *Aid Under Fire: An Evaluation of the Mozambique–Nordic Agricultural Programme (MONAP)*, SIDA Evaluation Report 1991/1, Stockholm: SIDA.

14. Bräutigam, *Aid Dependence and Governance*, p. 32.

15. Valdelin, J. (1998) 'Aid management' in L. Wohlgemuth and others (eds), *Institution Building and Leadership in Africa*, Uppsala: Nordiska Afrikain-stitutet and African Development Bank, p. 206.

16. Moris, J. (1981) *Managing Induced Rural Development*, Bloomington, IN: International Development Institute, p. 49.

17. Therkildsen, O. (2001) 'Efficiency, accountability and implementation of public sector reform in East and Southern Africa', *Democracy, Governance and Human Rights Programme Papers*, No. 3, Geneva: UNRISD, web address: http://www.unrisd.org/cgi-bin/.

18. Burgess, R. and others (1997) 'Contemporary policies for enablement and participation: a critical review' in R. Burgess and others (eds), *The Challenge of Sustainable Cities*, London: Zed Books, p. 147.

19. For evidence regarding water privatization see Hall, D. (2001) *The Public Sector Water Undertaking – a Necessary Option*, Public Services International Research Unit (PSIRU), University of Greenwich, web address: http://www.psiru.org/.

20. Aubrey, L. (1997) *The Politics of Development Cooperation: NGOs, Gender and Partnership in Kenya*, London: Routledge.

21. Koenig, D. (1997) 'Competition among Malian elites in the Manantali Resettlement Project: the impacts on local development', *Urban Anthropology*, 26 (3–4): 369–411.

22. Sainath, P. (1996) *Everybody Loves a Good Drought: Stories from India's Poorest Districts*, London: Penguin Books India, p. 338.

23. Helmore, K. (1994) 'Development moves downstream in Nepal', *Choices*, New York: UNDP Division of Public Affairs, December, p. 24.

24. Holdcroft, L. (1982) 'The rise and fall of community development in developing countries 1950–1965', in G. Jones and M. Rolls (eds), *Progress in Rural Extension and Community Development*, Vol. I, London: Wiley, pp. 207–31.

25. In Bénin, more than half the deputies in the National Assembly run or take part in hometown development associations. Hibou, B. and R. Banégas (2000) 'Civil society and the public space in Africa', *Codesria Bulletin*, 1, pp. 39–47. In Indonesia, President Suharto and his family founded close to twenty *yayasans* with links to family business holdings.

26. McMillan, D. (1997) 'Renegotiating development partnerships: a case

study of national execution of a UNDP program in the Gambia', *Urban Anthropology*, 26 (3–4): 314.

27. See, for example, Uphoff, N. and others (1998) *Reasons for Success: Learning from Instructive Experiences in Rural Development*, West Hartford, CT: Kumarian Press; and Bonnet, B. (2001) 'Shared management of common resources: strengthening local skills', Montpellier: Institut de Recherches et d'Applications des Méthodes de Développement (IRAM), web address: http://www.iram-fr.org/.

28. Biekart, K. (1999) *The Politics of Civil Society Building: European Private Aid Agencies and Democratic Transitions in Central America*, Utrecht: International Books.

29. See Carlsson, J. and L. Wohlgemuth (eds) (2000) *Learning in Development Cooperation*, Stockholm: SIDA. On organizational learning, see Argyris, C. and D. Schön (1996) *Organizational Learning II*, Reading: Addison-Wesley.

30. Hulme, D. (1994) 'Does the World Bank have a learning disability? A reply to Venkatesan', *Public Administration and Development*, 14: 93–7; and Standing, G. (2000) 'Brave new words? A critique of Stiglitz's World Bank rethink', *Development and Change*, 31, especially pp. 752–8.

31. Walkup, M. (1997) 'Policy dysfunction in humanitarian organizations: the role of coping strategies, institutions, and organizational culture', *Journal of Refugee Studies*, 10: 37–60; and Edwards, D. (1997) 'Organizational learning in non-governmental organizations: what have we learned?', *Public Administration and Development*, 17: 235–50.

32. See Wallace, T. and others (1997) *Standardising Development: Influences on UK NGOs' Policies and Procedures*, Development Studies Series No. 1, Oxford: WorldView Publishing and Development Administration Group, University of Birmingham.

33. In the 1990s small networks of researchers and agency staff began dismantling some barriers and build an 'academic–practitioner interface' (Alan Fowler, personal communications). Further progress will depend on the setting: official and private aid agencies and academics in the UK tend to be more engaged with applied research than their counterparts in the Netherlands, for example.

34. Pieper, U. and L. Taylor (1998) 'The revival of the liberal creed: the IMF, the World Bank, and inequality in a globalized economy', in D. Baker, G. Epstein and R. Pollin (eds), *Globalization and Progressive Economic Policy*, Cambridge: Cambridge University Press, p. 62.

35. Karl Deutsch, cited in Wendt, A. (1999) *Social Theory of International Politics*, Cambridge: Cambridge University Press, p. 331.

36. 'Crowded out by the competition', *Guardian Weekly*, 7–13 December 2000.

37. Fowler, A. (1982) 'Temperatures in development funding: the hot money model', *Development: Seeds of Change* (2): 81–2.

38. Lancaster, C. (1999) *Aid to Africa: So Much to Do, So Little Done*, Chicago: University of Chicago Press, p. 118.

39. See Hunter, G. (1969) *Modernizing Peasant Societies*, London: Oxford University Press; Morss, E. (1984) 'Institutional destruction resulting from donor and project proliferation in the sub-Saharan countries', *World Development*, 12 (4): 465–70.

40. Moore, M. (1997) 'Aid and tax effort in developing countries', unpublished IDS paper cited in Mosley, P. and M. Eeckhout (2000) 'From project aid to programme assistance', in F. Tarp (ed.), *Foreign Aid and Development*, London: Routledge, p. 140.

41. 'Aid inflows account for half of budgets and half of imports in the poorest countries, so that aid volatility generates fiscal and macroeconomic instability. Further, the recipient agencies cannot make long-term plans to improve health, education and infrastructure if future resource flows are uncertain. This leads to microeconomic inefficiency and a tendency to "take everything that is offered".' FitzGerald, V. and A. Cobham (2000) *A Waste of Development? The Volatility and Pro-Cyclicality of Official Flows to Developing Countries*, Oxford: Finance and Trade Policy Research Centre, Queen Elizabeth House, for DfID White Paper on Globalization.

42. Hopkins, R. (2000) 'Political economy of foreign aid', in F. Tarp (ed.), *Foreign Aid and Development*, London: Routledge, p. 430.

43. As noted in Tvedt, T. (1998) *Angels of Mercy or Development Diplomats? NGOs and Foreign Aid*, Oxford: James Currey.

44. Maina, W. (1998) 'Kenya: the state, donors and the politics of democratization', in A. Van Rooy (ed.), *Civil Society and the Aid Industry*, London: Earthscan, pp. 134–67.

45. For an optimistic overview see Arndt, C. (2000) 'Technical co-operation' in F. Tarp (ed.), *Foreign Aid and Development*, London: Routledge, pp. 154–77; for an anthropological view of power plays in technical assistance see Crewe, E. and E. Harrison (1998) *Whose Development?*, London: Zed Books.

46. Of the 700 aid workers contracted by the Dutch semi-governmental aid agency SNV as of 2000, for example, about 40 per cent were from Southern countries.

47. See, for example, Khor, M. (2001) 'A South–South meeting to face

up to global forces', web address: http://www.twnside.org.sg/title/2136.htm.

48 Cook, L. and J. Sachs (1999) 'Regional public goods in international assistance' in I. Kaul and others (eds), *Global Public Goods: International Cooperation in the 21st Century*, New York, Oxford: Oxford University Press for the UNDP, pp. 436–49.

49. Schuman, M. (1994) *Towards a Global Village: International Community Development Initiatives*, London: Pluto Press.

50. Raffoul, M. (2000) 'La cooperation décentralisée, nouveau champ de la solidarité internationale', *Le Monde Diplomatique*, July.

51. Foster, M. and others (2000) *The Status of Sector Wide Approaches*, London: ODI, web address: http://www.odi.org.uk/.

52. See Samoff, J. (1999) 'Education sector analysis in Africa: limited national control and even less national ownership', *International Journal of Educational Development*, 19, pp. 249–72. Less pessimistic is Engberg-Pedersen, P. (1998) 'Successful capacity assistance for sector development', in L. Wohlgemuth and others (eds), *Institution Building and Leadership in Africa*, Uppsala: Nordiska Afrikainstitutet and African Development Bank, pp. 214–30.

53. See Schacter, M. (2001) *Sector Wide Approaches, Accountability and CIDA: Issues and Recommendations*, Ottawa: Institute on Governance, web address: www.iog.ca. Thanks to John Saxby for calling attention to this paper.

54. Jones, S. (2001) *Increasing Aid Effectiveness in Africa: The World Bank and Sector Investment Programmes*, Oxford Policy Management, web address: http://www.opml.co.uk/.

55. For UNCDF experiences see website: http://www.uncdf.org/. An overview of Ibis in Mozambique, written by the author, appears at: http://www.um.dk/danida/ngostudier/Kapacitetsanalyse/8_ibis/mozambique/.

56. Kanbur, R. and others (1999) 'A radical approach to development assistance', *Development OUTREACH*, 1(2); Griffin, K. and T. McKinley (1993) *A New Framework for Development Cooperation*, Occasional Paper 11, New York: UNDP web address: www.undp.org/hdro; Edwards, M. (1999) *Future Positive: International Co-operation in the 21st Century*, London: Earthscan; Hyden, G. (1995) 'Reforming foreign aid to African development: the politically autonomous development fund model', *Development Dialogue*, 2, Stockholm: Dag Hammarskjold Foundation, web address: http://web.africa.ufl.edu/asq/v2/v2i2a1.htm.

57. Cornia, G. A. (2001) 'Social funds in stabilization and adjustment progammes: a critique', *Development and Change*, 32: 1–32.

SIX
Governance without Politics?

Lack of accountability in international affairs has cost millions of people their lives, condemned billions to extreme poverty and threatens our environment.[1]

It is a commonplace to deplore foreign aid's links with politics. The high moral ground is supposed to belong to aid leaders, not to cynical strategists and their *realpolitik*. Aid managers like to depict it as apolitical, a branch of applied rationality inspired by humanitarianism. Aid is supposed to be a kind of antiseptic medicine, free of impurities, prescribed by benevolent professionals. Politics are unfortunate pollutants spread by meddlesome non-professionals: politicians, NGOs, and foreign policy mandarins at the upper ends of the aid chain, or by manipulative, parasitic authorities at the lower ends.

But consider the case of aid to Yugoslavia. In 1989–90, when officials from Washington, DC were assembling a new aid package for that country, they may have sincerely believed that the conditions they demanded in exchange for aid were merely self-evident economic truths. Whatever their intentions, their prescriptions took no account of the fears Yugoslav citizens had about their livelihoods and well-being. Indeed, aid officials ignored clear warnings about the inflammable state of politics in the Balkans. Claiming apolitical intentions, they insisted on wholesale public sector cutbacks, mass sackings of enterprise workforces, reduced pay for the armed forces, and radical decentralization. Predictably, these policies helped trigger a violent backlash by ethnic-nationalist forces bent on breaking up the country.[2]

So began Yugoslavia's descent into the abyss of warlord rule, upheaval and mass murder. Did it fall or was it pushed? Direct evidence is scarce because details of IMF negotiations are secret. But to the extent that they set the stage for politico-military conflict, those at the top of the aid system were seriously – perhaps criminally – negligent.

Setting the Stage

The portrayal of development aid as apolitical and non-ideological, like a kind of engineering, is mythology. Doctrines propagated by the US Treasury, IFIs and the OECD are deeply political, as are the Market Leninist methods used to apply them. Yet for decades the camouflage of technical benevolence has served both givers and receivers well.

Some modernizers may continue in their optimism that better-managed and more autonomous bureaucracies are the key to success. Their claim is that aid professionals can come up with the right formulas and achieve their development mission – but only if elected officials and lobbies keep their distance and let the experts get on with the job. Better management and technical knowledge are of course desirable. But it is doubtful that aid's chief shortcomings are found at this level. In any case, claims for the efficacy of aid's 'technical fix' look exaggerated. As policy activists have long insisted, and as some agencies now tacitly accept, it is naive and even self-defeating to keep pretending that politics are not at the heart of aid. The real issue is: politics on whose terms?

This chapter considers aid against the background of its zig-zag political career. It reviews a shady past: paying off anti-democratic rulers, beefing up governments and re-engineering whole societies. It tells several stories of the 1980s and 1990s: the counter-revolution in aid policy and the drive to overcome recipient resistance by re-engineering governance. It concludes by suggesting that the point is not to continue dreaming of a politically chaste, technocratic form of aid, but rather to bring politics to the surface and democratize them.

A FEW REMARKS ABOUT POWER The interplay of aid and power can be profound, but power is not one thing. The political economist Susan Strange distinguished two kinds of power in global affairs: relational power, which tends to be coercive, direct and consciously applied, and structural power, which tends to be indirect and even unconscious.[3] The first is at an episodic, cause-and-effect level, such as in sanctions, trade negotiations, small wars, aid conditionality and other kinds of international arm-twisting.

The second, structural power, works at levels where norms and ideas are made and where domination does its quiet work. Gender studies have contributed to an understanding of it. Outcomes may be unmistakable, but perceiving how they came about is not easy. Spheres of influence illustrate this kind of power. Canadians are constantly aware of the shadow cast by their hegemonic neighbour to the south. Simmering popular anger in the Islamic world towards US power may, as of September 2001, have begun to register in Western consciousness. Powers of those disembodied things, The Markets, to punish governments is another example common in business-page editorials. Nevertheless, structural power is rarely the stuff of headlines.

Most writing about aid draws attention to the episodic cause-and-effect levels of power. Here aid serves simply to reward or punish recipients, controlling their behaviour in the short term. Depending on the giver, aid can indeed buy political support. UN votes, for example, can be bought where the USA does the buying.[4] Japan makes no secret of its use of aid to deflect political problems, such as criticism of its whaling policies. In 2001, aid was the Serbian government's reward for delivering ex-President Milosovic to the UN War Crimes Tribunal. Yet the long lists of those not complying with loan conditionalities, or of the collapsed states that were once major aid clients, suggest that aid's powers to change behaviour may be overrated. However, failure to achieve advertised effects does not mean that aid's political effects are nil.

ROGUES' GALLERY In the public imagination, foreign aid has tended to keep bad company. In its past is a rogues' gallery of political clients ranging from slightly buffoonish figures like the 'Emperor' Bokassa of the Central African Republic to the sinister Marcos and Duvalier dynasties in the Philippines and Haiti. In the patron–client politics binding rich and poor country elites, the top of the aid system regarded such figures in much the same way that a US president once regarded a Latin American *caudillo*: 'He may be a son of a bitch, but he's *our* son of a bitch.'

Perhaps because of this dubious past, mainstream writings on aid often gloss over its interplay with politics. Optimists today see aid helping to sweep the villains out and usher in Good Governance. Political institutions are now considered ripe for reform. Terms such as 'empowerment' and even 'rights' have begun to compete with 'growth' as leading aid system by-words.

Today we are asked to believe that those bad old clientelist practices are things of the past. If only that were true. A recent cross-country study addressing the question 'Do corrupt governments receive less foreign aid?', concluded that:

> there is no evidence that less corrupt governments receive more foreign aid. On the contrary, according to some measures of corruption, more corrupt governments receive more aid. Also, we could not find any evidence that an increase in foreign aid reduces corruption. In summary, the answer to the question posed in the title is 'no'.[5]

After Alberto Fujimori came to power in Peru in 1990, Washington's aid (and Japan's) shot up and continued backing that increasingly authoritarian and corrupted regime to the bitter end, ten years later. In the case of Russia, the attitude at the top of the aid system in Washington was, '"We wanted Yeltsin re-elected.

WE DON'T CARE if it's a corrupt election."'[6] Telling these kinds of truths cost Joseph Stiglitz his job in 1999 as chief economist at the World Bank. His dismissal at the behest of the US Treasury suggests how the top of the aid system itself is governed.

Today's expressions of moral indignation about oligarchs and dictators suggest selective memory, or haste to forget the past. That is understandable, for the top of the aid system has frequently colluded in bad governance. That is not only because it helped keep the Marcos and Mobutu regimes in power, but also because it helped re-configure whole societies.

SOCIAL ENGINEERING Shaping social strata and geographies has been among aid's important if usually unspoken purposes. A former senior aid official summarized the overall logic of Western policy as follows: 'economic growth would create a middle class with property interests which, however small, would make its beneficiaries hostile to political instability in general and Communism in particular'.[7]

Yet, in a couple of early instances, Western powers were unwilling to wait for markets to work their magic on class structures. They intervened politically to put redistribution before growth. The marginalization of big landowners and creation of small farmer systems helped put Korea and Taiwan (see Box 6.1) on successful capitalist growth paths. Foreign aid played important parts at decisive moments.

The historical moment was special. Early Cold War drives for security required stable, broadly shared growth in Japan and other Asian satellites. The egalitarian model of social engineering in mainland China posed a competing alternative. Economic thinking in the West was not yet in the grip of market fundamentalism. The USA in particular applied its aid as one element of a broad, coherent political strategy to strengthen Asian economies. Its motto was roughly: To keep things the same, things have to change. It cleared a path for Asian capitalism crucially by helping redistribute assets, especially land, then helping shelter internal

Box 6.1 Redistribution before growth:
Taiwan and Korea

Those running foreign aid for East Asia in the 1950s did things that today's aid doctrine outlaws. They used massive and coercive state power to take from the haves and give to the have-nots. The USA feared that without guided redistribution from the top down, change would come from the bottom up. 'U.S. assistance produced changes in rural Taiwan that, in magnitude and complexity, approached a social revolution.'[8] Once broken up and in new hands, land and other assets became the means by which millions could earn a living, start saving, pay taxes and begin to consume more. As a case of applied political economy it worked well.

Korea and Taiwan used state power to protect infant industries, control foreign investment, and import know-how. The US opened its huge consumer market to Asian exports without insisting that the Asian doors swing open to US products. Protected local capitalists gladly ploughed profits back into the home market. Having flattened out pyramids of income, political leaders further boosted everyone's life chances, and the quality of workforces, by investing in health and education. That required strong public sectors and government planning. As a result, national economies began to take off.

These and other East Asian 'miracles' had huge shadow sides. Until the 1990s the political classes in Korea and Taiwan ruled with iron fists. They were ugly, but those governments did deliver broadly rising living standards during a phase of intense accumulation. That is in contrast to today's aid-led doctrine, which merely promises to deliver improvements at some vague future time. The economic historian Irma Adelman concludes bluntly: 'had the neo-liberal "Washington Consensus" been enforced on the East Asian miracle countries during the 1950s, 1960s and early 1970s, there would not have been an East Asian miracle'.[9]

markets in which purchasing power was broadly based across a narrow band of income levels.

Yet the redistribution–before–growth strategy was not to be repeated, although there were plenty of other opportunities. In Latin America between 1930 and 1955, agrarian reform had built up political momentum. The USA might have helped this movement, thus ending a highly unequal, and un–dynamic, pattern of land–holding, as in Taiwan and Korea. The Cuban revolution forced agrarian reform on to the agenda in the 1960s. Aid-supported studies and policy utterances began drawing attention to the importance of agrarian systems led by small producers. This meant taking tough political positions.

The USA responded in two ways. It used aid to domesticate politics. In the north east of Brazil, where poor peasants and farm labourers were joining a movement for social justice, the USA mounted a massive aid programme to kill it. The episode was later termed 'the revolution that never was'.[10] The other, less overtly political approach was to promote technical fixes such as Green Revolution agriculture and the private market in land. This fitted well with polarized agrarian systems whose centre-pieces were big farms and ranches. Aid technocrats and local allies argued that wholesale land reform would depress output. Here, as in so many other cases, the short term pushed aside the long term.

Talk about poverty and redistribution–with–growth was reaching a climax in the mid-1970s, but it ended in a whisper. The World Bank insisted on respect for 'the existing social system' and for the need of 'avoiding opposition from powerful and influential sections of the rural community'.[11] In the 20 years that followed, serious talk of asset redistribution was not heard in aid corridors of power. The benefits of growth would eventually trickle down. Patience was the by-word.

Farm surpluses exported as foreign aid led to social engineering spontaneously via markets for food and labour. Food aid meant lower costs for wage-earners, but deeper and wider rural poverty and rising displacement of poor people to the urban periphery.[12] Of course food aid sometimes helped people in distress. But by depressing prices and introducing new diets and tastes (such as for bread) it helped speed up the destruction of small-scale farming and raise the import bill. Aid did nothing to stop, and in some cases actively helped promote, the polarized, hyper-urbanized and unjust societies that market forces also promoted, but without the pretence of helping anyone.

Aid has been part of coarser forms of social engineering. Hearts-and-minds campaigns in wars from Vietnam to Guatemala exemplify coercion. Ethiopia's Dergue government in 1985 enjoyed a rapidly rising tide of aid from the USA and others. While pursuing a brutal war against sub-groups in the population, the regime forced over four million people to quit their homes and to resettle far away in villages of exactly one thousand persons each. A 1973 World Bank memo on resettlement probably inspired the scheme. Foreign aid did not support it directly, however, thanks to an international outcry. But aid then pouring into Ethiopia proved 'fungible', that is, it released government resources for the purpose.[13] Aid agencies were not leading actors in these tragedies, but they did play supporting roles.

More benign but still coercive was the case of Tanzania, where in 1973–76 five million people were bullied into model communal settlements, backed by aid resources. Here too the government, not the aid agencies, took the initiative. But as the political anthropologist James C. Scott notes in a powerful study of modernization and social engineering:

> Setting people into supervised villages was emphatically *not* uniquely the brainchild of the nationalist elites of independent Tanzania. Villagization had a long colonial history in Tanzania and elsewhere, as program after program was devised to concentrate the population. The same techno-economic vision was shared, until very late in the game, by the World Bank, United States Agency for International Development (USAID), and other

development agencies contributing to Tanzanian development. However enthusiastic they were in spearheading their campaign, the political leaders of Tanzania were more consumers of a high-modernist faith that had originated elsewhere much earlier than they were producers.[14]

Aid in these African cases did not trigger coercion like a switch turning on an electric current. Rather it helped spread, validate and promote ideas. It set agendas. Its power was permissive. Aid's plentiful presence made such massive social engineering seem affordable. The creation of 'state peasantries' is a further example of social engineering in Africa, where rural schemes stressed micro-management of people's lives:

> An even more thorough form of social and political organization imposed from above has been the numerous but widely scattered integrated rural development schemes favoured by the World Bank and other international lenders in the 1970s. In a cotton scheme in Burkina Faso, settlement pattern, house design, and pattern of work were all designated by the scheme … In Zambia similar controls were exercised, although some representation from scheme members was built into the scheme … The limit is probably reached with the sugar schemes in Kenya, where the members sign contracts with the scheme management, setting out in great detail the work of the members.[15]

Many of these schemes rest on a triple alliance of the state, local labour, and private capital co-financed by official aid agencies. Western firms, not necessarily the giants, have been the preferred business partners for aid. Local residents are not partners or even clients, but mere means of production. The effect is to deny people control over their lives. A detailed study of one such triple alliance notes the frustrated local 'attempts to establish some form of control, in a situation where the … villagers as a whole had experienced a sharp decline in their control over their own society'.[16]

Aid and (Dis-) Empowerment

Power also operates by removing issues from the realm of politics. Some cases from Africa suggest why many continue to welcome the aid and development enterprise even when its projects fail.

In a detailed study of a failed multi-million-dollar programme in Lesotho, the anthropologist James Ferguson argues that the aid system has a two-edged effect. First, it 'is a machine to reinforce bureaucratic state power, which incidentally takes "poverty" as its point of entry'. Second, in the guise of 'a neutral, technical mission to which on one can object' it de-politicizes both poverty and the state. Like the 'anti-gravity machine' of science fiction, the aid and development apparatus is able to 'suspend politics from even the most sensitive political operation' and thus to function as an 'anti-politics machine'.[17] This begins with definitions of reality. Aid planners could represent Lesotho as 'a nation of farmers, not wage laborers; a country with a geography, but no history; with people, but no classes; values, but no structures; administrators but no rulers; bureaucracy, but no politics. Political and structural causes of poverty in Lesotho are systematically erased and replaced with technical ones.'[18]

In the Lesotho case, aid's advertised purpose of poverty reduction came to little. Does it matter? Ferguson argues that failure does not matter much to national and local authorities because, whatever its impact on poverty, aid reinforces their reach and patronage powers. For this reason 'it does become less mysterious why "failed" development projects should end up being replicated again and again'.[19]

Something similar, but more tragic, emerges from a meticulous study of aid in Rwanda up to the genocide in 1994. Using the concept of structural violence, the political scientist Peter Uvin reaches similar conclusions:

> Unfortunately, the development aid system is not simply in-effective, unsustainable, limited and uncertain in its impact — unsatisfactory as that may be. It also contributes to processes of

structural violence in many ways. It does so directly, through its own behavior, whether unintended (as in the case of growing income inequality and land concentration) or intended (as in the condescending attitude toward poor people). It does so indirectly, but strengthening systems of exclusion and elite building through massive financial transfers, accompanied by self-imposed political and social blindness.[20]

In post-communist Eastern Europe and the ex-Soviet Union, political 'big men' have shrewdly used aid to tighten their grip through systems of patronage and coercion.[21] The evidence and arguments just reviewed are compelling. But they skirt some important areas where the aid regime has worked deliberately, if not always observed, to re-engineer public sectors and governance.

PUBLIC SECTORS   At one time long ago, strengthening the state was one of aid's main purposes. In the 1950s and 1960s, before they began applying budgetary fire and sword to public sectors, donors actively favoured state intervention. They helped public sectors to grow and supply goods and services. Foreign economists helped draw up comprehensive national five-year plans, and, at more practical if gender-blind levels, manpower plans. The Ford Foundation promoted the cause of public sector management, investing in institutes of public administration, forerunners of today's capacity-building programmes.[22] Bilateral donors backed higher education, funding expansion of universities in the South and bursary programmes in Northern institutions for the best and brightest students from the South. The aim was to build effective, modernizing states.

State ownership, according to earlier aid doctrine, could be a good thing. In 1969 the government of Zambia nationalized the copper mines – as advised by seasoned British development economists. Rudimentary urban welfare schemes, inspired by Fabian socialism in the case of Britain, also appeared. Prevailing development thinking left little room for doubt: the state, helped by aid agencies and private banks, should expand the scope of its activities in the economy and beyond.

Meanwhile, across the post-colonial world, thousands of trade unionists, journalists, religious activists, students, intellectuals and others were calling for good governance and opposing abuse of state power and public revenues by donor darlings such as Hasting Banda in Malawi and Zia ul-Haq in Pakistan. Towards the critics and reformists, however, a typical gesture among aid providers was a shrug of the shoulders. For aid managers, criticism of sitting regimes was just left-wing rabble-rousing.

COUNTER-REVOLUTION: SEND IN THE TANKS Recipient countries were thus poorly prepared for the about-face in aid doctrine in the 1980s. Reaching full flower in the Thatcher and Reagan administrations, the counter-revolution in economic thinking had been brewing since the 1930s, when right-wing intellectuals and businessmen in the USA and Britain began 'thinking the unthinkable' against prevailing Keynesian paradigms of the regulating, active state.[23]

'Shrink the state' became a donor battle-cry, with the World Bank, IMF and USAID leading the assault. Aid to the public sector was cut back on the disputable grounds that it might crowd out private sector investments.[24] In conditions attached to hundreds of structural adjustment loans, aid providers required governments to sell off enterprises, slash payrolls and cut public sector spending. The axe sometimes fell where it hurt only a privileged few, such as national airlines. It may of course be no bad thing to end public subsidies to automobile assembly plants and luxury hotels whose chief purposes are prestige or mere convenience for elites. But many cuts came down in ways that hurt millions, such as in food subsidies, social security systems, schooling, medical supplies, and public power and transport. Aid system leadership assumed, correctly in most cases, that consumers of public services, and the suddenly impoverished employees that provided them, could not mount effective resistance.

To avoid unpleasant surprises on that front, donors and lenders promoted two kinds of political measures. One, well-advertised, was the creation of social funds, especially for wage-earners hit hardest by austerity. These were, in the words of a development bank official, the 'ambulances' sent in after the 'tanks' (structural adjustment programmes) had done their work.[25] In the end these social safety-nets have had little impact on poverty, although they may have helped defuse discontent in urban areas.[26] A second measure came with much less fanfare. IFI loans were given on the implicit condition that protection of waged labour would be weakened.[27] This meant crippling trade unions – in some places the most effective actors in civil society.

By the mid-1990s, across much of Africa, the ex-Soviet Union and other countries, these aid-driven measures, and general economic decline, had helped push public sector management towards collapse. Corruption spread, reaching down into citizens' daily lives, where medical orderlies managed queues of patients or where teachers graded students' exams. In many places non-state actors, from criminal mafias to big companies, began pushing aside the enfeebled state and its weakened police, judiciary and tax authorities. Whatever give-and-take there may have been between citizens and states began to crumble. As intended, the state had been well and truly shrunk.

ON SECOND THOUGHTS ... But then aid system leaders changed their minds again. In the mid-1990s, after nearly two decades in earnest pursuit of downsizing, Washington began to cool its hostility to the state. It claimed that its real mission all along had been to build more effective and efficient public sectors. This shift was an act of self-preservation, for no aid agency can survive unless it can move its money safely and in bulk. That cannot happen in the absence of a functioning state at the receiving end. Without public systems, legitimate private businesses run for the exit, viable projects evaporate, civil society organizations shrivel up, and loans become uncollectable. In its enthusiasm to shrink the public sector, the top of the aid system had turned into a dead-end street. Chastened, aid leaders started talking about 'right-sizing' government. In 1997 the World Bank issued a book-length statement of its revived faith in the state.

Market fundamentalism was meant to rescue the economy from the dead hand of the state and put it in the safe hands of bankers, technocrats and the thrusting new class of entrepreneurs. But in the ex-Soviet Union, Ghana, Mozambique and Uganda, the enrichment of foreign asset-strippers and domestic political cronies disguised as entrepreneurs has been a main outcome of privatization.[28]

As of the late 1990s, even doctrinaire insiders were adjusting their views of aid's power politics. Elliot Berg, one of the early architects of austerity, looking back on more than fifteen years of failure, offers compelling testimony: 'To a degree unparalleled in history, outsiders have introduced, even imposed, reforms intended to change the way that sovereign governments organize themselves and spend their money. Donor agencies crafted the reforms, financed them, and played a big role in their implementation.'[29] He deplores the 'hubris to which World Bank staff is prone' and their 'natural tendency to resort to off-the-shelf solutions' shown in the pursuit of an elusive sacred knowledge called 'best practice'.[30] Yet the fault, according to Berg, was not with the basic ideas of 'reform', but with the lack of donor cunning in packaging them. The name of the game is how recipients can be made to 'own' the policies donors want.

CONDITIONALITY AND THE PRETENCE OF 'OWNERSHIP' Although aid agreements have always included conditions, only in the 1970s did conditionality crystallize into formal demands for structural adjustment. Presented as expert and neutral advice from bodies with global, multilateral standing, World Bank and IMF conditionalities were in fact highly political and coercive.

Resistance to aid conditionality, and efforts to break that resistance, have been sources of drama in country after country.

Whether this drama takes the form of tragedy or farce is not always clear, as most episodes take place behind closed doors; actors on both sides tend to keep quiet about who capitulated to whom. As coercive processes carried out in the name of expanding freedom, they are symptomatic of aid's incoherence.

Yet while the donors' agendas were political, their approach betrayed a certain innocence of political strategy. For their borrowers rapidly learned to play the game, out-manoeuvring aid managers for years on end – without, of course, calling attention to that embarrassing fact. *The Economist* sketched the following picture in 1995:

> Over the past few years Kenya has performed a curious mating ritual with its aid donors. The steps are: one, Kenya wins its yearly pledges of foreign aid. Two, the government begins to misbehave, back-tracking on reform and behaving in an authoritarian manner. Three, a new meeting of donor countries looms with exasperated foreign governments preparing their sharp rebukes. Four, Kenya pulls a placatory rabbit out of the hat. Five, the donors are mollified and the aid is pledged. The whole dance starts again.[31]

By shutting expatriate aid minders out of the loop of information, gaining special exemptions and simply postponing things, recipient governments could sidestep many of the conditions they didn't like. Lenders refused to impose sanctions.[32] To paraphrase the wisecrack about working and getting paid under state socialism: borrowers pretended to comply with aid conditionalities while lenders pretended to enforce them.

Recipients know that aid providers are unlikely to take their marbles and go home. At the end of the day, the aid system has to move its money. If lenders/donors cannot roll over old debts with new loans, their very existence will be in question. In the aid regime, threats to cut off funding are about as powerful as threats in geo-politics to use a nuclear bomb – possible, but so unlikely as to lack any credibility.[33]

By the late 1980s, donors were frustrated. Recipient resistance was working, conditionality was not. A World Bank official is said to have burst out, 'You know, we just can't get the government to take ownership of our policies!' There came a crescendo of talk about 'partnership'. Yet power-sharing was not the intention; aid providers wanted compliance. An aid official in Africa is reported to have said, '"we want them to take ownership but of course they must do what we want. If not they should get their money elsewhere."'[34]

In response, aid system leaders resolved to advance on two fronts. They moved further to perfect ways of motivating and supervising 'first generation' conditionality, chiefly around the four Ds: devalue, decontrol, deflate and denationalize.[35] They also launched 'second-generation' conditionality, in the complex realm of politics and governance. This thrust has had two main components. The newer and well-advertised component seeks to build ownership or broad social consensus around economic policies. A basic aim is to get governments to clean up their acts and show more competence in order to boost popular consent to policies agreed. The second, less well-advertised component involves remodelling the state to insulate power from popular demands, and to lock in policies desired by donors.

RE-ENGINEERING GOVERNMENT Frustration with non-compliance led officials of the World Bank, USAID and some major US foundations to commission studies about recipient resistance and how to overcome it. The diagnosis[36] held that politics at the receiving end were vulnerable to anti-reform interests, mainly 'populist' politicians and organized labour. Moreover, friendly technocrats were not yet in key positions in sufficient numbers, nor did they have sufficient political backing. The proposal boiled down to political re-engineering, mainly to:

- shift the locus of power over major economic issues away from parliaments and public politics; use statutory changes and binding international agreements to put those powers irrevocably

in the hands of finance ministries, central banks and currency
boards and insulate those authorities from further local interference;

- build up the skills and authority of policy technocrats; boost
  their allegiance to market fundamentalism through training,
  internships, conference-going, a continual flow of reading
  material, and other means of inserting them into international
  policy networks; and

- restructure relationships between government and the private
  sector in order to amplify the voices of outward-oriented
  business interests; those interests should monitor state decisions
  in order to set off 'fire alarms' if the technocrats begin to
  backslide or defect from the outward-looking market fundamentalist policies.

In some cases these were less proposals than endorsements of
measures already under way. Furthest advanced was the recruitment of policy-makers into transnational policy alliances
pivoting on Washington, DC. By the 1970s, technocrats trained in
fundamentalist economic doctrine had assumed key positions in
their home governments; the Chicago Boys in Chile were the
most notorious, although US-trained economists dominated
almost every finance ministry in Latin America. The World Bank-
led donor consortium for Indonesia never had to apply coercive
conditionality because US-trained technocrats, the Berkeley Mafia,
were already in key positions and never entertained other ideas:
'On the contrary, their ideas were virtually identical.'[37] In Russia
in the 1990s, collusion between US consultants and Russian
technocrats was so close that they could substitute for one another
in certain circumstances.[38] The ways of weaving together aid
systems and national political systems are many.

Elsewhere it has not been easy to recruit skilled allies into
policy networks. 'In low-income countries,' wrote one researcher
of the resistance-to-adjustment issue, 'the creation of a technocratic core, short of reliance on expatriates, has become a major

obstacle to the creation of a firm transnational alliance.'[39] Basing
their policies on such diagnoses, the IFIs have put more emphasis
on training and dissemination of doctrine.

In 1990 the World Bank and UNDP created the African
Capacity Building Initiative, which by 2001 was supporting major
training efforts for central bank and finance ministry staff throughout the continent, economics training at 33 African universities, as
well as research dissemination and joint projects with the private
sector and civil society.[40] For its part, the IMF since 1964 has
trained more than ten thousand officials in its policies and practices.
Every year it sends around six hundred technical assistance missions
to borrower countries.[41] Operating from a monopolistic position,
they quietly insert fundamentalist orthodoxies into national policies
in the name of competition, openness and freedom.

However, the political bases of finance ministries and central
banks are much too narrow. Hence getting civil society groups
on board the market fundamentalist bandwagon has become an
important strategy. Amidst the hullabaloo about public-spirited
civil society, its pro-business segments are often overlooked. The
USA has strongly backed chambers of commerce and other
associations of business and professional people sympathetic to
the orthodoxies.[42] In Egypt, for example, it has supported efforts
to marshal such groups behind structural adjustment.[43]

Curbing the powers of parliaments over economic policy has
been a delicate but largely successful gambit. Parliamentary democracy may never have been strong; client strongmen from Mobutu
to Fujimori to Yeltsin have seen to that. Aid chains have tended
to hollow out sovereign powers still further. The IMF and World
Bank have occasionally conditioned their loans on parliamentary
enactment of specific laws. They might as well use recipients'
constitutions to wipe their boots.

A lot of aid flows in off-budget, beyond central government
authority and public debate. In Mali, at least one-third of all aid
(and probably much more) is not recorded in national accounts.[44]
In Tanzania 70 per cent of projected aid flows did not appear in

the 1996/97 budget. In Ukraine, extra-budgetary aid flows were equivalent to 12 per cent of GDP in 1992.[45] Of the tens of thousands of activities and billions of dollars provided by private aid agencies, only a fraction is subject to recipient parliamentary approval and oversight.

By keeping big economic policy issues off parliamentary and public agendas, the aid system has helped create what one African political observer has termed 'choiceless democracies'.[46] The top of the aid system proclaims the virtues of political competition but holds that there are no alternatives to its doctrine. It emphasizes social consensus and broad 'ownership' of policies, but requires supervision by powerful outsiders in Washington, DC, who have the last word.

Coercion, social engineering, reduced public services and leadership indifference to citizen wishes have provoked cynicism and alienation. From ex-Yugoslavia to Ecuador to West Africa, these factors have triggered violence. State legitimacy has been weakened, if not shattered altogether. The external orientation that the aid system has demanded of these countries' economies reinforces external steering of their politics. In many aid-affected countries, rulers account chiefly to donors, not to citizens. These trends set limits on the donors' new endeavour, good governance.

Governance as an Export Product

Good governance is a term typical of aid's plastic words: popular catch-phrases serving a coalition of interests because they admit many definitions while at the same time sounding clear, positive, and morally beyond reproach. Aid officials have used the concept to promote a wide range of activities in the fields of human rights, anti-poverty policy, deregulation and de-bureaucratization, decentralization, multi-party democracy and civil society. Anti-corruption is probably the most common denominator. After the Cold War, bad behaviour by Western clients ('our sons of bitches') did not have to be tolerated any longer since those regimes had done their job – that is, they had kept out left-wing elements.

Good governance helps Western publics and elites feel good about themselves and their triumphant system. But the top of the aid system viewed pro-democracy elements abroad with some ambivalence, as they were not necessarily loyal allies in the forward march of the market. Therefore some steering was required. Thus second-generation conditionalities around good governance can often look like mere management gimmicks to achieve the first-generation economic aims.

As with other kinds of foreign policy sanctions, the use of double standards has further hurt donor credibility. Donors have used aid carrots and sticks mainly in sub-Saharan Africa, where few major interests are at stake. Human rights abuses and denial of democracy in Egypt, Turkey, Colombia and most of East Asia, on the contrary, rarely figure in official aid talk about those countries. In general terms, as one researcher concludes, 'human rights and democracy principles appear to be always at the bottom of the pile'.[47]

At the end of the 1990s, development banks began to condition their soft loans on recipients' meeting specific criteria of governance. These conditions have teeth. If a country shows no progress, its funding via soft-loan windows will be cut. Of 20 criteria applied by the World Bank and the African Development Bank in annual Country Policy and Institutional Assessments (CPIAs) to determine eligibility for aid, six criteria concern governance. These cover matters such as anti-corruption, property rights, tax collection and public consent for policies. Although reflecting to some degree new donor interest in anti-poverty efforts, these criteria are mainly about promoting the conditions for investor confidence.

The CPIA is one more detailed and intrusive instrument for steering the affairs of aid-dependent governments. Accompanying it in most cases is a far more detailed list of measures recipient governments must adopt; in the period 2000–03, for example, the government of Benin had to meet 159 specific aid conditions.

Whatever the merits of these criteria – and principles of transparency, clean government, and adequate public sector working conditions have obvious merit – the fact remains that they are imposed by powerful bodies from outside, not by publics from within. The stage continues to be set for outcomes like those of first-generation conditionality: pantomimes of compliance masking cynicism and resistance. Supported by revenues neither derived from taxpayers nor used with their active knowledge and approval, national political leaders lack anchoring in political processes responsive to citizens.

If the USA, France, Italy and Japan were models of impeccably clean and fair politics, such donor conditionality might be easier to swallow. But people in the South and East may be forgiven if they ignore pious lectures from governments whose policies are heavily influenced, if not bought outright, by large vested interests.[48]

Beyond the cynicism, doubts arise about the deeper logic and practical viability of rapid democratization through conditions imposed from outside and above. For the Makerere University academic and legal scholar John-Jean Barya, 'the very idea that people can be forced to be democratic and/or free is quite startling. Freedom and liberation from autocratic rule, as well as democracy and accountability cannot be decreed. They must have a social basis in which they arise, are nurtured and sustained.'[49]

Donors may agree that reforms cannot be imposed and must be anchored socially. But they remain steadfast in their faith that aid can help engineer them. Recent initiatives in 'democracy-building', another strategy for good governance, suggest that those engineering hopes continue to triumph over experience.

DELIVERING DEMOCRACY Efforts to shore up the popular legitimacy of client regimes began to appear in the 1960s. 'Demonstration elections' and 'low-intensity democracy'[50] were preferred instruments in Latin America, Vietnam and other lands where anti-communist military juntas needed political legitimacy. In the

1990s such programmes grew explosively. New think-tanks, quangos and private agencies emerged, while older ones expanded their programmes. From an early date the USA was directly active on the ground, whereas European donors chose to spread funds among Southern and Eastern human rights and democracy bodies. Groups and movements for democracy in Eastern Europe, Korea, South Africa and elsewhere had sustained themselves for decades, often under dangerous circumstances, with little or no help from the aid system. In the 1990s, they were joined by hundreds of new NGOs emerging to catch the democratization wave.

Official democracy assistance by the USA illustrates the problems of this kind of aid intervention. European donors take a softer, subtler approach, but display some of the same features. American promoters of Good Governance see their political system as unsurpassed, and willingly prescribe it for others. The main thrust of this evangelical mission has been to build US-style institutions – electoral competition between two major centrist parties, a three-part governmental structure (legislature, executive and judiciary), active private media and lobbying NGOs as watchdogs on the politicians.

The approach 'stays clear, however, of the more result-oriented, socio-economic models which maintain that democracy must entail a certain level of social justice and economic dignity for all citizens'.[51] The approach doesn't require attention to problems of power underlying political life or existing institutions; such things can be tackled by force of political will by elites and the obvious superiority of the Western model. Programmes to export the US model of government have an 'artificial technical quality' in which

> Political change is treated as a desiccated, pseudo-scientific process dominated by manuals, courses, 'log frames' specifying intended outputs, and outside consultants. The stubborn reality that politics involves competing interests, struggles over power, conflicting ideologies and clashing values is ignored until it asserts itself, unwanted, at some later stage. Democracy assistance projects often founder on the shoals of this reality.[52]

In short, pre-packaged democracy export can resemble the theatre of the absurd, ripe for parody. But because it is so well-funded and strongly backed, it threatens to crowd out meaningful ways of stimulating political thinking and action.

Two important terrains thus present themselves for deeper comparative study, reflection, and action by policy activists, academics and those concerned within the aid system itself.

One, the terrain of democratic politics, where struggles over purposes and meanings take place. The building up of formal institutions has captured the imagination and resources of most of the aid system, largely to the exclusion of real political expression and processes.[53] *Two*, the terrain of the aid system itself, where claims to promote good governance may be challenged. Responsive ideas and forms of aid are more likely to emerge where the top of the aid system loses its monopoly powers, faces competing institutions and ideas, and becomes subject to normal rules of democratic accountability.

In conclusion, the problem is not how to help the aid technicians realize their dream of keeping politics at a respectful distance. Rather, it is how to bring political workings of aid to the surface and to democratize them.

Notes

1. Charter 99 (2000) *Global Accountability: How to Improve International Decision-making*, London: Charter 99, web address: http://www.charter99.org.

2. Woodward, S. (1995) *Balkan Tragedy: Chaos and Dissolution after the Cold War*, Washington, DC: Brookings Institution; Gowan, P. (1999) 'The NATO powers and the Balkan tragedy', *New Left Review*, 234: 83–105.

3. Strange, S. (1996) *The Retreat of the State: The Diffusion of Power in the World Economy*, Cambridge: Cambridge University Press, pp. 16–30.

4. Lebovich, J. (1988) 'National interests and United States foreign aid: the Carter and Reagan years', *Journal of Peace Research*, 25: 115–35; Wittkopf, E. (1973) 'Foreign aid and the United Nations votes: a comparative study', *American Political Science Review*, 67: 868–88.

5. Alesina, A. and B. Weder (1999) *Do Corrupt Governments Receive Less*

Foreign Aid? Working Paper No. W7108, Cambridge: National Bureau of Economic Research, web address: http://papers.nber.org/papers/W7108.

6. 'IMF's four steps to damnation', *The Observer* (UK), 29 April 2001.

7. Burnham, J. (2000) *Understanding the Multilateral Development Banks*, London: Adam Smith Institute, web address: http://www.bus.duq.edu/faculty/burnham/London2.htm.

8. Jacoby, N. (1966) *U.S. Aid to Taiwan: A Study of Foreign Aid, Self-Help and Development*, New York: Praeger, p. 163.

9. Adelman, I. (2000) 'The role of government in economic development', in F. Tarp (ed.), *Foreign Aid and Development: Lessons Learnt and Directions for the Future*, London: Routledge, p. 71.

10. Page, J. (1972) *The Revolution that Never Was: Northeast Brazil, 1955–1964*, New York: Grossman.

11. Lappé, F. M. and others (1980) *Aid as Obstacle: Twenty Questions about our Foreign Aid and the Hungry*, San Francisco: Institute for Food and Development Policy, pp. 79–84.

12. See for example de Janvry, A. (1981) *The Agrarian Question and Reformism in Latin America*, Baltimore, MD: Johns Hopkins University Press; van de Walle, N. (1996) 'The politics of aid effectiveness', in S. Ellis (ed.), *Africa Now: People, Policies and Institutions*, The Hague: DGIS (Dutch Aid Ministry), pp. 232–50.

13. Scott, J. C. (1998) *Seeing Like a State: How Certain Schemes to Improve the Human Condition Have Failed*, New Haven, CT and London: Yale University Press, pp. 247–52; de Waal, A. (1997) *Famine Crimes. Politics and the Disaster Relief Industry in Africa*, Oxford: James Currey, pp. 106–32.

14. Scott, *Seeing Like a State*: p. 247.

15. Barker, J. (1989) *Rural Communities Under Stress. Peasant Farmers and the State in Africa*, Cambridge: Cambridge University Press, p. 182.

16. Mackintosh, M. (1989) *Gender, Class and Rural Transition: Agribusiness and the Food Crisis in Senegal*, London: Zed Books, p. 104.

17. Ferguson, J. (1990) *The Anti-Politics Machine. 'Development', Depoliticization and Bureaucratic Power in Lesotho*, Cambridge: Cambridge University Press, pp. 255–6.

18. Ibid., p. 66.

19. Ibid., p. 256.

20. Uvin, P. (1998) *Aiding Violence: The Development Enterprise in Rwanda*, West Hartford, CT: Kumarian Press, p. 143.

21. Wedel, J. (1998) *Collision and Collusion: The Strange Case of Western Aid to Eastern Europe 1989–1998*, New York: St Martin's Press.

22. Berman, E. (1980) 'The foundations' role in American foreign policy: the case of Africa, post 1945', in R. Arnove (ed.), *Philanthropy and Cultural Imperialism: The Foundations at Home and Abroad*, Boston: G.K. Hall, pp. 203–32.

23. Cockett, R. (1995) *Thinking the Unthinkable: Think-tanks and the Economic Counter-Revolution, 1931–1983*, London: Fontana Press.

24. Toye, J. (1987) *Dilemmas of Development: Reflections on the Counter-Revolution in Development Economics*, Oxford: Blackwell, p. 191.

25. Cornwall, A. and others (2000) 'From users and choosers to makers and shapers: repositioning participation in social policy', *IDS Bulletin*, 31 (4): 50–62.

26. Cornia, G. (2001) 'Social funds in stabilization and adjustment programmes: a critique', *Development and Change*, 32: 1–32.

27. Lloyd, V. and R. Weissman (2001) 'Against the workers. How IMF and World Bank policies undermine labor power and rights', *Multinational Monitor*, 22 (9), web address: http://www.essential.org/monitor/mm2001/01september/sep01corp1.html.

28. See for example Tangri, R. and A. Mwenda (2001) 'Corruption and cronyism in Uganda's privatization in the 1990s', *African Affairs*, 100: 117–33.

29. Berg, E. (2000) 'Aid and failed reforms. The case of public sector management', in F. Tarp (ed.), *Foreign Aid and Development*, London: Routledge, p. 298.

30. Ibid., p. 308.

31. Kanbur, R. (2000) 'Aid, conditionality and debt in Africa', in F. Tarp (ed.), *Foreign Aid and Development*, London: Routledge, p. 416.

32. Detailed in Killick, T. (1998) *Aid and the Political Economy of Policy Change*, London: Routledge and ODI.

33. Collier, P. and others (1997) 'Redesigning conditionality', *World Development*, 25(9): 1399–407.

34. G. K. Helleiner, cited in Mukandala, R. (1999) 'From proud defiance to beggary: a recipient's tale', in G. Hyden and R. Mukandala (eds), *Agencies in Foreign Aid: Comparing China, Sweden and the United States in Tanzania*, Basingstoke: Macmillan, pp. 31–67.

35. Lipton, M. and J. Toye (1990) *Does Aid Work in India? A Country Study of Official Development Assistance*, London: Routledge, p. 101.

36. Key texts are: Bates, R. and A. Krueger (eds) (1993) *Political and Economic Interactions in Economic Policy Reform*, Oxford: Blackwell; Haggard, S. and R. Kaufman (eds) (1992) *The Politics of Economic Adjustment: International*

Constraints, Distributive Conflicts and the State, Princeton, NJ: Princeton University Press.

37. Schulte Nordholt, N. (1995) 'Aid and conditionality: the case of Dutch–Indonesian relationships', in O. Stokke (ed.), *Aid and Political Conditionality*, London: Frank Cass, p. 136.

38. Wedel, J. (1998) *Collision and Collusion: The Strange Case of Western Aid to Eastern Europe 1989–1998*, New York: St Martin's Press.

39. Kahler, M. (1992), 'External influence, conditionality, and the politics of adjustment', in S. Haggard and R. Kaufman (eds), *The Politics of Economic Adjustment: International Constraints, Distributive Conflicts and the State*, Princeton, NJ: Princeton University Press, p. 130.

40. African Capacity Building Foundation May 2001, web address: http://www.acbf-pact.org/noframe/facts_and_figures.htm.

41. Scholte, J. (1998) 'Civil society and the International Monetary Fund', The Hague, mimeo, p. 5.

42. Lucas, J. (1997) 'The politics of business associations in the developing world', *Journal of Developing Areas*, 32 (1): 71–96.

43. Miskin, A. (1992) 'Aid's "free market" democracy', *Middle East Report*, November–December, pp. 33–4.

44. Naudet, J. (2000) *Accounting for Aid Flows to Mali*, Paris: OECD Club du Sahel, web address: http://www.olis.oecd.org/olis/2000doc.nsf/LinkTo/SAH-REFA(2000)2.

45. Bräutigam, D. (2000) *Aid Dependence and Governance*, 2000: 1, Stockholm: Almquist & Wiksell for the Expert Group on Development Issues, p. 31. web address: http://www.egdi.gov.se/pdf/2001pdf/2000_1.pdf. In Mozambique, bilateral donors and the government colluded in channelling aid off-budget, where it escaped the ceiling on aid imposed by the IMF. There could be no clearer illustration of how aid institutions work to defeat each other's purposes and at the same time hinder democratic control over public investment. See Hanlon, J. (1996) *Peace without Profit: How the IMF Blocks Rebuilding in Mozambique*, Oxford: James Currey.

46. Mkandawire, T. (1998) *Crisis Management and the Making of 'Choiceless Democracies' in Africa*, The Oslo Symposium, Oslo: United Nations Office of the High Commissioner for Human Rights, web address: http://www.undp.org/hdro/Oslorep6.html#mkandawire.

47. Crawford, G. (1997) 'Foreign aid and political conditionality: issues of effectiveness and consistency', *Democratization*, 4 (3): 103. See also Olsen, G. (1998) 'Europe and the promotion of democracy in post Cold War Africa: how serious is Europe and for what reason?', *African Affairs*, 97: 343–67.

48. A longtime US television publicist and Washington insider, Bill Moyers, someone not known for strident left-wing views, summed up the state of democracy in the United States in 2001 as follows: 'Big money and big business, corporations and commerce, are again the undisputed overlords of politics and government. The White House, the Congress and, increasingly, the judiciary reflect their interests. We appear to have a government run by remote control from the US Chamber of Commerce, the National Association of Manufacturers and the American Petroleum Institute. To hell with everyone else.' 'Journalism and democracy. On the importance of being a "public nuisance"', *The Nation*, 7 May 2001, p. 13.

49. Barya, J.-J. (1993) 'The new political conditionalities of aid: an independent view from Africa', *IDS Bulletin*, 24(1): 16–23.

50. Gills, B. and others (1993) *Low-intensity Democracy*, London: Pluto Press.

51. Carothers, T. (1997) 'Democracy assistance: the question of strategy', *Democratization*, 4 (3): 115–16.

52. Ibid., p. 123.

53. See Luckham, R. and others (2000) *Democratic Institutions and Politics in Contexts of Inequality, Poverty and Conflict: A Conceptual Framework*, Sussex: IDS web address: http://www.ids.ac.uk/ids/publicat/wp/Wp104.pdf; J. Hippler (ed.) (1995) *The Democratisation of Disempowerment*, London: Pluto Press; Abrahamson, R. (2000) *Disciplining Democracy*, London: Zed Books.

SEVEN
When Money Talks, What Does It Tell Us?

[T]he ideas of economists and political philosophers, both when they are right and when they are wrong, are more powerful than is commonly understood. Indeed the world is ruled by little else. Practical men, who believe themselves to be quite exempt from any intellectual influences, are usually the slaves of some defunct economist. Madmen in authority, who hear voices in the air, are distilling their frenzy from some academic scribbler of a few years back. I am sure that the power of vested interests is vastly exaggerated compared with the gradual encroachment of ideas.[1]

When wealthy foreign donors come calling, recipients are not supposed to squirm in their chairs and put off accepting any money. Yet in the USA, officials of major universities have shown just that kind of uneasiness towards some big donors from abroad. Governments, business foundations and wealthy individuals from Taiwan, Korea, Singapore, Mexico, Turkey – donors not known as resolute defenders of academic freedom – are offering millions to promote research and teaching about their respective lands. Academics may welcome the money, but they face serious misgivings about the benefactors and their motives. One seasoned US professor of East Asian studies said bluntly: 'They are out to get over a point of view. They are paying to win support for their government.'[2]

Americans object because they fear the agendas driving those monies will close off genuine inquiry. They can mount opposition, however, with few risks to themselves or others; indeed, they may gain status by standing up for scholarly autonomy. When institutions prostitute themselves – think of the many universities getting handsome payments for research results favouring the products of pharmaceutical firms – there is reason for serious alarm. Alongside such big and dangerous domestic pay-offs, those foreign millions look like minor threats to intellectual integrity.

How analogous, but how different are the vulnerabilities in countries of the South and East. There, policy agendas of big donors and lenders, once plucked of their rhetorical feathers, are also unmistakable. But to challenge them is to run serious risks. Too much is at stake. Virtually every aid offer is one that cannot be refused, especially if it comes from Washington, DC. After decades of aid given only on condition that aid providers' ideas are accepted, refusal is no longer an option – except perhaps from a few dissenters, who can be easily quashed. Where ideas are run towards goals under aid sponsorship, the playing fields are anything but level.

Ideology has long been at the heart of foreign aid. Producing and transmitting policies and discourse, and filtering out and de-legitimizing others, are essential vocations of aid's most powerful players. It is not by caprice that the World Bank is positioning itself as the world's mightiest think-tank. As the leading producer of doctrine and knowledge about how the planet should develop, it aims to achieve the supreme instrument of power – power to define the alternatives.[3]

Those at the top of the aid system faithfully transmit the dominant ideas of business and political elites, but they also routinely research and develop their own. They often roam about plundering ideas of rivals and critics. In the 1990s, aid-speak at the top became saturated with terms such as 'sustainability', 'civil society' and 'empowerment'. These ideas sprang from the emancipatory camp of social movements, but they found themselves cast in supporting roles in market fundamentalist scripts.

This chapter suggests that the aid system's most important instruments and outcomes are in the realm of ideas. In the hands of sophisticated users, aid-driven ideas have leveraged change far out of proportion to the monies applied. The World Bank, the endowed foundations, think-tanks and policy activist NGOs all know this. Surprisingly, only a few private aid agencies have begun to go beyond the charity micro-project to engage in battles of ideas.

Ideas (Almost) All the Way Down

Beliefs, models of cause-and-effect, shared knowledge, norms and vocabularies all refer to ideas. In matters of foreign aid, a synonymous term would be ideology, in the neutral sense of belief system. Depending on context, ideas can do many kinds of work. They define and rank the categories by which we pay attention to issues or overlook them. They frame problems and solutions, label identities and assign value. They may descend like fog over all policy, as with market fundamentalism, or cast a sharp spotlight on specific terrains, as with the Gini coefficient of income inequality.

How do ideas figure in international relations? Some theorists assign them only minor roles. According to the dominant Realist school, each nation's material interests (military assets, finance, access to oil and to markets) drive global politics; ideas are merely residuals. Against that school of thought, a challenge comes from the Constructivist school. It holds that big ideas such as anti-communism, free trade and political Islam can come to construct or constitute interests that generate and channel power. The approach draws on discourse analysis and feminist theory about how power works at deep levels. 'The central thesis', according to one of this school's major theorists, Alexander Wendt, 'is that the meaning of power and the content of interests are largely a function of ideas.'[4] World politics, he argues, consist of 'ideas (almost) all the way down'.

For a study of foreign aid, this has optimistic implications. For if ideas rather than fixed material interests constitute the system – including the system of foreign aid – then ethically preferable alternatives open up. The routes to transformation are shorter, and knowledge-based work can help create the vehicles and roadmaps to get there. Wendt argues that we should 'begin our theorizing about international politics with the distribution of ideas, and especially culture, in the system, and then bring in material forces, rather than the other way around. The importance of this ultimately lies in perceived possibilities for social change.'[5]

Ideas do their work through institutions, including networks. Business associations, protest movements and single-issue groups promote their causes through routine methods such as lobbies, campaigns and cash contributions. Sometimes they act through non-routine methods of protest. Today attention has swung to deeper levels of politics, where influence flows through institutions whose stock-in-trade is conceptual: think-tanks, expert networks, and the material and virtual media for transmitting and consuming ideas. The World Bank and its allied banks and donors make up a semi-formal network of policy-makers who produce, legitimize and transmit ideas in fields as general as governance and as specific as the warehousing of farm chemicals.

New approaches into how people think and talk about politics today allow better insight into policy-making.[6] However, the roles of donors in the marketplace of policy ideas have not been studied in depth. One scholar, in an overview article about concepts of development, after citing the phrase 'where colonialism left off, development took over', adds that 'it is surprising how little work has focused on the invention of institutions which produce, transmit and stabilize regimes of development "truth"'.[7] Given the far-reaching impact of the 'truths' guiding foreign aid for half a century, this neglect is astonishing. The following paragraphs briefly note a few markers in this history of ideas.

EARLY DONORS IN THE MARKETPLACE OF IDEAS The vanguard of today's aid system were the philanthropic foundations built on the fortunes of some early giants of Anglo-Saxon capitalism: the Rockefeller funds, the Ford Foundation, the

Carnegie and Russell Sage foundations in the USA and the Rowntree trusts in Britain. From the outset of their work in the first two decades of the twentieth century, they shunned conventional philanthropy, that is, charity via small-scale, short-run activities with palliative intent. Instead they pursued what John D. Rockefeller termed wholesale philanthropy: longer-term, substantial support to activities with constructive or preventive intent by way of strategic institutions, particularly those creating and transmitting policy. They saw themselves in the business of applied rationality, science and public uplift through social planning.[8]

The endowed foundations emerged in a period like our own: wealth was piling up fabulously, inequality was growing explosively. In the realm of ideas, the establishment faced competition. Public gatherings, pamphlets and thousands of small newspapers enabled socialists, reformists and reactionaries to battle away in civil society. For disquieted members of the elite, the foundations were obvious vehicles to help steer policy. In the USA, 'they vigorously intervened in the era's vibrant marketplace of ideas, putting their vast resources at the disposal of only some of the groups promulgating ideologies, furthering only these groups' capacities to produce and disseminate world-views supportive of the status quo'.[9]

In what has been termed 'ideology-in-action', the Russell Sage Foundation in 1907 began promoting a movement of voluntary social action groups (service delivery NGOs of that era) by way of a didactic national magazine, community surveys of social conditions, and the new profession of social work. The Foundation itself became a policy institute. In 1903 the Carnegie Institute of Washington, DC was set up to focus on economic and social issues including labour-management and regulation of big business. This first major Washington think-tank portrayed its work as non-ideological, but its job was clearly to counter a threatening red tide of socialism by way of pragmatic measures for mild reform.[10]

From an early hour, foundations invested in ways to produce and disseminate ideas. They needed allies and contractors. Universities and semi-official laboratories were main grantees. *Laissez-faire*, equivalent to today's market fundamentalism, was present, but by no means the orthodoxy of the age. Lacking an off-the-shelf formula to apply everywhere, policy-makers had to learn about social contexts. Foundations therefore put money into applied social research. They supported British social anthropology, for example, because colonial administrations needed to avoid trouble in the non-Western societies they were governing.

Foundation influence has rarely been heavy-handed. Instead it has worked like the imaginary hand of the market. By 1930, their discreet influence had drawn the acid pen of the academic and publicist Harold Laski, then at the London School of Economics:

> [T]he foundations do not control, simply because, in the direct and simple sense of the word, there is no need for them to do so. They have only to indicate the immediate direction of their minds for the whole university world to discover that it always meant to gravitate swiftly to that angle of the intellectual compass.[11]

Foundation thinking has sometimes been ahead, but seldom radically ahead of its time. In the late 1920s Carnegie funds supported a major inquiry into poverty in South Africa – the poverty of white people. The aim was to promote means (later adopted by successive racialist governments in South Africa) to reintegrate poor whites with the rest, and thus 'prevent the "ultimate nightmare" of a class movement that would unify the poor across racial lines'.[12]

These early episodes of strategic philanthropy foreshadow foreign aid practices. Driving and shaping the donors' use of funds were:

- concerns to curb threats to the status quo and to promote Third Way reform somewhere between unregulated capitalism and redistributive socialism;
- emphasis on designing and replicating practical measures rather than on comprehensive theories;

- emphasis on rational, value-neutral, 'scientific' intellectual production immune to the charge of ideological bias;
- concerns to generate policy-relevant knowledge accessible to decision-makers, preferably in close proximity to them;
- interest in higher education, the seedbed of intellectual and political leadership; and
- readiness to create new institutions in civil society, appealing mainly to emerging white-collar classes, often in order to compete with or control membership-based organizations based on blue-collar wage-earners and the unwaged poor.

Essentially the foundations aimed to 'mobilize bias' in civil society towards their models of reform, to the exclusion of competitors' models.[13] In doing so they helped create a knowledge and idea market resembling the highly skewed, monopoly-centred capitalism of that era.

IDEAS IN EARLY AID DECADES   As the Western aid regime took shape after 1945, it could build on what the endowed foundations had pioneered. Channels of official aid began serving as channels of ideas – without, however, calling attention to that fact. Indeed, overt use aid as a policy lever went into eclipse. Aid agencies faced incentives to be 'practical'; they had to spend big, and rapidly, on tangible things and activities. Hence they largely ignored strategic advice, such as that given USAID in 1966 by two leading academics: 'In the long run, aid's "influence potential" is much more important than its resource contribution.'[14] Instead, most agencies put the accent on action. That meant projects and resource transfer. In its early decades, official aid was largely a cargo cult.

    In aid's very early years, development officials could promote ideas that today would sound like four-letter words in church. Officials of the British Colonial Office, for example, strongly advocated central planning and the internationalization of welfare. Some of them voiced doubts about the blessings of private capital in Africa. Beginning in 1950, the United Nations' Economic

Commission for Latin America (ECLA), promoted a paradigm of inward-oriented development. It opposed rapid economic integration of peripheral countries in the Northern-dominated economic order. ECLA defended these ideas for four decades. It finally jettisoned them after years of political repression, the collapse of communism, the advance of market fundamentalism, and its own intellectual self-doubt.[15]

Not all development ideas depend on aid system backing to gain attention. But without that backing, their lifespans will usually be short. A new assertiveness in the South, including muscle-flexing by oil-producers, led in 1974 to a proposal for a New International Economic Order (NIEO). Much less radical than the ECLA positions, the idea was largely a non-starter under opposition from major donor countries. Although disputed, the NIEO enjoyed considerable 'ownership' among elites in the South. But it lacked an institutional home or heavyweight patron in the aid system.[16]

A set of alternative ideas critical of mainstream modernization models crystallized in the mid-1970s in an initiative of the Swedish Dag Hammarskjöld Foundation and the UN Environment Programme. Leading intellectuals from the South, and figures such as Jan Pronk, then aid minister in the Dutch government, expressed doubts that there was only one path to development. They posed development as a contested matter for the North as well as for the South, and argued that 'the primacy of economics is over'. Echoing Swedish positions, they advocated that foreign aid 'be directed above all to states which undertake to reduce internal inequalities, and withheld from those which do not respect human rights'.[17] Despite the backing of some courageous 'like-minded' donor agency leaders, this initiative made no further headway in the official aid system. Its early death ended chances that a second Western aid regime might emerge to compete with the dominant one centred in Washington. A quarter-century later, such ideas are unwelcome in the corridors of power; the UN secretary-general today speaks unequivocally in favour of 'a single economic model'.

Meanwhile the endowed foundations, later joined by branches of the official aid system, pressed ahead with their idea-centric approaches. Box 7.1 itemizes a number of the better-known initiatives.

Box 7.1 Aid-driven ideas: a sampler

MODERNIZATION   This big idea continues to circulate today, although it has lost the allure it once had as a leading paradigm. Seemingly a common-sense notion with no identifiable origins, it was in fact created and inserted into development discourse, mainly to answer communist narratives of history and the future. Its seedbeds were research, publications and conferences begun in the 1950s and managed by international and area studies programmes at selected universities, largely at the instigation of the Ford Foundation. Such ideas were self-reinforcing: like most other agencies, the foundations used the modernization concept as a template for their own work.

POPULATION SCIENCE   Overcoming nervousness about the politically charged issue of birth control, academics and population activists (notably John D. Rockefeller III) set up the Population Council in 1953 with funds from the Ford Foundation and Rockefeller Brothers Fund. From that initiative emerged new professional fields of demography and reproductive health. Donor-backed research, training and policy-making set the stage for major national and international population programmes.[18]

PUBLIC HEALTH IN THE TROPICS   Donor agencies have actively influenced approaches to health. The Rockefeller Foundation targeted specific diseases such as hookworm and yellow fever with technology- and specialist-intensive investments. These vertical strategies do help account for successful aid-backed campaigns against smallpox and polio, and for recurring optimism about other inoculation efforts. The technical fix, often linked with big pharmaceutical companies, remains a favourite of the World Health Organization. Such approaches have frustrated more promising ones linking health with poverty and equity, such as strong versions of primary health care.[19]

GREEN REVOLUTION The Rockefeller Foundation vigorously pursued a strategy of research, training and institution-building to promote high-yielding varieties of rice, maize and other crops. It is often claimed as one of foreign aid's rare triumphs, but those claims are hotly disputed. Yet aid agencies are drawn to this kind of technology like moths to a flame. The Green Revolution's polarizing socio-economic impacts in many (though not all) places underscore the validity of precautionary principles, and of healthy scepticism about aid's frequent claims for the virtues of the technical fix.[20]

DESERTIFICATION For decades an informal alliance of official aid agencies, national governments and scientists had promoted a narrative of advancing ecological catastrophe caused by rural dwellers' mismanagement of woodlands and pastures. As a frightening slogan, the idea served to justify the bullying of rural people and the generous funding of aid institutions and their chains of projects and clients. In the 1990s, research from largely outside the aid system eventually demolished the narrative of locals' mismanagement. Exposed as a gross distortion, it nevertheless remains one of those simplifying cause-and-effect ideas that refuse to die.[21]

LAW AND DEVELOPMENT Backed by the Ford Foundation and USAID, this initiative of US legal professionals took the missionary position to transplant US legal models abroad. Following the idea's collapse in the 1970s, a Ford Foundation official wrote a book blaming its failure on ethnocentrism, the legal branch's 'perceiving and assisting the Third World in its own self-image'.[22] Despite this débâcle, the IMF, World

Bank, UNDP, US State Department and American Bar Association have today cooked up an analogous scheme to export standardized laws to low-income countries, ignoring existing contexts and the importance of anchoring legal systems in political processes.[23]

INFORMAL SECTOR Concepts of dual labour markets and micro-enterprise were around at the dawn of the aid system. Ever since, the icon of the small entrepreneur who solves her or his own unemployment problem has carried enormous ideological baggage. In the 1970s and 1980s this cluster of ideas was born again under the ill-defined term 'informal sector'. Around it grew a broad coalition of interests led by the ILO and World Bank. Projects multiplied. With backing from centre-right European foundations and USAID, a host of think-tanks emerged after 1980 to promote this and related ideas, which have assisted various social strata, but rarely the poorest.[24]

The list in the box is far from comprehensive. A host of others, from 'human resources' to appropriate technology to the model of privatized urban transport, could have been mentioned. Nevertheless, even this small sample illustrates some of the abiding features of aid-driven ideas:

- Optimism about the suitability of the Northern model, whether in technology, law, or an entire historical trajectory of growth, shows respect neither for actual problems in their contexts, nor for local processes in problem-solving and policy-making. In its crudest form, the aid system sends out a solution in search of problems; the main concern then becomes one of operations, not of the definition of problems and alternative responses to them.
- The system avoids ideas that open up spaces for public control

of technical policies or development processes. Despite occasional lip-service to public participation, it gives preference to control by scientists/technicians, national decision-makers and donors.

- There is an inability to see how local people would define things. Such blinkered attitudes lead outsiders to re-cast serious problems such as precarious livelihoods and impoverishing labour markets as a booming and benign informal sector that magically solves unemployment without major public costs or risks.

- There is pessimism about local know-how, such as the view that local crop varieties are hopeless or that rural dwellers are incompetent managers of natural resources.

- There is inattention to conditions or boomerang effects that undercut aid efforts, such as social polarization leading to violent conflict; aid-subsidized producers facing no incentives to produce because imports destroyed their markets; and bad public sector management hit by aid-driven austerity, leading to a bad environment for private investment and for aid itself.

Put into practice, many aid-driven ideas proved impotent. Resistance and re-negotiation lower down aid chains deflected some harmful effects. Failure sometimes led to better understandings of social contexts, and to progressive initiatives. For example, attention to the informal sector allowed a closer look at precarious livelihoods; those insights have since informed thinking and experimentation in sustainable livelihoods and such things as trade unions of market women. Ideas emerging from population science catalysed action in women's reproductive rights – largely thanks to a women's movement promoting its ideas both inside and outside the aid system.

Ideas trigger critique and counter-ideas. Against the pessimism about local know-how, for example, activists and academics concerned about the rights of indigenous people (including their rights over seeds and useful plants) joined with sympathetic aid system staff to promote understanding of indigenous knowledge. Similar cycles of debate and renewal have taken place where outsiders' criticisms have triggered rethinking about gender, the role of the state, complex political emergencies, and social service delivery, to name only a few topics. In these ways, concepts and practice in the aid system have seen real improvement.

Appearing in these debates is a striking pattern, sometimes hidden under a fog of aid-speak about management, monitoring, partnership and best practice. Aid-driven ideas, whether techno-cratic ones such as the Green Revolution or political ones such as anti-communism, tend to produce negative knock-on effects. In 2001, the 'blowback' of conflict, displacement and hostility towards US global dominance – of which foreign aid was an important part – began to reach terrifying proportions.[25]

A rethinking of the aid system nested in contexts of power is long overdue. If the objects of aid are to become subjects and active agents in its use, their interests and ideas will have to form points of departure. But that is unlikely to happen where intended beneficiaries or their representatives lack parity with those wishing to develop, rescue or empower them. In the balance is whether aid system backers of new ideas, once they start investing in them, can anticipate and tackle these disparities of power.

'The Intellectual/Financial Complex of Foreign Aid'

Policy ideas emerge from bubbling soups heated by public and bureaucratic political struggles. There, contingent factors such as an active leader, a media gatekeeper or a protest campaign can influence outcomes. A rock music star can unblock legislation to write off debt; a dynamic minister can rouse an aid bureaucracy from its lethargy. Yet in today's aid system, much effort goes towards buffering such contingencies. In competing kitchens of research, communication and persuasion, aid policy cooks carefully super-vise how ideas and knowledge are selected, prepared, served up and digested – and *then* given favourable reviews.

'Research shows that ... ' is one of the stock phrases in policy discussions. While research may reflect genuine inquiry, its actual uses in the aid system can be manipulative. Those who decide have to legitimate their decisions and win arguments. Research reports are trump cards. Therefore the World Bank has invested heavily in research. Such practices are at the heart of what Joel Samoff, a specialist in education policy, calls the 'Intellectual/Financial Complex of Foreign Aid'.[26] Aid influence on education policy illustrates patterns seen in other fields. Accompanying the widespread deterioration of education in Africa, according to Samoff, has been the widespread imposition of standard policy measures to:

- reduce the central government role in providing education;
- decentralize;
- increase school fees;
- encourage and assist private schools;
- reduce direct support to students, especially at tertiary level;
- introduce double shifts and multi-grade classrooms; and
- favour in-service over pre-service teacher education; etc.

These policies originate in the World Bank, which has powerfully influenced education policy in Africa, chiefly through its command of research agendas and results. It behaves with limitless self-assurance. As its president reported smugly in 1996, the Bank deals only in 'the best' ideas: 'We are a global clearinghouse that identifies and seeks out the best ideas, develops their practical applications, and get them to end users in time to apply them to the real problems people face.'[27] The problem here is not know-it-all arrogance, but an unchecked power to define truth and falsehood. The net effect is to intimidate, cut off debate and close off alternatives. That is dangerous. For some of the Bank's earlier 'best' ideas have proved damaging – as the World Bank itself now tacitly admits.

The World Bank is not alone in gearing research to suit its doctrines, but it has unrivalled powers to do so across a broad front. While talking of demand-driven aid and recipient partnership and ownership, the Bank and other donors/lenders unilaterally determine the purposes, scope, issues and methods of research, and who has access to the results. Because jobs, contracts and careers depend on funding by Bank-led donor consortia, the audience and users of this knowledge have little choice but to go along quietly.

In South Africa in the 1990s, however, the Bank and other donors faced something they rarely meet: an outspoken challenge to their intellectual authority. Education policy was one of several terrains where they met resistance. Local institutes affiliated with the country's democratic movement had investigated and consulted widely, generating a massive amount of policy research. But the Bank and other donors insisted on commissioning their own research, which unsurprisingly backed what the Bank wanted, namely proposals for bricks-and-mortar and technocratic management. With some exceptions, official aid bodies ignored South African findings and proposals that would have broken with past patterns and expanded educational access for the poor.[28] This case is consistent with findings by researchers on aid in South Africa, who have detected a rise in technocratic optimism and a decline in the quality of EU aid, and general mediocrity of US aid efforts.[29]

The Bank itself carries no financial risks, nor liabilities for policy failure. In Africa, it has presided over an erosion of educational performance, but it can disclaim any responsibility for harm done (although it can claim credit for success). Limited debates, often reflecting struggles over turf and position, take place within it, but even mild dissenters such as Herman Daly, Joseph Stiglitz and Ravi Kanbur have been rigorously purged.[30] Beyond its walls, it has powers to ignore or rubbish knowledge produced by others. Selected outsiders publicly review some of its own research, but there is no genuinely independent assessment. It is a closed world, the world of an unregulated monopolist. Samoff's assessment of education sector analysis in Africa is probably valid for other fields and countries: 'massive research that contributes more to legitimacy than to understanding'.[31]

The Bank's communication strategies aim to win. It targets audiences carefully, aiming at four key categories: policy-makers, especially in the South and East; researchers and analysts; students likely to become policy-makers and analysts; and 'members of the development community, including journalists and non-governmental organizations'. By the mid-1990s the World Bank was producing from 350 to 500 publications annually, 70 per cent of them based on research.[32] By 2001 it was moving strongly into production for television and the Internet.

The Bank is clearly proud of its position in the marketplace of ideas – and with reason, for that position is awesome. Reader surveys, indices of publications cited in professional journals, and uptake in mainstream media all point to the pre-eminence of Bank ideas. Their presence is evident in policies not only about economic development but also about social services, agriculture, governance, education and the environment.

Intellectual bullying via the aid system is widespread, but poorly documented, as neither the bully nor the bullied wish to see it exposed. A researcher at the South Centre, a Geneva-based think-tank associated with the Non-Aligned Movement, concludes that intimidation and fear are part of this intellectual hegemony, resulting in 'the image of apparent harmony, consensus and broad acceptance of the status quo at the public level'.[33] Those earnest policy papers churned out by technocrats in recipient countries to reflect 'ownership' of dominant ideas may well be mere cardboard façades – today's Potemkin villages.

THINK-TANKS AND POLICY COMMUNITIES The aid system has also given rise to other centres and circuits of knowledge. The policy research institute is the most common model. Some are based at universities. They range from the specialized and contract-driven, such as the Land Tenure Center at the University of Wisconsin, to the broad-gauged and institutionally subsidized, such as the Institute of Development Studies at the University of Sussex. Government funds helped set up quasi-private bodies for development policy research such as the Overseas Development Institute in Britain (1960), and the Centre for Development

Research in Denmark (1969). Others have had, in addition to their own research tasks, mandates and funds to improve research capacity in the South; the International Development Research Centre in Canada (1970), and SIDA's Department for Research Cooperation (SAREC) in Sweden (1979) are chief examples.

Many United Nations agencies developed in-house units for research, statistics and publications. Best known for conceptual work have been UNICEF and the UNDP, whose annual *Human Development Report*, begun in 1990, remains influential. UNCTAD has argued for a fairer deal for economies of the South. Beyond the aid agencies is the Geneva-based UN Research Institute for Social Development (UNRISD) and the Helsinki-based World Institute for Development Economics Research (WIDER). Both have focused on globalization and inequality. Research within the UN system is vulnerable, however, to pressure by member countries and multinational enterprise. A dramatic illustration was the dismantling in the early 1990s of ECOSOC's policy research Center on Transnational Corporations, set up in 1974 to keep an eye on big business and press for corporate responsibility. In 1994 it was reincarnated under UNCTAD with mandates not to monitor but to *promote* global corporations.[34]

In the South, non-profit research centres began appearing in the 1970s. Promoted at first by endowed foundations and then by official aid agencies, these private think-tanks multiplied rapidly in Latin America, where they 'displaced public universities as the region's leading producers and disseminators of social science and policy research ... They employ, without doubt, a disproportional share of the best talent, including many of Latin America's foremost intellectuals.'[35]

Most think-tanks position themselves at the centre of political spectrums. They present themselves as non-ideological and technocratic. USAID and some centre-right European political foundations have promoted market fundamentalism through think-tanks specially created for the task. European private aid agencies have financed a smaller number of think-tanks, including some in Latin America focused on poverty, human rights and democratization. In South and South East Asia, governments have been more active promoters of policy research centres; private policy activist think-tanks are less common. In Africa, with the exception of South Africa, private policy research centres are thinly spread, as universities and government units were historically tasked with research.

These centres, policy units in aid institutions, individual academics and laboratories can form influential networks. From micro-credit to early childhood education to land tenure to the lowly sweet potato, aid monies have been invested to attract and weave together practitioners, academics, publicists and policy-makers into specialist communities. In some of them experts hammer out consensus and define world standards. These networks

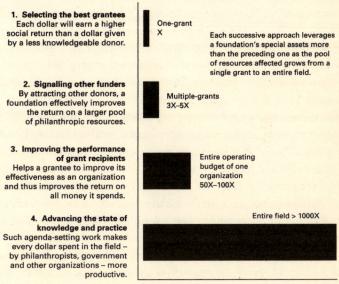

1. Selecting the best grantees
Each dollar will earn a higher social return than a dollar given by a less knowledgeable donor.

One-grant
X

Each successive approach leverages a foundation's special assets more than the preceding one as the pool of resources affected grows from a single grant to an entire field.

2. Signalling other funders
By attracting other donors, a foundation effectively improves the return on a larger pool of philanthropic resources.

Multiple-grants
3X–5X

3. Improving the performance of grant recipients
Helps a grantee to improve its effectiveness as an organization and thus improves the return on all money it spends.

Entire operating budget of one organization
50X–100X

4. Advancing the state of knowledge and practice
Such agenda-setting work makes every dollar spent in the field – by philanthropists, government and other organizations – more productive.

Entire field > 1000X

Dollar value of resources affected by foundation activity

Source: Porter, M. and M. Kramer (1999) 'Philanthropy's new agenda: creating value', *Harvard Business Review*, November–December, p. 124.

Figure 7.1 Foundations create value in four ways

can carry powers to filter norms and methods, designating some as 'best practice' and excluding the rest.

Official agencies and especially endowed foundations have been cultivating policy networks and investing in new ideas (or recycling old ones) for decades. As a result, more often than not, they have successfully 'mobilized bias'. This strategy has been compared with three other strategies: one-off grants, multiple grants, and 'capacity-building' for one organization. The analysts present their comparisons graphically as shown in Figure 7.1.

In the meantime, where were those non-governmental agencies of aid, those most vocal about poverty, hunger, the grassroots – and innovation? With some important exceptions, they have mobilized little besides compassion for children and victims of disaster, and large streams of income. Most agencies stick by their old, tested model: transferring resources through micro-projects. Some agencies, looking for the exit, are concerned about the future of their projects after their support ends. A result is stepped-up attention to 'capacity-building', which tends to focus on revenues and how to keep them coming in from the aid system.

Since the 1980s, pressures have intensified to scale up organizations and their projects. Under the old aid axiom Bigger is Better, the usual path has been expansion: more fields of activity, more staff, more management layers, more financial turnover. Staffs of some NGOs in Bangladesh today number in the thousands, and manage far bigger budgets than local governments. Bigger can mean more influential, especially with the powers that be. But this does not necessarily mean more effective in generating changes, or in anchoring them among those whose poverty and exclusion justify an organization's existence and funding.

The other path to scaling up involves, paradoxically, curbing tendencies to grow. It may even mean smaller, more focused organizations. The point is to insert new approaches into public sector practice on a wider scale. This is so-called mainstreaming.[36] Historically, public sectors have adopted social innovations in schooling, housing and health started by non-profit bodies. Yet despite the historical record of acorn-into-oak-tree models, few aid agencies pursue this strategy. They prefer the sure, visible, well-financed path of direct delivery – even in the face of evidence that non-profit delivery is far less efficient and effective than broad public programmes.

Policy Activism

To scale up social innovations is one thing. It is another to shift rules of the games of debt, trade, financial flows and property rights. Policy advocacy towards governments and big business is a knowledge-intensive pursuit. To do it well, organizations need intellectual depth, communication skills and networking strategies – all informed by political savvy. Many aid agencies, especially private ones, lack these capacities and shrink from the thought of developing them. Some are willing to play only the safe role of ventriloquist's dummy, as some NGOs have done on behalf of governments at international conferences.

Inspired by the success of focused policy campaigns begun in the 1970s (such as on infant formulas promoted by food multi-nationals, and on debt) and discouraged by the meagre results of micro-projects, more private aid agencies have today begun exploring policy leverage. In Britain, where the official aid ministry favours NGO policy activism, a recent report for that ministry confirmed that many private aid agencies 'see their shift to advocacy coming about in recognition of the limited and short-term impacts of traditional operational development work, and in an effort to "scale up" their impact. As one interviewee put it, it is felt that "advocacy work can deliver a bigger bang for your buck".'[37]

Public pressure about injustice in faraway places has a long and honourable tradition, from the Anti-Slavery Society (1839) to various anti-war and pro-environment efforts in our times. Activism promoted by those within the aid system is more recent and sporadic, and reflects many shades of political opinion. A number of US-centred agencies such as CARE and World Vision, and a few European ones such as Médecins Sans Frontières France, were active anti-communist crusaders in the Cold War years.

The endowed foundations, as noted earlier, have generally favoured domesticated, Third Way reform rather than transformation. Faced with the non-routine politics of rebellion and protest in the US movement for civil rights in the 1960s, they provided millions to promote interest-group advocacy – that is, political action through routine channels.[38] Meanwhile, right-wing foundations have invested massively and effectively to put across their alternatives and rubbish the rest.[39]

Several private aid agencies in Britain – Oxfam, Christian Aid and Action Aid – have shown what can be accomplished beyond the micro-project, in the battle of ideas. These agencies have paid attention to the larger contexts of their work and developed conceptual handholds to grasp them. Among the results: global policy agendas from debt to farm pesticides to environment–poverty links have been permanently re-cast and concrete measures taken. Knowledge-based policy activists are building alliances with social movements, thus setting the pace of policy debates in the South and North. Media editors have an authoritative stream of critical views and alternative proposals. All this turns up the heat on the bubbling soup of policy ideas.

Yet the list of private aid agencies pursuing policy change is still not terribly long. Most continue to avoid engagement. They depict their tasks as doing, not thinking. Indeed, they are criticized for 'anti-intellectual tendencies'[40] and for severe learning disabilities, the 'failure to learn from failure'.[41] Such self-limitation can also be traced back to those who control revenues. In private charities, the fundraisers and marketing boys usually disapprove of taking public stands. Funding authorities in parliaments and ministries, sometimes backed by interests pressing to de-fund the left, have more often curbed than promoted policy activism.

FROM DELIVERY TO LEVERAGE? Realistically speaking, most official and private agencies are not about to transform themselves into knowledge-based innovators or proponents of fresh policies, let alone active combatants on the front-lines in the battle of ideas. The rewards of simply transferring resources are satisfying, and the risks of tackling issues of power and inequality are intimidating. Yet a number of trends may force a rethink, and for some a shift from delivery to leverage.[42] Briefly noted, these trends include:

Official encouragement Some official aid agencies in the past have encouraged non-profit policy activism on such issues as food aid and apartheid. Today a few of them are nudging non-profits further. Funding authorities in Britain, Denmark and the Netherlands have recently revised spending rules to make possible policy activism on wider fronts. The UNDP and UNICEF have begun to cast development policy in terms of social and economic rights.

'Participation' in aid-driven processes Worried by the shallow anchoring and legitimacy of policy conditions, and thus lack of borrower compliance with them, the IFIs and some donors have begun insisting on public participation in loan approval processes. Genuinely participatory they are not, but these processes might create some space for public comment and some skirmishing, if not battles, of ideas. Civil society bodies from the for- and non-profit branches, and media commentators will be airing views.

Demand from social movements Organizations of wage-earners, environmental activists, and others pressing for accountable and regulated capitalism and beyond show no signs of diminished need for policy knowledge; a problem is their lack of money to translate those needs into effective demand for policy research and dissemination. The World Social Forum, a gathering of activists and intellectuals held in Porto Alegre, Brazil, in early 2001, got most of its financial backing from progressive Brazilian local governments, but also got aid from Dutch and German quango donors and the Ford Foundation. Senior figures in the official aid system are clearly concerned about this movement's growing leverage and resistance to co-optation into the big tent of foreign aid.

Conclusion

By cornering and shrewdly backing the production, transmission and legitimation of knowledge and ideas, an elite corps of agencies – some endowed foundations, the World Bank, and a few UN and bilateral bodies – have made a little money go a long way. For decades, those investments have shaped paradigms, the public policies nested in them, and the debates about those policies. And that was the intention. As one of the economists present at the 1944 Bretton Woods meeting said, 'One of the most important functions of a development assistance institution is to influence the politics and strategies of aid recipient countries.'[43] This is deliberate, but it is not high conspiracy. There is no control room steering the flow of ideas from a secret location. Yet what a Harvard professor wrote about his own branch of area studies suggests the limits to freedom in the marketplace of ideas:

> Hence, as always, the main drive comes from Washington itself and from the shift in the way in which policymakers view America's role in international affairs. As always, major shifts of this type work their way through the system with remarkable speed, soon causing the heads of federal agencies, private grant-making foundations and university presidents to all speak with one voice.[44]

Notes

1. Keynes, J. M. (1936) *The General Theory of Employment, Interest and Money*, London: Macmillan.

2. Chalmers Johnson, quoted in 'Universities find foreign donations sometimes carry price. Foreign-studies aid scoured for political strings', *New York Times*, 9 December 1996.

3. Schattschneider, E. E. (1961) *The Semi-Sovereign People*, New York: Holt, Reinhart and Winston.

4. Wendt, A. (1999) *Social Theory of International Politics*, Cambridge: Cambridge University Press, p. 96.

5. Ibid., p. 371.

6. See Apthorpe, R. and D. Gasper (eds) (1996) 'Arguing development

policy: frames and discourses', *European Journal of Development Research* (Special Issue), 8 (1).

7. Watts, M. (1995) '"A New Deal in Emotions", theory and practice in the crisis of development', in J. Crush (ed.), *Power of Development*, London: Routledge, p. 55 (citing Kothari).

8. Howe, B. (1980) 'The emergence of scientific philanthropy 1900–1920', in R. Arnove (ed.), *Philanthropy and Cultural Imperialism*, Boston: G. K. Hall, pp. 25–54.

9. Slaughter, S. and E. Silva (1980) 'Looking backwards: how foundations formulated ideology in the progressive period', in R. Arnove (ed.), *Philanthropy and Cultural Imperialism*, Boston: G.K. Hall, p. 56.

10. Ibid., especially pp. 57–78.

11. Laski, H. (1930) 'Foundations, universities and research', *Dangers of Obedience and Other Essays*, New York: Harper & Brothers, p. 174.

12. Bell, M. (2000) 'American philanthropy, the Carnegie Corporation and poverty in South Africa', *Journal of Southern African Studies*, 26 (3): 493.

13. Schattschneider, *The Semi-Sovereign People*.

14. Nelson, J. and G. Ranis (1966) 'Measures to ensure the effective use of aid', USAID discussion paper, quoted in Wood, R. E. (1986) *From Marshall Plan to Debt Crisis: Foreign Aid and Development Choices in the World Economy*, Berkeley: University of California Press.

15. Sikkink, K. (1997) 'Development ideas in Latin America: paradigm shift and the Economic Commission for Latin America', in F. Cooper and R. Packard (eds), *International Development and the Social Sciences: Essays on the History and Politics of Knowledge*, Berkeley: University of California Press, pp. 228–56.

16. Rist, G. (1997) *The History of Development*, London: Zed Books, pp. 143–54. The NIEO did, however, gain some support from the leadership of UNCTAD in the 1970s.

17. Ibid., p. 155, citing *What Now: The 1975 Dag Hammarskjöld Report*, published in *Development Dialogue*, Stockholm.

18. Sharpless, J. (1997) 'Population science, private foundations, and development aid', in F. Cooper and R. Packard (eds), *International Development and the Social Sciences*, pp. 176–200.

19. Packard, R. (1997) 'Visions of postwar health and development and their impact on public health interventions in the developing world', in F. Cooper and R. Packard (eds), *International Development and the Social Sciences*, pp. 93–115.

20. Shiva, V. (1991) *The Violence of the Green Revolution*, London: Zed Books;

and Chambers, R. and J. Pretty (1994) 'Are the international agricultural research centres tackling the crucial issues of poverty and sustainability?', *International Agricultural Development*, November/December. In mid-2001 the UNDP issued a report extolling the virtues of genetically modified crops designed, it claimed, for poor farmers. Policy activists condemned the report for misdirecting attention away from issues of distribution. 'UN agency champions GM food crops for poor', *Guardian Weekly*, 19–25 July 2001.

21. See Leach, M. and R. Mearns (eds) (1996) *The Lie of the Land: Challenging Received Wisdom on the African Environment*, Oxford: James Currey, especially Swift, J., 'Desertification: narratives, winners and losers', pp. 73–90.

22. Gardner, J. (1980) *Legal Imperialism: American Lawyers and Foreign Aid in Latin America*, Madison: University of Wisconsin Press, p. 9.

23. A researcher at Harvard University's Kennedy School of Government has exposed many conceptual flaws of this initiative. See Pistor, K. (2000) 'The standardization of law and its effect on developing economies', *G-24 Discussion Paper Series*, 4, Geneva: UNCTAD.

24. Peattie, L. (1987) 'An idea in good currency and how it grew: the informal sector', *World Development*, 15 (7): 851–60.

25. Johnson, C. (2000) *Blowback: The Costs and Consequences of American Empire*, New York: Henry Holt and Company.

26. Samoff, J. (1992) 'The intellectual/financial complex of foreign aid', *Review of African Political Economy*, 53, pp. 60–87.

27. James Wolfensohn, cited in Standing, G. (2000) 'Brave new words? A critique of Stiglitz's World Bank rethink', *Development and Change*, 31: 737–63.

28. Samoff, J. (1999) 'Education sector analysis in Africa: limited national control and even less national ownership', *International Journal of Educational Development*, 19: 249–72.

29. SPM Consultants (1996) *Evaluation of the European Special Programme on South Africa* (for the European Commission DG8), Stockholm; and Tilton, D. (1996) *USAID in South Africa*, Washington, DC: Africa Policy Information Centre.

30. The economist Daly resigned in 1994 after a frustrating six years trying to promote ideas of sustainable development. Stiglitz was forced out as chief economist in late 1999, and in mid-2000 Kanbur resigned as editor of the Bank's flagship publication, the *World Development Report*, mainly because the US Treasury did not like their apostasy towards fundamentalist doctrine.

31. Samoff, 'Education sector analysis in Africa', p. 249.

32. World Bank (1996) 'World Bank research in the marketplace of ideas', *World Bank Policy and Research Bulletin*, 7 (1).

33. Gosovic, B. (2000) 'Global intellectual hegemony and the international development agenda', *International Social Science Journal*, 166: 452.

34. Europe-Third World Centre and others (2000) *Relations entre les Nations Unies et les sociétés transnationales, Statement to Human Rights Sub-Commission, United Nations*, Geneva: CETIM. Web address: http://www.cetim.ch/2000/00FS04W4.htm.

35. Levy, D. C. (1996) *Building the Third Sector: Latin America's Private Research Centers and Nonprofit Development*, Pittsburgh: University of Pittsburgh Press, p. 1.

36. Uvin, P. and others (2000) 'Think large and act small: toward a new paradigm for NGO scaling up', *World Development*, 28 (8): 1409–19; and Wils, F. (1995) 'Scaling up, mainstreaming, and accountability: the challenge for NGOs', in M. Edwards and D. Hulme (eds), *Non-Governmental Organisations – Performance and Accountability*, London: Earthscan, pp. 53–62.

37. Hudson, A. (2000) *Linking the Levels? The Organisation of UK Development NGOs' Advocacy, End of Grant Report for DfID (ESCOR)*. Web address: http://www.alanhudson.plus.com/dfidreport.pdf.

38. Minkoff, D. (1994) 'From service provision to institutional advocacy: the shifting legitimacy of organizational forms', *Social Forces*, 72 (4): 943–69.

39. George, S. (1997) 'How to win the war of ideas. Lessons from the Gramscian right', *Dissent*, September–December.

40. Burnell, P. (1991) *Charity, Politics and the Third World*, London: Harvester, p. 275.

41. Smillie, I. (1993) 'Changing partners: Northern NGOs, Northern governments', in Smillie, I. and H. Helmich (eds), *Non-Governmental Organisations and Governments: Stakeholders for Development*, Paris: OECD, p. 18.

42. Edwards, M., D. Hulme and T. Wallace (1998) *NGOs in a Global Future: Marrying Local Delivery to Worldwide Leverage*, NGOs in a Global Future Conference, January 1999.

43. Raymond Mikesell, cited in Caufield, C. (1996) *Masters of Illusion: The World Bank and the Poverty of Nations*, New York: Henry Holt and Company, p. 193.

44. Owen, R. (1997) 'Globalisation of area studies in America', *The Middle East at Harvard: Newsletter of the Center of Middle East Studies*, 11, Summer, cited in I. Grendzier, 'Following the flag', *Middle East Report*, October–December 1997, pp. 10–11.

EIGHT
Outcomes in Four Dimensions

The stories of the hunt will be tales of glory until the day when the animals have their own historians. (popular saying, Zimbabwe)

Happy endings are the trademarks of good foreign aid stories. Plots are preferably simple: people are in distress; beneficent problem-solvers intervene; the distress is relieved; life gets a little better. Such narratives are told and retold because, as an anthropologist once remarked about myths and legends, they are 'good to think'. Aid narratives gratify needs to feel good. Those needs are powerful and widespread. They boost political backing for official aid. And their commercial payoff is apparent in the spectacular boom for charities specializing in telling stories about people far away for whom aid is salvation.

Simple, upbeat narratives have long been criticized, however, even from within the aid industry. By over-simplifying matters, they make aid look too good to be true, fuelling doubts about the aid industry's honesty. Environmental activists – among them some of the World Bank's most effective opponents – enjoy far higher credibility; indeed, they are regarded as more trustworthy than almost anyone else in Western public life. Today the industry faces rising pressures to tell it like it is – or risk further exposure by research and journalism not under its control. In the late 1990s, industry leaders began to acknowledge not only aid's lack of success, but also its propensity to do harm.

An example of candour and self-criticism is a report, issued in 2000, by one of the citadels of aid, the OECD.[1] It presents results of a major inquiry about aid in Mali, a country heavily dependent on aid for decades, and subjected to aid-driven structural adjustment programmes since 1981. Among its main findings:

- Aid 'weakens national institutions' because it bypasses public sectors via parallel structures managed by or answerable to donors; aid is exempted from taxes and duties; it hires away the best local staff; it fails to take into account Malian contributions to development initiatives; for these and related reasons, most of its benefits are unlikely to be sustained.
- There is a discrepancy between the amount of aid provided (more than $50 per head per year for the last two decades) and the rise in living standards – which in general have hardly risen at all.
- The amounts of money provided 'on behalf of Mali' are significantly greater than the 'sums actually injected into the economy'.
- The adjustment programmes had severe social effects for some population categories. Findings from household surveys also point to an increase in poverty over this period.
- In most cases the structural adjustment programmes were not 'owned' to any great degree by the Malian authorities and the managers assigned to carrying them out.
- Donors were quite satisfied with the success and relevance of their projects, while Malians think otherwise: 'local people had the impression that aid took no account of their priorities'.
- Serious reform of aid is essential. That will require 'a sort of "revolt" against certain aspects of the way in which the aid system works. To put it another way, one of the keys to success may lie in how indignant, or how indifferent, the leading actors are about widely acknowledged cases of wasted resources and inefficiency.'

Proposals for revolt are hardly commonplace in publications of the OECD, but otherwise this report contains no surprises. Gaps between the optimistic narratives of foreign aid and its complex, ambiguous and often disappointing realities have long been known. Often these gaps are deliberately concealed. But getting to the 'truth' about aid outcomes can be genuinely difficult. Hard conclusions remain out of reach for a number of reasons:

- Managers in aid chains pay attention chiefly to internal operations and spending, and then only during a programme's lifespan; they rarely look hard at outcomes; indeed, they may be discouraged from doing so by the risks of embarrassment, threats of funding cuts, and political sensitivity of results.
- Impact evaluation is a young, inexact science hampered by theoretical and practical problems, notably in conceptualizing and measuring three things:[2]
  - contributions of each segment of an aid chain, posing the issue of whose performance is being evaluated;
  - conditions before an aid intervention, and the relevance and accuracy of the indicators of the situation after; and
  - relations of cause and effect, especially when a host of other factors – from weather to markets to personalities – also influence outcomes in complex, hard-to-measure ways.

  Some specialists hold that the complexities make it impossible to reach hard conclusions about outcomes.
- Lack of independence and thus objectivity of the evaluator.
- Dependence on resources at the receiving end discourages full and open responses; intended beneficiaries, for example, may fear trouble if they give 'wrong' answers to inquiring outsiders.

In the swamp of loose and watery knowledge about aid outcomes, there are few hard places on which to stand. The industry's mainstream often dismisses as merely anecdotal the findings by outsiders – journalists, academics, policy activists or fearless local citizens at the receiving end. Yet their information has often helped to build what solid footing there is in the swamp.

The following observations about aid outcomes are based on findings by industry insiders and outsiders. These are clustered under four objective interests that, according to international relations theorist Alexander Wendt, countries must satisfy over the long run in order to be secure in the world: physical survival; economic well-being; political autonomy or self-determination; and collective self-esteem.[3]

Survival

Foreign aid's finest hours are thought to be those in which lives were saved and suffering relieved on a large scale. An official Dutch report on relief aid in Somalia 1991–93, for example, credits the International Committee of the Red Cross (ICRC) with having saved hundreds of thousands of lives. In most African settings, food relief usually accounts for only a small fraction of what famine victims manage to consume. During most crises, host governments and citizens – not the foreign aid system – shoulder the biggest burdens of care and protection. Nevertheless, the conclusions about relief aid in Somalia's violent crisis, even if exaggerated, are impressive; they testify to great effort and courage. Yet these stories have shadow sides, involving the suffering of hundreds of thousands, if not millions.

In the Somali crisis, aid agencies such as the ICRC together paid out tens of millions of dollars in protection money to warlords, the very authors of the violence, who then pursued their crimes in anticipation of yet more aid – rewards that the aid system had always conferred on previous Somali strongmen. Similar cases have appeared in Zaire and West Africa. With some exceptions, humanitarian agencies and the media at first ignored those perverse outcomes. Journalists and researchers later brought them to the surface, provoking lively debates and some agency rethinking. Today the ICRC stands out among humanitarian agencies for drawing public attention to the economics of today's civil wars and to the risks that aid can fuel them.[4]

The complex political emergencies of Central America, Afghanistan, the Balkans and so many corners of Africa may be home-grown, but they were also seeded and cultivated over years of foreign intervention, including aid, with corrosive effects on local institutions.[5] The perverse outcomes arising from some humanitarian aid efforts stem from long-term process of political decay. Earlier development aid, for example, has often helped destroy reciprocal norms of give and take between rulers and ruled. Alex de Waal, a close observer of famine and the aid industry, reaches the following conclusions, ending on an exceptional African case where a political contract between state and citizens worked to *prevent* catastrophe:

> Overall, relief aid appears not to contribute to the development of a form of governance that is likely to promote the struggle against famine. The basic elements of a political contract against famine are not there in the aid encounter. On the contrary, aid can often be an obstacle to the development of the political awareness and political processes needed for such a contract to emerge. Where a contract already exists, however, aid can achieve its humanitarian goals without adverse political impacts. For example, the Botswanan drought relief programme is essentially an indigenous relief and rehabilitation programme based on a national political contract.[6]

While aid has sometimes helped groups to survive, it has only occasionally been a major factor in the survival of an entire nation. Massive aid to Mozambique's government and its opponents (as part of a peace deal) did help stabilize a fragile situation after 1990. The survival of the Palestinian nation, albeit in dreary refugee camps, could be credited in part to the UN Relief and Works Agency, probably the oldest single humanitarian endeavour on earth.

A more striking outcome is collapse. Under aid auspices, a number of nations have been polarized and made politically fragile. Rwanda, Somalia and Congo-Kinshasa, to name merely three cases from the 1990s, suffered widespread breakdown. Afghanistan's collapse as a viable state was partly due to massive support to anti-Soviet Islamic guerrillas and aid benefits to Pakistan. In 1996 this was termed one of the great successes of US aid.[7] Many have paid a high price for this 'success'.

How can aid prevent fragility and collapse? As economic openness is a central tenet of their doctrine, the World Bank and IMF unsurprisingly claim that greater integration into the world economy reduces conflict. But they appear to be projecting fact from doctrine, for the contrary may be closer to the truth. Numerous studies now show that as global economic integration advances unevenly in low-income countries, social fabrics are torn and competitive scrambles for survival intensify.[8] The economist Valpy FitzGerald identifies three factors that can trigger violent conflict and put national survival in jeopardy:[9]

- sudden widening of disparities in wealth and income, either vertically between social strata or horizontally between territorial/ethnic groups, generating a collective sense of injustice and resentment, undermining legitimacy of local institutions;
- increasing uncertainty about the livelihoods and assets of dominant or subordinate groups, generating collective insecurity;
- weakening of the capacity of the state to provide public goods in ways seen to be fair, undermining the legitimacy of the public sector and government as a whole.

Does foreign aid help or hinder such processes? Aid-driven austerity measures are known to cause sharp increases in inequality. Such shifts have often provoked violent instability, of which so-called IMF riots are only one instance.[10] Feelings of collective insecurity are not easy to survey, but the volatility of aid flows correlates strongly with peaks and dips in economic output, provoking uncertainty for investors and consumers alike.[11]

Ups and downs in world markets can affect societies severely. By demanding that poor economies stake their futures on world markets, aid industry leaders commonly ignore the risks and who will lose if things go badly. In the 1980s USAID and the World Bank vigorously promoted coffee farming among poor smallholders in Rwanda. But having pushed that crop in other countries too, aid experts forgot a bit of elementary economics, for the composite result was a glut of coffee on world markets and a price collapse. Tens of thousands of Rwandan farmers suddenly fell into even deeper poverty. Social tensions grew and within a few years exploded. With cocoa the story was much the same, though mercifully without major violence: insistence on exports above all else, enticement of poor farmers to take the risks, world over-production, and price collapse. This 'immiserizing growth' – unstable mixes of a few winners and many losers – is not an inevitable outcome of aid-driven doctrine, but it has been a common outcome.[12]

'Current international arrangements', writes FitzGerald, 'are not "responsible" or "the cause of" such conflicts, but they can exacerbate or ameliorate the domestic political tensions and state failures leading to conflicts.'[13] As leading designers of economic strategies, the IMF and World Bank should have paid attention to the risks of violent conflict, just as building architects are required by law to pay attention to fire and earthquake risks. But there is no evidence of such attention. Indeed, in the early 1990s, just before Rwanda and Burundi toppled into violence, the IFIs had praised those countries as good performers in terms of market fundamentalism. Only around 1997 did the IFIs begin to revisit their policy incoherence.[14] Meanwhile the rest of the world is facing increased political fragility, insecurity, anger and violence made worse by growing millions with precarious livelihoods.

Economic Well-being

One of the industry's key suppositions is that aid promotes growth. Does it? The question has absorbed much computer time and printer's ink, yet a definitive answer remains elusive. Most studies conclude that if all recorded growth rates are taken together, aid does nudge growth – a little. But where fast-growing Malaysia and Sri Lanka are lumped together with troubled Malawi and Congo, important differences will be concealed. The economist and aid expert Paul Mosley split up recorded growth data by major regions, correlating them with aid flows over the 1960s, 1970s and 1980s. His conclusion: 'the net impact of aid [on GDP growth] is neutral overall, probably positive in most Asian countries and almost certainly negative in most African countries'.[15] That aid probably hinders growth where it has been most intense, such as in Africa, is consistent with a recent econometric study showing a 'significant impact of aid on growth, as long as the aid to GDP ratio is not excessively high'.[16]

Has market fundamentalism made a difference to growth? Recent history suggests that it has made a big difference – largely for the worse. Recorded growth in the period 1960 to 1980, before the doctrine was enforced, has been compared with growth in the period 1980–98, when the doctrine ruled. In Latin America, per capita GDP increased by 75 per cent in the first period, but in the second it grew by a mere 6 per cent. In sub-Saharan Africa per capita GDP grew by 36 per cent in the first period, but *fell* by 15 per cent in the second.[17] Even orthodox *Business Week* found these figures disturbing.[18]

Is the aid system's main policy package then simply perverse, frustrating its own objective, rapid growth? According to the current mainstream consensus, there are no significant effects one way or another.[19] The truth may be harder. A recent, exhaustive, study concludes that the effect of IMF programmes is in fact negative.[20] Putting the best possible light on market fundamentalism – aid's holy gospel since 1980 – it is now clear that it has failed to show a positive balance of outcomes, even on its own terms. That doctrine is, in short, a bogus idea.

Perplexed, aid industry economists have revisited the numbers and dusted off some old books. They have rediscovered what economists like Veblen, Keynes, Myrdal and Hirschman have argued: abstract, universal models of growth don't work well, 'even when playing the far easier game of explaining past growth rather than improving future growth'.[21] That is, growth is a more mysterious process, more dependent on complex dynamics of specific times and places, than the aid industry has assumed. One conclusion is clear: growth is not driven by one predominant factor. The one true path does not exist. In terms of history, theory and practice, the assertion that 'there is no alternative' to market fundamentalism is nonsense on stilts.

Whose well-being is improved by foreign aid? Both high and low on aid chains, that question has made people uneasy. A lot of fuzzy words, talk of the future, and outright camouflage have concealed evidence about the matter. Since the late 1990s, however, the study of inequality has gained momentum, generating insights into foreign aid's contribution to a fairer world.

Income inequality tends to increase under aid-driven structural adjustment, especially where an economy is growing and aid conditionalities are tough and applied rapidly and fully – that is, 'shock therapy'.[22] Other studies show that income inequality worsens with greater economic openness, which also exposes the poor to trade-related shocks.[23] Standard IFI measures redistribute income upwards. The share of income going to labour drops, that going to capital rises. In addition, cutbacks in public services and food subsidies, the social wage, have hit the poor far harder than middle- and upper-income groups. Using a lens of political economy, two economists reached the following summary. Winners of structural adjustment have tended to be:

> industrialists in a position to gain from liberalization and an export push (by no means comprising the total of national firms), financial speculators, households in the top 10–20 percent of the income distribution who can afford an ample array of new consumer goods in a liberalized trade regime, and a local economic technocracy that put the new policy packages in place. The losers included people in the bottom 80 percent of the distribution, some important industrialists, and old political elites.[24]

Especially where aid has been long and intense, it can worsen social stratification. In Burkina Faso and Mozambique, for example, elites have captured aid benefits to gain productive assets, especially land.[25] With its emphasis on private social services and other forms of upward redistribution, fundamentalist policies have helped pull up the ladders by which poorer children can gain higher social status. Thus, in the scramble to get ahead, children of the better-off crowd out the poorer. Social mobility tapers off, social castes solidify.

Yet aid has sometimes helped hold the line against worsening inequalities. In Mozambique, local organizations subsidized by politically astute aid agencies mounted a successful campaign to redefine the land law, and thus preserve some land access for the poor. Aid from a few private aid agencies probably helped at crucial moments in countries such as Brazil and South Africa, where unions and other social movement organizations created a political climate that tipped balances against austerity measures affecting the poor.

There is a further twist in the tale of inequality. Contrary to what trickle-down or 'horse-and-sparrow' economics[26] predicts, a fairer distribution of income and wealth tends to *improve* growth and general economic well-being, and to reduce rates of poverty. Studies have shown that inequality is bad for growth – a finding that even some in the World Bank now accept.[27] Such findings make intuitive sense. Growth in South Africa, a highly unequal society, is sluggish. Its torpor contrasts sharply with the economic dynamism in Vietnam, a relatively egalitarian land. Plausibly, where aid promotes inequality – as it has done under market funda-mentalism – it can put a brake on growth. Since economic openness tends to worsen income inequality and to expose the poor to shocks, there are probably trade-offs between outwardly oriented growth and pro-poor growth.

Aid to low-income countries does not automatically yield aid to low-income people. Take the case of Bangladesh. Anti-poverty talk saturates aid rhetoric about that country. Yet studies by senior Bangladeshi researchers tell a different story. In the three decades from independence in 1971 up to 2000, foreign aid had been distributed roughly as follows:

- 25 per cent to foreign suppliers, agents, consultants, etc;
- 30 per cent to domestic Bangladeshi bureaucrats, politicians, commission agents, consultants and contractors;
- 20 per cent to higher-income groups in urban and rural areas; and
- 25 per cent to lower-income people, chiefly in rural areas.[28]

Elsewhere, distribution of aid benefits may be even worse. In Rwanda, a study concludes that aid beneficiaries are not among the poorer half of the population, but are rather 'heavily weighted in favor of the wealthiest and the well-connected'.[29]

Information about debt also speaks to the question of aid distribution. In 23 countries for which estimates were made in the late 1990s, 57 per cent of the foreign debt (about $451 billion, mostly aid-derived) stems from dictatorships of recent decades; much of that money simply made a 'round trip' back to Northern financial circuits. Of Indonesia's $126 billion debt in the late 1990s, an estimated 98 per cent was incurred by the family and close associates of the Suharto regime, a donor darling.[30] At about $600 per person, that debt was equivalent to Indonesia's 1998 per capita GNP.

Plausibly, aid's immediate or first-round distributional effects are not the last word in the distribution story. Public goods such as roads and waterworks built by contractors, for example, may benefit low-income people by increasing the demand for labour or lowering food costs. Paul Mosley tested this hypothesis in the 1980s, but reached pessimistic conclusions. Although exceptions were identified – mainly cases where national or lower-level governments pursued deliberate policies of redistribution – aid was not very good at downward redistribution.[31]

In many sectors little is known about long-term outcomes. Take university scholarship programmes, some of them aid-supported since the 1960s. What is the balance of benefits to individuals versus benefits to the low-income societies from which they came? Despite personal knowledge of this field and an extensive search,[32] the present writer is not aware of any systematic information on the question.

Aid to basic education and to basic health may be rising slightly, but in 1999 those two sectors received a pitiful 1 and 2 per cent respectively of bilateral aid commitments. Spending in other sectors is even less oriented towards poverty reduction. The outspokenly anti-poverty UNDP, for example, spends more than 60 per cent of its transport programme funds on civil aviation.[33] Yet even pro-poor activities are regularly captured by the non-poor. Micro-finance, a major aid fashion of the 1990s, has proved on closer examination to be riddled with distributional problems, contrary to claims of its enormous advantages for the very poor and women.[34]

Foreign aid's outcomes for the physical integrity of the planet – water, air, soils and living species – are mixed to the point of paradox. Here too, aid institutions have seldom used the late-comer's advantage to leapfrog over known error and make a fresh start. Instead the aid industry has generally muddled along with other industries to reproduce 'modernization' and 'development'. Thus it more often complicates environmental problems than resolves them. Nevertheless, aid has made some concrete contributions: in many tropical cities, foreign aid financed the humble drainage and sewerage systems, thus improving public health for poor and rich alike.

More striking, however, are the perverse outcomes: dams that create 'development refugees' and epidemics of water-borne disease; irrigation schemes that deplete water supplies and destroy more livelihoods than they create; urban transport systems based on the automobile, a cause of grossly inefficient cities, drains on foreign exchange, and high costs to human health from bad air and accidents.

Neglect of institutions and politics is a common failing. The Inter-American Development Bank successfully promoted US-style protected natural areas in countries like Brazil. But US-style institutions – social and governmental watchdogs – do not exist in sufficient strength in Brazil to enforce genuine protection. As a result, so-called protected areas are exposed to destruction by what were once legitimate timber companies now operating illegally, having corrupted the public sector in the process.[35]

A different kind of unintended consequence of IFI policy has been popular resistance. In struggles around mega-projects to dam rivers and raze forests, environmental activists have been among the most consistent and effective challengers to non-account-ability at the top of the aid system. One result has been the World Bank's decision in 1994 to set up an Inspection Panel to assess public complaints. In Brazil, a major environmental battle-field, citizens' experience with that panel has been disappointing.[36] Yet the creation of such a panel marks a democratic victory: a powerful, arrogant and hitherto non-transparent aid agency was forced to accept the principle of public accountability to those affected by its power.

Political Autonomy

Western foreign aid helped defeat communism, thus achieving one of its primordial goals. Aid has sometimes enabled coherent states to emerge. In a few cases – Korea, Taiwan, Botswana – national government and politics took over as the intensity of aid fell. Often, however, aid has tended to rob states and citizens of political power and self-determination. Outcomes include:

- fragile, hollow and corrupted public institutions that have lost legitimacy and reciprocal links with citizens;
- decay or destruction of instruments to steer public policy and to mobilize public revenues; and
- political accountability upwards and outwards, effectively a surrender of sovereignty.

A study correlating aid flows to 80 countries with indicators of the quality of their governance – corruption, bureaucratic quality, and the rule of law – reveals a shocking pattern: as aid intensity increases (that is, as aid accounts for a larger share of a country's recorded GNP), the quality of public institutions worsens. The direction of causation runs from aid to bad institutions.[37] Such conclusions sound plausible. Before Tanzania, Mozambique, the Ukraine and Nicaragua began getting massive doses of aid, their public sector management and legal systems may have been basic and unimaginative, but at least they were not ravaged by corruption, loss of good staff, demoralization, legal decay and rampant gangsterism.

Aid has created winners and losers. Where, as in a number of African countries, the aid industry is the second-largest employer (after the public sector), social outcomes are easy to attribute; they show up in the rise of a well-paid technocratic stratum and the mushrooming of thousands of NGOs. It also has less direct effects. Where aid has promoted the downsizing of public sectors and the selling off of public assets, winners include domestic private investors and officials who straddle public and private sectors. Losers include former wage-earners now trapped in precarious livelihoods. Trade unions will have shrunk and lost clout. In short, aid has helped reconfigure the social basis for politics.

How such social shifts play out in political life depends on paths laid down over generations, if not centuries. Path dependence can be illustrated in the case of Italy. In its northern regions, diverse but often horizontal patterns of civic and political life are more open and participatory than the vertical, patronage-based political traditions of southern Italy. Measures to improve governance throughout Italy in the 1970s and 1980s followed those old patterns; unsurprisingly, outcomes were much better in northern regions.[38] Political change thus tends to follow very old paths.

Where governance centres on personal rule and weak public oversight, external linkages such as to donors will usually reinforce the status quo – as dealings with outsiders occur only with the blessing of a 'big man' politician. Where politics are anchored in publicly accountable institutions, on the other hand, outside reinforcement of patronage can be avoided. Bearing such differences in mind, the following tendencies are often detected among political outcomes of aid:

- Development policy issues are portrayed and managed as technical matters, thus kept outside public political discussion.
- Power over most economic issues shifts upwards and outwards, away from representative bodies such as parliaments and towards technical units in finance ministries and central banks insulated from public politics; thus politicians account upwards to donors/lenders (mainly in Washington, DC), not downwards to citizens.
- Downward linkages are limited to groups – businesses, non-profits and technocrats – with strong immediate stakes in the outward orientation of the economy and polity, while accountability to the public is reduced to hollow events, such as manipulated elections.
- Organizations in civil society face funding incentives and ideological pressure to drop political mobilization and protest and take up service delivery or domesticated 'lobbying' activities.

Problems sharpen when these trends combine with weakened public sector abilities to deliver basic social services, physical security and legal protection on a broad and fair basis. The incapacity of public institutions to provide these things undercuts their legitimacy and the willingness of citizens to pay taxes and fees. Aid can worsen these trends to the extent that it becomes the chief source of power and legitimation for elites.

Research suggests that rulers who rely on offshore revenue sources such as oil are not very good at converting those riches into public goods. By contrast, rulers relying on production onshore tend to be more successful at converting available resources, however modest, into rising living standards for the poor.[39] Aid can act like oil revenues, driving a wedge between rulers and ruled. Authorities can feed cities, fit out their armies and police, reward their constituents and punish rivals without having to rely on the output, taxes and fees of farmers and wage-earners.

When the donors speak, they get full attention; when citizens voice complaints or smuggle their production abroad, they can still be safely ignored. For in the end aid pays the bills.

Foreign debt is a major outcome of foreign aid. At first sight that is not surprising, since the IFIs are after all in the business of selling loans, while various bilateral agencies also deal in loans (accounting for about 18 per cent of total net ODA in 2000). Yet viewed over the long term this is an astonishing result. For the main purpose of most of the loans was to boost countries' capacities to repay. But in places of greatest aid intensity that capacity is weaker than ever. Table 8.1 shows the stock of foreign debt to aid system lenders.

The graph in Appendix D illustrates for each region the absolute levels of debt by type of lender. Private debt is highly significant in Latin America and the Caribbean, whereas sub-Saharan Africa's debts are largely to official aid bodies.

Debt is obviously an economic issue. It puts long-term claims on surpluses that would otherwise be usefully invested. It also discourages long-term investors who fear taxation and inadequate public goods because governments have to pay foreign creditors before anything else. Negotiating and renegotiating debt puts heavy demands on the scarce time and attention of officials. Debt also puts claims on foreign aid itself: currently large chunks of ODA go not to the South or East, but to creditors at upper ends of aid chains, that is, into the shell game of debt roll-overs.[40] Much of this lending is defensive: it protects bankers by keeping the system turning over, concealing bad performance, forestalling default and maintaining the fiction that low-income nations will some day pay back what dictators and technocrats borrowed in their name.

Among 62 countries classified as low-income in 2000, debt repayment (mainly to official agencies) claimed about 19 per cent of recorded export earnings. For the severely indebted countries among them, debt servicing claimed about 24 per cent of earnings. Among severely indebted middle-income countries such as

TABLE 8.1 Stock of debt owed to bilateral and multilateral lenders in 2000

	Sub-Saharan Africa	South Asia	North Africa and Middle East	E. Europe and Central Asia	Latin America and Caribbean	East Asia
As % of total debt	78	72	66	37	25	38
As % of exports of goods and services	113	108	46	34	36	23

Source: World Bank (2001) World Development Finance.

Argentina, Russia and Turkey, a whopping 81 per cent of export earnings on average went towards servicing debts.[41] Such repayment levels are not set naturally, but negotiated over years with creditors. Terms are severe compared with those negotiated after the Second World War for Germany, whose repayments never exceeded 3.4 per cent of export earnings. Indeed, for borrowers over their heads in debt, today's terms are unrealistic, being set for political rather than economic reasons.

Debt is at bottom a political outcome. It is a social construction. The cascade of post-war political decisions to deregulate capital flows and orient weaker economies outwards set the stage for debt control as a means of political surveillance. Indebted states have much less freedom to respond to citizens. They will tend to cut spending on social protection and public services for fear of capital flight, donor strikes and denial of investment. Debt draws economic surpluses upwards and outwards, and does much the same with political power. It has helped shatter sovereignty and frustrate the emergence of public, democratic control over the economy.

The hollowing-out of national sovereignty gathered pace under structural adjustment programmes, although the IFI leadership for years kept saying with straight faces that the borrowing governments were in charge. Debt shifts control even further away from borrower hands. In the case of sub-Saharan Africa, economists associated with IFIs recently did some arithmetic in political economy. In 1998, of about $16 billion received from the aid system, only $3 billion went to general government budgets; the rest went to projects. In that year, however, African governments paid $9 billion to service their debts; for their national budgets, the aid balance was a net negative $6 billion. Of course some aid to projects may have afforded governments a little 'fungibility', that is, freedom to spend on other purposes. But the main freedoms are enjoyed by those who call the shots about projects, that is, the donors and lenders. Financially and politically, where donors and lenders assign higher priority to debt servicing and projects than to direct aid for national budgets, they effectively deny recipient governments powers to make decisions and to take responsibility for their actions.[42]

Around 1999, in response to concerted civil protest and eroding credibility North and South, the IFIs repackaged their structural adjustment lending. They hoped thereby to put recipients in the drivers' seats. The accent is on anti-poverty action – a field in which the IFIs are not noted for success. Debt reduction and soft loans for the heavily indebted are to be conditioned on recipient government preparation, with IFI help, of Poverty Reduction Strategy Papers (PRSPs). To ensure local 'ownership' of them, governments must promote policy-making in concert with bodies in the civil and the for-profit sectors.

This strategem requires a willing suspension of disbelief. For the top of the aid system now insists that borrowing governments become anti-poverty crusaders and promoters of open, participative, extra-parliamentary policy-making – roles that major lenders/donors had never played themselves, and indeed for decades had actively discouraged among borrowers. Donors/lenders may be applauded for accepting principles of public consultation, but their actual practice has been hollow, even deceptive. An independent, comprehensive review of that practice concludes as follows:

> Reviews of World Bank CASs [Country Assistance Strategies], and our knowledge of other donors' assistance strategies, suggest that civil society 'participation' in them rarely extends beyond information-sharing and consultation to shared agenda-setting, decision-making or any kind of empowerment for participants.[43]

Initial assessments of the new IFI approach to policy-making were not optimistic. Organizations watching PRSP processes at close range in Africa have rejected them as the old fundamentalist conditionality, now dangerously broadened to include governance, repackaged for better public relations.[44] At the same time a senior mainstream economist with in-depth knowledge of the IFIs noted the large gaps between the theory of the PRSPs and the practice, which show many of the hallmarks of donor, not recipient, ownership.[45]

Creating space for genuine participation in policy-making is of course not easy. Gaps between talk and practice are found not only where big agencies are at work, but also where private aid agencies interact with their end-of-chain recipients.[46] One researcher concludes that the participation agenda 'has been organized around a highly moral rhetoric and is located in an NGO movement which has been unwilling to acknowledge the role that power and interests plan in its agenda'.[47]

Collective Self-esteem

Does foreign aid enable nations and peoples to feel good about themselves, to enjoy respect and status? In so far as cooperative attitudes and behaviour depend on positive self-images, that is not a trivial question, since many in the aid industry refer to their work as 'cooperation'. On the face of it, aid is not a prime candidate to promote collective self-esteem. It tends to locate 'the problem' in the incapacities (underdevelopment, backwardness, and so on) of the people it is supposed to help. Their shortcomings demonstrate the need for aid and even trusteeship.

Such points of departure risk stigmatizing and patronizing people. They can boost the prestige of the outsider's solutions and belittle local solutions. In both crude and subtle ways the aid encounter exposes differences in wealth, status and power, fostering feelings of humiliation and powerlessness. From there it is but a few steps to fear, loathing and aggression. These issues may be well known in social work and other helping professions, but in matters of international relations, group self-esteem appears to be poorly studied.[48] Only fragmentary evidence is available about aid's outcomes for self-esteem.

From rugby games to conclaves of world leaders, moments of palpable national pride for South Africans were numerous and vivid following the country's first democratic election in 1994 and its re-admission, with high status, to the world community. Yet the most powerful branch of the aid system had *delayed* that outcome. Up to 1967 the World Bank loaned apartheid South Africa far more money than to any other land in sub-Saharan Africa. The IMF kept up its support for 16 more years, and remained influential even after 1983, when the US Congress outlawed IMF lending to apartheid.[49] Another group of aid agencies took a different line. From the early 1970s to 1994, aid from Scandinavia, India, some Eastern Bloc countries, Western solidarity groups and later the European Community modestly *advanced* a democratic outcome by supporting South Africa's movement for majority rule.

From Tehran to Monrovia to Khartoum, with support from the top of the aid system, ruling elites have offended or oppressed racial and ethnic groups or religious minorities. Some of those regimes ended in firestorms of public anger. People know who the donors' darlings are. 'Israel receives more US aid per capita annually than the *total annual* GNP per capita of several Arab states, including Egypt, Mauritania, Sudan, Yemen and Morocco.'[50] Such biases provoke feelings of injustice and rage, thereby swelling the ranks of political Islam.

Aid can undercut self-esteem in everyday ways. In Rwanda, where the 'development enterprise' in its pre-genocide years has been studied in depth, it reinforced feelings of exclusion and impunity, thereby teasing out and inflaming prejudice. Aid contributed to a system that humiliated and infantilized people, robbing them of their self-respect and their creativity.[51]

But the aid encounter may at times spark rejection and a turn inwards. A sociologist of African churches writes:

> For many, self-esteem and self-confidence have been the first casualties of Africa's decline. We heard Otabil begin his preaching in Zambia: 'When you look at yourself as an African, it is easy to think that God has cursed you ... We are a people who feel

inferior and wallow in our own inferiority.' It was this that led him to develop his theology of black pride.[52]

Outcomes may thus be highly mixed: greater dependence and subservience, compensated (for some) by greater self-confidence and entrepreneurship. Clearly the booming response to donor demand for NGOs – many tens of thousands of them having sprung up in low-income countries – does not indicate a lack of pep and optimism. Granted, most of those NGOs would vanish without a trace if donors were to pull the plug. But recent histories of civil societies in Brazil, South Africa and the Philippines suggest the effects that small, hardy minorities of politically aware NGOs can serve as training grounds and launching-pads for self-confident emancipatory action.

If a publication of the OECD can call for revolt against the aid system, and if African observers draw hope from 'collective insubordination' detected in their continent, then there are grounds for optimism. But much remains to be overcome. Two statements on aid's effects in Africa, by African researchers, conclude this chapter:

> The aid–recipient relationship in Africa has developed into one that neither generates mutual respect nor synergetically harnesses the capacities of all those involved. Instead, it has generated the dependency syndrome, cynicism, and 'aid fatigue'.[53]

> In the long run, and all other things being equal, foreign assistance dependence, like drug addiction, destroys rather than enhances the institutional capacities of the users, paralyses national initiatives, diminishes peoples' faith and confidence in their abilities, and erodes the very basis of national sovereignty.[54]

Notes

1. Damon, J. and others (2000) *Improving the Effectiveness of Aid Systems: The Case of Mali*, Paris: OECD Club du Sahel and UNDP web address: http://www.oecd.org/sah/products/mali.htm.

2. Adapted from Fowler, A. and K. Biekart (1996) 'Do private aid agencies make a difference?', in Sogge D., K. Biekart and J. Saxby (eds), *Compassion and Calculation*, London: Pluto Press, pp. 107–35.

3. Wendt, A. (1999) *Social Theory of International Politics*, Cambridge: Cambridge University Press, pp. 233–7.

4. ICRC (2000) *War, Money and Survival*, Geneva: International Committee of the Red Cross (ICRC).

5. See for example Uvin, P. (1998) *Aiding Violence: The Development Enterprise in Rwanda*, West Hartford, CT: Kumarian Press; de Waal, A. (1997) *Famine Crimes: Politics and the Disaster Relief Industry in Africa*, Oxford: James Currey; Middleton, N. and P. O'Keefe (1998) *Disaster and Development: The Politics of Humanitarian Aid*, London: Pluto Press.

6. de Waal, A. (2000) *Who Fights? Who Cares?*, Trenton, NJ: Africa World Press, p. 153.

7. Zimmerman, R. and S. Hook (1996) 'The assault on U.S. foreign aid', in S. Hook (ed.), *Foreign Aid Toward the Millennium*, Boulder, CO: Lynne Rienner, p. 66.

8. See for example Duffield, M. (1999) *Internal Conflict: Adaptation and Reaction to Globalisation*, Briefing 12, Sturminster Newton: The Corner House, web address: www.icaap.org/Cornerhouse/; and UNRISD (1995) *States of Disarray: The Social Effects of Globalization*, Geneva: UNRISD.

9. FitzGerald, V. (1999) 'Global linkages, vulnerable economies and the outbreak of conflict', *Development*, 42 (3): 57–64.

10. Dessus, S. and others (1998) 'A politico-economic model for stabilisation in Africa', *Journal of African Economies*, 7(1): 91–119; Adekanye, J. (1995) 'Structural adjustment, democratization and rising ethnic tensions in Africa', *Development and Change*, 26: 355–74.

11. FitzGerald, V. and A. Cobham (2000) *A Waste of Development? The Volatility and Pro-Cyclicality of Official Flows to Developing Countries*, Oxford: Finance and Trade Policy Research Centre, Queen Elizabeth House, for DfID White Paper on Globalization.

12. Raffer, K. and H. Singer (1996) *The Foreign Aid Business*, Cheltenham: E. Elgar, p. 160–1.

13. FitzGerald, 'Global linkages', p. 61.

14. Boyce, J. K. and M. Pastor (1998) 'Aid for peace. Can international financial institutions help prevent conflict?', *World Policy Journal*, Summer, pp. 42–9.

15. Mosley, P. (1997) 'The World Bank, "global Keynesianism" and the distribution of gains from growth', *World Development*, 25 (11): 1951.

16. Hansen, H. and F. Tarp (2000) 'Aid effectiveness disputed', in F. Tarp (ed.), *Foreign Aid and Development: Lessons Learnt and Directions for the Future*, London: Routledge, p. 118.

17. Weisbrot, M. and others (2000) *The Emperor Has No Growth: Declining Economic Growth Rates in the Era of Globalization*, Washington, DC: Center for Economic and Policy Research (CEPR). For evidence that progress in health and education also suffered, see Weisbrot, M. and others (2001) *The Scorecard on Globalization 1980–2000: Twenty Years of Diminished Progress*, Washington, DC: CEPR. Web address: http://www.cepr.net/.

18. 'Global Capitalism: Can it be made to work better?' (cover story), *Business Week*, 6 November 2000.

19. Easterly, W. (2001) *The Effect of IMF and World Bank Programs on Poverty*, WIDER Development Conference on Growth and Poverty, Helsinki: WIDER. Web address: http://www.wider.unu.edu/.

20. Przeworski, A. and J. Vreeland (2000) 'The effect of IMF programs on economic growth', *Journal of Development Economics*, 62: 385–421.

21. Kenny, C. and D. Williams (2000) 'What do we know about economic growth? or, why don't we know very much?', *World Development*, 29 (1): 1–22.

22. Garuda, G. (2000) 'The distributional effects of IMF programs: a cross-country analysis', *World Development*, 28 (6): 1031–51; Easterly, *The Effect of IMF and World Bank Programs on Poverty*.

23. Lundberg, M. and L. Squire (2000) 'The simultaneous evolution of growth and inequality', Washington, DC: World Bank, mimeo, cited in Maxwell, S. (2001) 'Treatment of redistribution', *Journal of International Development*, 13: 337.

24. Pieper, U. and L. Taylor (1998) 'The revival of the liberal creed: the IMF, the World Bank, and inequality in a globalized economy', in Baker, D., G. Epstein and R. Pollin (eds), *Globalization and Progressive Economic Policy*, Cambridge: Cambridge University Press, p. 61.

25. Reyna, S. (1988) 'Investing in inequality: class formation in Upper Volta', in D. Attwood and others (eds), *Power and Poverty: Development and Development Projects in the Third World*, Boulder, CO: Westview Press, pp. 119–133; Hanlon, J. (1995) 'Supporting peasants in their fight to defend their land', London, mimeo.

26. 'Horse-and-sparrow economics – that is, if you feed the horse well, some will pass on through and be there on the ground for the sparrow.' MacEwan, A. (2001) *Dollars & Sense*, January–February.

27. See references cited in Norton, A., and S. Conlin (2000) *Globalisation Processes and the Implications for the Development of Global Responses in the Field*

of Social Policy, London: DfID/ODI, http://62.189.42.51/BackgroundPapers. htm; and Fielding, D. (2000) *Why is Africa so Poor? A Structural Model of Growth and Income Inequality*, Working Paper Series, Oxford: CSAE. Web address: http://www.economics.ox.ac.uk/CSAEadmin/workingpapers/pdfs/2001–05text.pdf.

28. *The Independent* (Dhaka), 11 February 2001, citing a paper by Professor Abul Barkat of Dhaka University.

29. Uvin, P. (1998) *Aiding Violence: The Development Enterprise in Rwanda*, West Hartford, CT: Kumarian Press, pp. 142, 146.

30. FitzGerald, V. and A. Cobham (2000) *Capital Flight: Causes, Effects, Magnitude and Implications for Development*, Oxford: Finance and Trade Policy Research Centre, Queen Elizabeth House, p. 24.

31. Mosley, P. (1987) *Overseas Aid: Its Defence and Reform*, Brighton: Wheat-sheaf, especially 'Aid as a redistributive tool', pp. 155–208.

32. With thanks to Kees van Dongen of the Netherlands Organization for International Cooperation in Higher Education (NUFFIC), The Hague.

33. 'Corporate welfare of livable communities? Rerouting US foreign aid' (2001) *Sustainable Transport*, 12, New York: Institute for Transportation and Development Policy, p. 20. Web address: http://www.itdp.org/ST/index.html.

34. For a careful overview see Matin, I. and others (1999) *Financial Services for the Poor and Poorest: Deepening Understanding to Improve Provision*, Finance and Development Research Programme Working Papers, 9, Manchester: Institute for Development Policy and Management, University of Manchester. Web address: http://www.man.ac.uk/idpm/.

35. Rui Gonçalves, personal communication.

36. Barros, F. (ed.) (2001) *Banco Mundial, Participação, Transparência e Responsabilização. A experiência brasileira com o Painel de Inspeção*, Brasília: Rede Brasil sobre Instituições Financeiras Mulitlaterais.

37. Bräutigam, D. (2000) *Aid Dependence and Governance*, 2000: 1, Stockholm: Almquist & Wiksell for the Expert Group on Development Issues, pp. 16–20. Web address: http://www.egdi.gov.se/pdf/2000Ipdf/2000_I.pdf. The perceptions of 'experts' may not necessarily match those of local citizens, especially poor ones. Therefore some caution is required here.

38. Putnam, R. (1993) *Making Democracy Work: Civic Traditions in Modern Italy*, Princeton, NJ: Princeton University Press.

39. Moore, M. and others (1999) *Polity Qualities: How Governance Affects Poverty*, Brighton: IDS. Web address: http://www.ids.ac.uk/ids/.

40. Full data on defensive lending are hard to pin down. Currently about 20 per cent of bilateral grants for the 41 heavily indebted poor countries

(HIPCs) go towards 'debt forgiveness'. World Bank (2001) *Global Development Finance*, p. 105.

41. World Bank (2001) *Global Development Finance*, Washington, DC: World Bank.

42. Birdsall, N., and others (2001) *Will HIPC Matter?: The Debt Game and Donor Behavior in Africa*, Economic Reform Project Discussion Paper No. 3, Washington, DC: Carnegie Endowment for International Peace. Web address: http://www.ceip.org/files/Publications/HIPC.asp.

43. McGee, R. (2000) *Participation in Poverty Reduction Strategies*, Brighton: IDS. Web address: http://www.ids.ac.uk/ids/particip/information/recentpub.html.

44. *Jubilee South Pan-African Declaration on PRSPs*, Kampala, 10–12 May 2001, signed by 39 NGOs.

45. Jan Willem Gunning, remarks at a public hearing, Amsterdam, 8 March 2001.

46. Eyben, R. and S. Ladbury (1995) 'Popular participation in aid-assisted projects: why more in theory than practice?', in N. Nelson and S. Wright (eds), *Power and Participatory Development*, London: Intermediate Technology Publications, pp. 192–200.

47. Bevan, P. (2000) 'Who's a goody? Demythologizing the PRA agenda', *Journal of International Development*, 12: 756.

48. Carr, S. and others (1998) *Psychology of Aid*, London: Routledge. This book's exhaustive literature list has few if any items about group or national self-esteem.

49. Ndungane, N. (2000) 'Defining the goals of the new struggle. Power of financiers versus power of the people', *Business Day* (Johannesburg), 23 October.

50. Zunes, S. (1997) *The Strategic Functions of U.S. Aid to Israel.* Web address: http://www.mepc.org/zunes.htm.

51. Uvin, P. (1998) *Aiding Violence: The Development Enterprise in Rwanda*, West Hartford, CT: Kumarian Press, especially pp. 127–36.

52. Gifford, P. (1998) *African Christianity: Its Public Role*, Bloomington: Indiana University Press, p. 324.

53. Mkandawire, T. and C. Soludo (1999) *Our Continent, Our Future: African Perspectives on Structural Adjustment*, Trenton, NJ: Africa World Press, CODESRIA and IDRC, p. 120.

54. Rugumamu, S. (1997) *Lethal Aid: The Illusion of Socialism and Self-Reliance in Tanzania*, Trenton, NJ: Africa World Press, p. 200.

NINE
End of the Beginning or Beginning of the End?

All human beings are bound by identical obligations, although these are performed in different ways according to the circumstances ... The obligation is only performed if ... expressed in a real, not a fictitious, way.[1]

Amidst global currents of politics and business, the aid regime may be a minor force, but it is none the less home to powerful institutions affecting the lives of hundreds of millions on the planet. Its two most visible institutions, the World Bank and the IMF, have become lightning-rods for a social movement calling for a gentler, more inclusive, just and democratic world. That movement wants fairer sharing of income, wealth and knowledge – the very thing foreign aid is popularly thought to do. By targeting the top of the aid system, and coalescing around the slogan, 'another world is possible', it implies the need for alternatives to the current aid system.

Faced with such proposals, political classes in most countries remain largely unmoved. From them are heard occasional pious utterances about poverty, but never serious talk of closing gaps between rich and poor. However, following the suicide attacks in September 2001, some public figures from the middle of the Anglo-Saxon political spectrum began to speak of the need to rethink 'the whole relationship between poverty, degradation and violence, between drugs and crime and violence, and trade and development and violence' and to redress the 'global imbalance in resources'.[2]

Were these just passing outbursts of worry and guilt, rapidly forgotten in the daily avalanche of mainstream opinion? Or might they signal a meeting of minds between a nervous policy-making establishment and a progressive social movement? Given surging unemployment and hate-mongering in civil society, policy elites are likely to give more attention to domestic problems than to foreign aid, not to mention the rejigging of global resource imbalances. Pushed on to the defensive by its mediocre record and by looming budget pressures, conventional foreign aid faces a difficult future.

Is foreign aid merely at a routine turning point, the end of the beginning? That is entirely possible. Throughout its zig-zag career, the industry has continually reinvented itself. As a carrot, stick, and high moral ground for powerful institutions, its utility in international power politics has not been exhausted.

Yet might its difficulties lead to a slow-motion collapse of foreign aid as we know it? Might this be the beginning of the end? That scenario could take quite different forms. In one of them, aid's trade war tasks of subsidizing exports and investments would be put where they in fact belong – under ministries for foreign trade and investment. Its non-mercantile tasks might, however, be limited to short-term caretaking action in zones of superfluous people, and potentially dangerous conflict, where armoured soup kitchens and humanitarian policing are the order of the day.

In another endgame scenario, policies to redress inequalities and exclusion would pivot on exchange but also on rights and obligations (taxes, services, transfers). In such a future, foreign aid would be transcended and replaced by much larger, statutory systems for genuine redistribution under public oversight and control. Aid chains would be shorter. Many would run horizontally, not vertically. Democratic deficits would be much reduced. There are few reliable roadmaps for the latter route; it is largely uncharted. In this concluding chapter, no map is offered, but rather some elements of a compass. To introduce these, it is useful here to recapitulate some of the themes informing this book.

A Summary Glance

Official aid and its institutions are vehicles of foreign policy. They may operate from a mixture of motives, but their mercantile and political purposes are never far from the surface of humanitarian and development discourse in which aid is packaged. Only rarely has official aid been harnessed to emancipatory purposes, such as to redistribute assets (Taiwan) or to bring about majority rule (South Africa). Official aid is but one of a number of foreign policy vehicles, and seldom the most important. Other instruments of trade, armed intervention and investment not only take precedence over aid, they can nullify it; policy incoherence is serious and widespread.

Incoherence becomes absurdly big in aid-driven efforts to roll back the public sector. Foreign aid has boomed in an era dominated by the money power of private financial firms and circuits. Their doctrine is market fundamentalism, which has driven the aid regime since 1980. The aid system is a major vehicle for the coercive re-engineering of economic and political life in lower-income countries according to this doctrine. It operates through long and tangled chains of agencies and firms whose added value by no means justifies their costs. Rarely are these chains transparent, accountable and responsive to public institutions at the receiving end. On the contrary, they often constrain and weaken them.

Where aid has been most intense, outcomes often include slow and erratic growth (in some cases followed by outright collapse), increasing inequality, decaying reciprocity between public authorities and citizens, causing social tension to rise. In the late 1990s, the World Bank and the IMF scaled back their assault on the state, in part to avoid shooting themselves in the foot. But they are under continuing, if inconsistent, pressures from funding authorities above and from activists in the North and the South below to end their harmful practices. Calls to curb their mandates and their funds, and thus radically to shrink their authority, are now heard across the political spectrum.

From its earliest decades, foreign aid has been exposed to attack. Failures at the receiving end are attributed to recipients, who are charged with incapacity, bad governance, foot-dragging on reform and aid dependence. The aid system itself is also under fire, even from within the industry, reflecting rivalries within and among agencies, banks and countries. Failure to find the right technical formula is a common type of criticism, as are over-centralization and subordination to *realpolitik*. Some of these criticisms are valid, but they begin to make greater sense when set against wider patterns of power — who wields it, and who doesn't — and the democratic deficits such controversies bring into the open.

The structure and workings of aid chains, and of the ideas that constitute and drive them, add to the democratic deficits. At the receiving end, the deficits tend to deepen and become more opaque. Pressure to tackle these problems, and thus to bring issues of power and powerlessness to the surface, has been growing in the South and North. Today, public processes of decision-making and how to promote them have at last come up for official discussion.

That is good news. Shifts are also detectable among a few aid agencies, such as those of Denmark and Britain, and the UNDP. Some units in them seem ready to grasp the nettle of emancipatory politics. The bad news is that the top of the aid system, while deploring (for some audiences) the 'top-down economic focus of the eighties',[3] is not about to abandon market fundamentalism, nor its powers to coerce and intrude at the receiving end.

Revisiting a Few Principles

Against underdevelopment and crisis, foreign aid used to be the remedy, the front-line of policy. No longer. Negotiating favourable policies on trade, corporate investment, capital stocks and flows, civic and social rights, security, the environment and governance are more important. That widening and re-ordering of perspective has brought more realism to debates about why poverty and inequality persist and what can be done about them. Useful resources from the aid system, even at the inflated levels reported officially, are dwarfed by other flows – mostly from poor to rich.

As this book has illustrated, the conventional aid system has not been a great success. Yet even failure has its uses. The aid system can't be consigned to the rubbish heap and ignored. It still represents a large and versatile constellation of money, expertise and networks that make and transmit ideas about how societies, polities and economies can be shaped and steered. Aid may no longer be first among equals, but it still counts.

It also enjoys a kind of residual popular indulgence. Public readiness to help the afflicted, act for the underdog, and even to accept some redistribution as the price of social cohesion are also, miraculously, still around in most countries. Public support for aid is still somewhat buoyant, despite leakage due to increasing doubts that it does much good. When ranked with other issues, foreign aid is not a high priority for Western publics. Yet majorities in rich countries ritually affirm their wish to see misery curbed, especially at moments of catastrophe. Such attitudes rest on shifting and culture-bound mixes of guilt, duty, despair, fear and the wish to be seen to belong to respectable society. They can hardly rest on solid convictions about aid effectiveness, or much knowledge of it. Popular backing for aid in most countries has a paradoxical and probably unstable fundament. For decision-makers, the opinions of publics at large appear to be far less important than the influence of action groups, policy specialists, firms and non-profits – in a word, the aid lobby.[4]

Pressing for the overhaul of foreign aid is unlikely to unleash a popular groundswell. But popular groundswells such as the 'another world is possible' movement mentioned in the opening of this chapter are today helping tilt the balance of power around and within key aid institutions. It is today's most active constituency for emancipatory change. The replacement of foreign aid by more effective kinds of solidarity is thus still a viable pursuit.[5] The following sections offer observations about ethical principles[6] worth taking into account in debates about foreign aid, and a set of topics worth developing further when setting out to transform it.

NON-DECEPTION   Full, straight-talking, non-manipulative communication about aid is not yet the norm, but there are efforts to make it so. Poverty pornography — the skeletal black child with a tearful face — turns up less frequently today in charity appeals. The World Bank no longer feeds gullible news editors with absurdly optimistic growth projections about countries that are in fact sinking deeper into poverty. But a fog of misleading concepts, data, financial accounts, catch-phrases and images continues to spew out of the aid industry, obscuring basic matters of inequality and power. Some p-words — participation, partnership, poorest of the poor — have been emptied of meaning. Ownership is a hollow slogan. Such terms drain issues of their political content, concealing what is actually going on, such as: 'state when we mean kleptocracy, market when we mean land-grabbing, community when we mean ethnic cleansing'.[7]

The politics appear in the patterns of the talk. Certain terms are loaded and then used — or not used — about certain kinds of events, relationships and people at certain times. The discovery of such patterns in the talk of the professions and the bureaucracies has advanced our understanding of aid processes and ideologies.

Deception goes well beyond the soothing, de-politicized babble of the agencies or the secrecy surrounding the outcomes of their work. Many political practices, such as the use of consensus rather than open voting in the IMF and World Bank, or the blurring of boundaries between lender and borrower, conceal what should be public information and hinder public accountability. Aid agencies will never overcome learning disabilities unless they stop fooling themselves. Their executives, for example, have to learn to deal with 'bad news' and criticism without going into states of denial or throwing tantrums.

To conceal who really gains, who loses, who takes the risks, and who takes decisions is to foster bogus understanding and bogus consent. From the official bodies to the charities, members of the aid industry need to revisit the ethics of communication.

NON-COERCION Complete freedom to steer policy and run institutions according to one's wishes is a rare thing in any circumstance. But seldom have members of the aid system – particularly its Market Leninists – actively expanded the degrees of policy freedom at the receiving end. Foreign aid managers have rarely risen above attitudes of trusteeship to treat people as adult subjects with responsibility for their own choices. In 1999 lenders began to add a human face of anti-poverty intentions to their loan conditionalities, but these remain an imposed, not a negotiated thing.

Coercive practice long ago began moving beyond crude, episodic threats; it now operates at deeper levels. Decision-makers have started to comply not because they fear punishment, but because they see the donors'/lenders' policies as being in their own interests.[8] And the rewards to policy technocrats can be royal indeed. At yet deeper levels, coercion is internalized: policy-makers schooled in conventional economics and then linked to well-positioned communities of experts accept the legitimacy of the donor/lender prescriptions with enthusiasm. 'If people were sharks,' wrote Bertolt Brecht,

the main question would be the moral education of the small fish. They would be taught that the greatest and most beautiful thing is to sacrifice oneself, and that they must believe and trust in the sharks, who determine their future. The small fish would have to understand that their future would be guaranteed only if they learned obedience.[9]

To force consent is to pre-empt choice among alternatives. Ownership, demand-driven and cooperation thus become bogus terms. One way to begin curbing coercion is to apply everyday competitive rules in the marketplace of ideas. Subsidized policy cartels should be broken up, idea gatekeepers dethroned and their 'one true path, no alternative' gateways dismantled. Today, conceptual toolboxes stocked by gender studies, Foucault and others have enriched understandings of what Brecht sketched in his parable. These have begun to inform the study of international relations, thus improving insights into aid's quiet coercive powers.

DO NO HARM   That foreign aid has great potential for harm is now beyond dispute. Even when intended to relieve suffering, aid has set the stage for more suffering, as in Somalia and Rwanda in the 1990s. Calls to apply the Hippocratic principle, Do No Harm, at first evoked indignation from the humanitarian branch of the aid industry. But as critical studies piled up, and as their worries grew about income, some humanitarian agencies have begun paying more attention to politico-economic contexts and to the rights, strengths and wishes of people affected by disaster. The need for precautionary measures is now accepted. Such changes would never have been achieved without outside pressure.[10]

Precautionary principles have gained ground. Before 1988 the World Bank had no policy to assess impacts on the environment and on people displaced by dams and other big projects. Today, donors and lenders face tougher codes of conduct and some public scrutiny. They insist, however, on policing themselves. As painfully demonstrated in the ex-Soviet Union and other places suffering aid-induced social collapse and destitution, the need for mandatory assessments of social impacts could not be clearer.

Aid decision-makers have to show greater respect for problems – their depth, their complexity and the non-linear, cumulative processes that surround them. The disasters produced by standardized, one-size-fits-all solutions have shown how aid system thinking can become dishonest, expedient and downright lazy.

Concluding his powerful study of 'how certain schemes to improve the human condition have failed', the social scientist James Scott proposes 'a few rules of thumb that, if observed, could make development planning less prone to disaster':

> *Take small steps.* [P]resume that we cannot know the consequences of our interventions in advance ... prefer wherever possible to take a small step, stand back, observe, and then plan the next small move. As the biologist J. B. S. Haldane metaphorically described the advantages of smallness: 'you can drop a mouse down a thousand-yard mineshaft; and on arriving at the bottom, it gets a slight shock and walks away. A rat is killed, a man broken, a horse splashes.'

> *Favor reversibility.* Prefer interventions that can easily be undone if they turn out to be mistakes ... Aldo Leopold captured the spirit of caution required: 'The first rule of intelligent tinkering is to keep all the parts.'

> *Plan on surprises.* Choose plans that allow the largest accommodation to the unforeseen ...

> *Plan on human inventiveness.* Always plan under the assumption that those who become involved in the project later will have or will develop the experience and insight to improve on the design.[11]

In short, learning, precaution and improvisation should underpin action. Amber lights of caution should start flashing when aid providers drone on about the purity of their intentions.

LIABILITY FOR DAMAGE   Can legal redress be sought for wrongful damage caused by aid agency policies and programmes? In most national settings, a firm or person may be sued for damages due to professional negligence. Malpractice suits against medical professionals and hospital administrators have been routine for decades. Yet redress for harm done is not (yet) an option open to those at the receiving end of aid. Aid agency impunity favours a perverse cycle: failures justify further grants and loans, thus reward institutions and careers more for failure than for success.[12] The incoherence of donor/lender policies – insisting on export-led growth while barring imports, funding university scholarships while luring professionals out of low-income countries – are also reasonable causes for compensation, as determined in law courts or otherwise.[13] To identify and track aid decisions and who made them would help improve the climate of accountability, and end the current climate of personal impunity. Some activists have begun watching policy-makers (in their public roles) as well as policies.[14]

OBLIGATIONS TO RESPECT CAPACITIES AND PROMOTE TAL-ENTS   In their earnest pursuits of improving the human condition, most aid actors' grasp of capacities at the receiving end has been poor – often over-pessimistic, occasionally over-optimistic, and almost always non-historical, de-politicized and gender-blind. It is therefore not surprising that aid often fails to respect capacities and talents. How can these blinkers be removed? On many prac-tical fronts, bookcases, hard-drives and workshop agendas are already full; there is no need to rehearse those discussions here. In the heading of this paragraph, however, the operative word is *obligation*.

The 1990s saw the forward march through aid institutions such as UNICEF, the UNDP and Oxfam of the notion that poverty should be fought on the basis not of beneficence, but of rights. UN covenants and scores of official and civil institutions continue building grounds to protect civil and political rights. However, social and economic rights (ratified internationally in 1948) and even a 'right to development' (1986) have met resolute opposition from the IFIs and the USA. That is no surprise. Market fundamentalist doctrine basically forbids anything that smacks of public claims by those disadvantaged by market forces – unless of course the claimants are rich and well-connected.

But are rights-based approaches all that robust? Generations of ethicists, from Bentham to Rawls, have found them insufficient, lacking hands and feet. A major problem with social and economic rights is that no one is tasked with their enforcement. They remain dead letters.

> A claim that the developed world, or a transnational corporation, or local landlords violate rights to life, food or subsistence in parts of the Third World may sound impressive. Since it speaks most forcefully to suffering claimants, the message may be inaccessible or half heard by those with power to bring change. Bentham was right when he observed that 'a *declaration of rights* would be but a *lop-sided job* without a *declaration of duties*'.[15]

More promising is the counterpart of rights: entitlements. These rest on political contracts between the state and citizens. Public institutions guarantee reciprocal rights and duties, but they extend beyond public services and taxation into the market (such as in regulating labour processes) and even the household (such as in juridical enforcement of paternity obligations).

Inspired by Nobel laureate Amartya Sen, the entitlement approach takes capacities and talents seriously as 'capabilities'. These include, but go beyond, the simple, and often Euro-centric, calculus of income and education levels. Where capabilities are denied or stunted because of market or other settings where bargaining strengths are unequal, the result is 'entitlement failure'.[16] Addressing that systemic failure should become the core business of a new regime of redistribution to replace the current regime of aid.

Is this hopelessly Utopian? There is a well-supported view that the consciences of Western publics have entered a 'twilight of duty'. There, Westerners expect to fulfil their obligations to help the disadvantaged only if it is in a painless way, and preferably fun, such as TV extravaganzas and rock concerts for charity.[17] Yet on wider planes of public policy, public sentiment is stronger. Principles of social solidarity and entitlement may be under attack, but they still underpin public policy in European social democracies.

Towards an Agenda

In light of these principles, what changes in the aid system would open ways towards emancipation from poverty and exclusion? What ways and means might be adopted, by whom, to secure whose entitlements?

PUBLIC ACTION NOT PRIVATE PRE-EMPTION   To halt the decay of governance and of reciprocal give and take between citizens and the state – problems at the heart of so many aid failures – two straightforward norms should be brought to bear:

- Promoting capabilities is, in general, a matter for *public* action.
- Aid matters are, in general, public matters.

The public action approach, as developed by Drèze and Sen and others, insists that for-profit, non-profit and community-based sectors have public roles alongside the state. 'Public action includes not just what is done for the public by the state, but also what is done by the public for itself. The latter includes not merely the directly beneficial contributions of social institutions, but also the actions of pressure groups and political activists.'[18]

Public action involves collective, openly accountable means to combat public bads such as pollution, crime and precarious livelihoods. It is also promotes public goods such as water and drainage, efficient small claims courts, criminal justice systems and affordable transport. It allows definitions of entitlement, and of who warrants them, to change over time. It frames how problems and alternative solutions are identified, who takes decisions, and how joint endeavours may be organized in combinations of state, for-profit and non-profit actors. Choices of investment and the loans needed to realize them, about fighting inflation and unemployment, about access to and use of 'the commons' and choices about how socially excluded or vulnerable people are to be protected are thus no longer matters of private actors nor of the state alone.

As a cluster of ideas, the public action approach has not yet crystallized. Thus far, national and sub-national settings have been its chief focus. For the aid system, a public action approach would mean paying attention to all levels, from the macro to the micro. Experiences from places such as India, the Philippines and Brazil (and also the ghettos of Chicago and the north east of Britain) suggest the ways public action can take root. Distilled and noted briefly here, focal points for overhaul of the aid system include the following.

Financial disarmament In proportion to their colossal means, private financial interests contribute little to *productive* investment either directly or in tax revenues. Rules favouring them, especially freedom from regulation and taxation, make possible dangerous criminal and military activities, and make impossible the fair sharing of rights and duties and reciprocity with public sectors. In short, they nullify aid's potentially positive effects. Those interests' influence over, among other things, the US Treasury, the IMF and the World Bank is unacceptable and should be broken.

Good governance is for aid-givers too Democratic control is the obvious counterpart to financial disarmament. If bankers and bond traders wish to continue running things in our name, let them compete openly for votes just like ordinary politicians. Sermons about good governance at the receiving end would carry far more conviction, and chances of success, if public policy of aid-providing lands were indeed more 'public', and political competition financed far less by vested interests.

Transformation of the IFIs Given their quasi-monopolistic positions in markets for development finance and public policy ideas, the IFIs should be subjected to norms analogous to competition (or anti-trust) rules. They should be broken up. Ideally, their main functions should be moved out of the USA; the lopsided influence of that country's elites is inconsistent with democratic principles that could be reasonably expected of institutions claiming to respond to the global community of nations, especially the poorer ones. Private, policy activist pressures for reform merit support, but other initiatives, such as to fill the large democratic deficits in parliamentary control over the IFIs, and public commissions of inquiry into IFI impacts, should be promoted.

Move towards bloc transfers Aid institutions must learn to let go, to end their preference for projects and hobbies, to smooth out the peaks and dips in flows, and to expand simple bloc grant transfers, exemplified today in publicly controlled local development funds. Expanded to national levels, such approaches could boil down to donor–recipient negotiation, and the writing of cheques to recipient authorities against publicly verified results, but without further agency involvement. Aid chains would be radically reduced, being maintained chiefly to ensure space for authentic public oversight and control. Aid can help protect and enlarge the political space where citizens can follow the money and results, and call those responsible to account if things go wrong. Such chains might preferably run via professional, municipal and membership organizations rather than private aid agencies.

Bloc transfers to redress regional inequalities, neighbourhood decay and disadvantage suffered by specific social groups is an old and hardly controversial idea.[19] Northern European countries spend more than one-third of their GDPs in redistributive programmes;[20] the bulk of the European Union's total budget rests on them. They also influence thinking about aid to some of Europe's neighbours to the east.[21] At global levels, official commitments reflected in anti-poverty targets agreed at conferences in the 1990s are but short steps away from public guarantees of effort (although they lack penalty clauses open to enforcement in courts of law); they are stepping-stones towards widening the global political constituency for entitlement-based approaches.[22]

REDISTRIBUTION DOWNWARDS, NOT UPWARDS Redistribution from rich to poor is not what foreign aid really does – nor what it is supposed to do. Today, however, obstacles to that purpose are weakening and movements in support of it are reviving. The proposition that inequality is an inevitable and probably necessary feature of growth – for 45 years a major pillar of trickle-down economics – has been demolished. Indeed, inequality has been shown to hinder growth. Promoting greater equality is a good thing for other reasons, including greater socio-political inclusion and reduced social tension, resentment and violence.

Redistribution downwards thus has both pragmatic and ethical arguments on its side. Concrete suggestions are emerging. The director of a major aid think-tank proposes, as an additional global development goal, a ceiling on inequality.[23] Political economists studying the feasibility of redistribution have identified seven types of policy instruments, and have estimated their usefulness in three kinds of settings: middle-income countries capable of redistribution with current income and assets; middle- and most lower-income countries in which policies would work under a growth-with-redistribution regime; and very low-income countries where policies are unlikely to make much difference, so that growth itself would have to carry the burden for the time being. The results are summarized in Table 9.1.

From this fairly coarse-grained matrix, further options can be worked out place-by-place. Social movements and analysts in many countries have many options worth pursuing; some have already begun testing them, such as land reform in Brazil and public job schemes in India. Cross-fertilization of these ideas and working alliances are clearly worth developing.

In every case a complex and delicate constellation of power factors will demand close attention. Targeting is one of them. If redistribution measures are to gain political momentum and be sustained, and if they are to avoid stigmatizing or marginalizing the poor as a distinct category, they will need support across social strata. Redistribution addresses poverty, but it is more than

TABLE 9.1 Feasibility of redistribution instruments by country category

Redistributive instrument	Redistribution of current income and assets (middle-income countries)	Growth with redistribution policies (middle- and most low-income countries)	Growth without redistribution policies (very low-income countries)
Progressive taxation	Yes	Yes, for some countries	No
Transfer payments	Yes	Yes, for some countries	No
Consumer subsidies	Yes	Yes	Yes, for some countries
Public job schemes	Yes	Yes	No
Land reform	Yes, but not always relevant	Yes	No, for most countries
Education and health	Yes	Yes	Yes
Infrastructure and public works	Yes	Yes	Yes

Source: Dagdeviren, H., R. van der Hoeven and J. Weeks (2001) Redistribution Does Matter: Growth and Redistribution for Poverty Reduction, WIDER Development Conference on Growth and Poverty, Helsinki: WIDER, web address: http://www.wider.unu.edu/.

merely 'anti-poverty'. Social welfare policies in richer countries are secure because they are politically anchored in the (lower) middle classes. This underscores the importance of a strategic aim: to 'lock in' pro-poor entitlements by anchoring them in the broadest political constituencies possible without their being 'captured' by the better-off.

End Trusteeship, Build Public Politics

Most of the above requires public politics, not merely administration, management and cookbook versions of 'good governance'. It requires filling democratic deficits. That is of course no simple thing. It needs great care and self-restraint. Where aid providers do not hold membership in emancipatory social movements (and most do not), they should avoid direct support to such movements. Rather, they can help expand the civic spaces in which emancipatory movements can flourish. Not blueprints but processes are needed. This means paying attention to settings, and improvising. A typical process moves step by step from achievement of small victories to the gaining of confidence and allies, to the winning of wider victories, thence to challenging the rules of the game and negotiating new ones.

Even in settings with no traditions of public decision-making about collective goods, ways are being found that enable citizens to steer outside resources (conventional aid, and, eventually, bloc grants) and local resources through public processes. The slow, culture-bound work of building institutions is vital. For outsiders the task is not, as in the conventional aid system, the imposition of models but the opening, analysing and testing of alternatives among institutional frameworks (land reform, water access, market licensing, social insurance coverage, and so on) known to improve poor people's entitlements.

Similarly, public authorities and social movements can be helped not to march to the beat of the donors' drums but to gain policy knowledge useful in campaigns and negotiations.[24] Public processes may be helped not by indoctrinating more technocrats in fundamentalist orthodoxies, but in promoting 'economic literacy' and the oversight of public choices by way of local media, civil society watchdog groups, international monitoring bodies within regions, and technical advisory bodies with autonomy from both business and government. These measures can be combined in ways that strengthen trust and public control at the receiving end. If trust between citizens and states improves, so too do the chances of give and take, of collecting taxes and fees, and thus of ending aid dependence.

It may be clear from a reading of this book that aid agencies are themselves part of an institutional framework – the aid regime – that continues to fall far short of its potentials. Conventional aid and its chains have too often been constraining, even crippling. Their replacement will not herald a millenarian end to suffering and injustice. A more modest, undramatic goal would be the mere provision, broadly and fairly, of that to which people are entitled.

Notes

1. Weil, S. (1949, trans. 1952) *The Need for Roots*, London: Routledge and Kegan Paul.

2. EU Commissioner and UK Tory politician Chris Patten, cited in 'Patten calls for redistribution as a weapon against terror', *Financial Times*, 17 September 2001.

3. World Bank chief of media relations, quoted in 'World Bank leader receives a critical accounting', *Washington Post*, 22 August 2001, p. A14.

4. Olsen, G. (2000) *Public Opinion and Development Aid: Is There a Link?*, CDR Working Paper 00.9, Copenhagen: Centre for Development Research. Web address: http://www.cdr.dk/working_papers/wp-00-9.pdf.

5. See Edwards, M. (1999) *Future Positive: International Co-operation in the 21st Century*, London: Earthscan, Chapter 10, 'Building constituencies for change'.

6. Inspired by O'Neill, O. (1986) *Faces of Hunger: An Essay on Poverty, Justice and Development*, Studies in Applied Philosophy, London: Allen & Unwin.

7. Bevan, P. (2000) 'Who's a goody? Demythologizing the PRA agenda', *Journal of International Development*, 12: 759.

8. Killick, T. (1998) *Aid and the Political Economy of Policy Change*, London: Routledge and ODI, Chapter 4, 'The "Ownership" problem'.

9. Cited in Achterhuis, H. (1993) 'Als haaien mensen waren. Moralisme als internationalisme', in H. Achterhuis and others (eds), *Het Orkest van de Titanic*, Brussels: VUB Press.

10. Anderson, M. (1999) *Do No Harm: How Aid Can Support Peace – Or War*, Boulder, CO: Lynne Rienner; for an overview of debates, see Collins, C. (1998) *Critiques of Humanitarianism and Humanitarian Action*, paper prepared for the UN Office for the Coordination of Humanitarian Affairs. Web address: http://www.reliefweb.int/library/documents/stock.html.

11. Scott, J. C. (1998) *Seeing Like a State: How Certain Schemes to Improve the Human Condition Have Failed*, New Haven, CT and London: Yale University Press, p. 345.

12. Raffer, K. (2000) *Memorandum*, Select Committee on International Development Appendices to the Minutes of Evidence, London: House of Commons. Web address: http://www.parliament.the-stationery-office.co.uk/pa/cm199900/cmselect/cmintdev/669/669ap01.htm.

13. Griffin, K. and T. McKinley (1993) *A New Framework for Development Cooperation*, Occasional Paper 11, New York: UNDP. Web address: www.undp.org/hdro.

14. For example, see *Watching the World Bank in Southern Africa*, a publication of the Alternative Information and Development Centre (AIDC), Cape Town. Web address: http://aidc.org.za.

15. O'Neill, *Faces of Hunger*, p. 120.

16. See Sen. A. (1993) 'Capability and well-being' in M. Nussbaum and A. Sen (eds), *The Quality of Life*, Oxford: Clarendon Press; Elson, D. (1997) 'Economic paradigms old and new: the case of human development', in R. Culpeper, A. Berry and F. Stewart (eds), *Global Development Fifty Years after Bretton Woods*, London: Macmillan, pp. 50–71.

17. Lipovetsky, G. (1992) *Le crepuscule du devoir. L'éthique indolore des nouveaux temps démocratiques*, Paris: Gallimard.

18. Drèze, J. and A. Sen (1989) *Hunger and Public Action*, Oxford: Clarendon Press, p. 61, cited in Elson, 'Economic paradigms old and new', p. 68.

19. It appears in Griffin and McKinley, *A New Framework for Development Cooperation*, and in South Centre (1999) *Financing Development: Issues for a South Agenda*, Geneva: South Centre. Web address: http://www.southcentre.org/publications/financing/.

20. van der Hoeven, R. (2000) *'Assessing Aid' and Global Governance: Why Poverty and Redistribution Objectives Matter*, Employment Paper, 2000/8, Geneva: ILO. Web address: www.ilo.public/english/employment/strat/download/ep8.pdf.

21. For example, European Union regional policy. Web address: http://inforegio.cec.eu.int.

22. See Deacon, B. (1997) *Global Social Policy: International Organizations and the Future of Welfare*, London: Sage Publications; Norton, A., T. Conway and M. Foster (2001) *Social Protection Concepts and Approaches: Implications for Policy and Practice in International Development*, Working Paper, 143, London: Centre for Aid and Public Expenditure, ODI. Web address: www.odi.org.uk/pppg/cape/papers/wp143.pdf.

23. The goal would be that no country's Gini coefficient should exceed 0.45. That would mean major assaults on inequality in countries where the Gini coefficient exceeds 0.5, notably Brazil, South Africa, Nigeria, Mexico and most of Central America. Maxwell, S. (2001) 'Treatment of redistribution', *Journal of International Development*, 13: 331–41.

24. Among important recent statements on this topic are: Luckham, R., A. Goetz and M. Kaldor (2000) *Democratic Institutions and Politics in Contexts of Inequality, Poverty and Conflict: A Conceptual Framework*, Sussex: IDS. Web address: http://www.ids.ac.uk/ids/publicat/wp/Wp104.pdf.; Moore, M. (2001) 'Empowerment at last?', *Journal of International Development*, 13: 321–9.

Appendix A: Major donors' top five recipients

Top five recipients of bilateral ODA at end of 1980s and end of 1990s (per cent of donors' total net bilateral disbursements in year for which data are available)

Australia	1988–89		1998–99
Papua New Guinea	23.3	Papua New Guinea	20.9
Indonesia	7.3	Indonesia	7.5
Malaysia	2.8	Vietnam	4.2
Philippines	2.5	Philippines	3.8
Thailand	2.4	Timor (East)	3.7

Belgium	1988–89		1998–99
Congo. Dem. Rep.	17.4	Tanzania	4.8
Rwanda	4.2	Congo. Dem. Rep.	2.8
Burundi	2.6	Rwanda	2.6
Indonesia	1.8	Côte d'Ivoire	2.3
Cameroon	1.5	Bolivia	2.2

Canada	1988–89		1998–99
Bangladesh	4.0	China	2.4
Pakistan	2.5	Bangladesh	2.4
India	1.9	Côte d'Ivoire	1.9
Jamaica	1.7	Cameroon	1.7
Indonesia	1.7	Haiti	1.4

Denmark	1988–89		1998–99
Tanzania	8.2	Tanzania	4.3
India	4.4	Uganda	3.7
Bangladesh	3.8	Mozambique	2.8
Kenya	3.7	Bangladesh	2.5
Sudan	2.5	Vietnam	2.3

France	1988–89		1998–99
French Polynesia	5.4	French Polynesia	5.7
New Caledonia	4.8	New Caledonia	5.3
Senegal	3.9	Côte d'Ivoire	4.7
Côte d'Ivoire	3.4	Egypt	4.3
Morocco	2.9	Morocco	3.8

Germany	1988–89		1998–99
Turkey	4.6	China	6.0
India	4.3	Indonesia	3.4
Egypt	3.9	India	3.3
Indonesia	3.0	Turkey	2.3
China	2.3	Egypt	2.0

Japan	1988–89		1998–99
Indonesia	13.1	Indonesia	11.1
China	7.4	China	9.6
Philippines	5.4	Thailand	6.1
Thailand	4.9	India	5.2
Bangladesh	3.9	Philippines	4.4

Netherlands	1988–89		1998–99
Indonesia	8.2	Netherlands Antilles	3.8
India	6.0	Bosnia-Herzegovina	2.4
Tanzania	3.3	Tanzania	2.1
Bangladesh	3.0	India	2.0
Netherlands Antilles	2.9	Bolivia	1.4

Portugal	1988–89		1998–99
Mozambique	17.1	Mozambique	31.3
São Tome & Principe	6.3	Timor (East)	10.9
Guinea-Bissau	6.1	Cape Verde	7.2
Cape Verde	5.8	Angola	7.1
Angola	4.6	Guinea-Bissau	4.0

Spain	1988–89		1998–99
Venezuela	5.4	Honduras	3.2
Ecuador	4.5	Morocco	3.1
Cuba	4.1	Côte d'Ivoire	2.8
Nicaragua	3.3	Peru	2.3
China	2.6	Angola	2.3

Sweden	1988–89		1998–99
India	7.8	Tanzania	3.3
Tanzania	5.8	Mozambique	2.7
Mozambique	5.6	South Africa	2.2
Nicaragua	3.2	Vietnam	2.1
Vietnam	2.6	Bosnia-Herzegovina	1.7

United Kingdom	1988–89		1998–99
India	5.3	India	4.5
Kenya	3.0	Tanzania	3.2
Bangladesh	2.9	Bangladesh	2.7
Ghana	2.4	Uganda	2.6
Tanzania	2.2	Ghana	2.3

United States	1988–89		1998–99
Israel	12.5	Egypt	8.6
Egypt	9.4	Bosnia-Herzegovina	2.2
Pakistan	3.9	Jordan	1.6
El Salvador	3.3	Peru	1.5
India	1.9	India	1.4

European Union	1988–89		1998–99
Côte d'Ivoire	6.6	Morocco	5.1
India	5.1	Egypt	3.7
Ethiopia	4.0	Bosnia-Herzegovina	3.5
Cameroon	3.5	Ex-Yugoslavia	3.0
Bangladesh	3.1	Algeria	2.6

All DAC donors	1988–89		1998–99
Indonesia	4.2	Indonesia	4.0
Egypt	3.1	China	3.7
India	3.0	India	2.6
China	2.8	Egypt	2.6
Israel	2.7	Thailand	1.8

Source: OECD (2001) *Major Recipients of Individual DAC Members' Aid* at web address http://www.oecd.org/dac/.

Appendix B: Five decades of foreign aid: political and economic highlights

1950s

Decade aims	Block communism; stabilize key regions; boost growth
Leading ideas	Containment of communism by colonial rule, local clients and war; community development; take-off, stages of growth; convergence theories; import-substituting industries
Modes and fashions	Policy leverage for land reform in Taiwan, Korea; support to anti-communist parties, unions etc.; big industrial and social overhead projects; food aid
Counter-trends	Nationalism rising; anti-colonial, anti-imperial insurgencies and non-violent movements; autarky and redistribution in China

1960s

Decade aims	Block communism; stabilize interests in ex-colonies; boost growth with good external balances
Leading ideas	Guided de-colonization; war in Southeast Asia; strong Keynesian developmental state; balance of industry and agriculture; inter-sectoral linkages; government planning
Modes and fashions	Continuation of 1950s but with emphasis on public sector management; technical assistance; start of policy-based loans and sectoral support to agriculture, education and scholarship aid; population control
Counter-trends	Strong versions of import-substitution industrialization in Latin America; doubts that peripheral economies will converge with core economies; critiques of growth without development

1970s

Decade aims	Stability in face of nationalism and weaker growth; compete more with communists on social fronts; boost growth and employment
Leading ideas	Social as well as military containment of communists;

some human rights rhetoric after 1976; multilateral banks
assume leading policy roles; IMF and WB become
enforcers of economic doctrine

Modes and
fashions
Shift to include poor: basic needs, integrated rural
development, informal sector, women in development,
appropriate technology; study but no serious promotion of
land reform

Counter-trends
Oil cartel, nationalism gain leverage; New International
Economic Order and collective self-reliance promoted in
UN and Non-Aligned group; insurgencies and political
Islam emerge

1980s

Decade aims
Rollback of Soviet allies on periphery; promote tough
pro-West regimes; curb Keynesianism; export-led growth;
open world for private investors; recycle oil monies; clear
path for and protect global finance

Leading ideas
Low-intensity war; low-intensity democracy; strong donor
steering; neoliberal counter-revolution and market
fundamentalism:
• orient economies outwards
• shrink the state, privatize
• get prices right
• reduce public consumption
• provide welfare safety-nets
  for austerity's politically
  troublesome losers

Modes and
fashions
Structural adjustment; austerity in public sectors;
promotion of exports, foreign business, NGOs and other
contractors; humanitarian boom; participation methods;
rise of micro-finance; in Europe, modest support to human
rights in Africa and Latin America

Counter-trends
Armed and passive resistance to Rollback; anti-apartheid
movement; Central American pro-democracy movements;
dissidence in Soviet bloc; decline, even collapse in Africa,
stagnation in Latin America, booms in East and SE Asia

1990–95

Decade aims
Extend powers over ex-Eastern Bloc; boost growth; extend
market systems; assure solvency of creditors

Leading ideas
Shift effective power to central banks and finance officials
insulated from politics; decentralize, privatize public

services; promote 'good governance'; shock therapy of neoliberal doctrine in ex-Eastern Bloc; civil society, social capital; sustainable development

Modes and fashions	Focus mainly on macro policy, beyond projects; capacity-building to create technocratic allies; democratization; decentralization fever; promotion of NGOs and business associations; conflict resolution
Counter-trends	Blowback problems (narco-regimes, insurgents etc.); growing criticism of aid, incoherence of Northern policies towards South; IMF and WB under attack from rising global campaigns on rights, environment, debt, and market fundamentalism

1996–2001

Decade aims	Same objectives as in 1990–95, but poverty reduction and spread of Western political model become key rationales
Leading ideas	Public sectors now brought in from the cold; accent on legitimation and recipient ownership of market fundamentalism and good governance; consensus on health, education priorities; concern grows about illicit economic circuits; revival of 'nation building'?
Modes and fashions	Conditionality shifting to policy dialogue including civil society; sector-wide approaches; development banks talk about poverty; search for coherence of trade and aid; some bilaterals and UNDP open towards policy activism and human rights
Counter-trends	IFIs under fire on all sides; export credit and tax havens under attack; rising talk of rights-based development;calls on humanitarian agencies to Do No Harm; activists show increased capacity and momentum; blowback terror

This overview was inspired by Hjertholm, P. and H. White (2000) 'Foreign aid in historical perspective', in F. Tarp (ed.) *Foreign Aid and Development: Lessons Learnt and Directions for the Future*, London: Routledge, p. 81.

Appendix C: Intensity of ODA over three decades

Significance of total net ODA in national economies (10-year averages)

	ODA as % of GNP			Annual ODA per capita in US$ 90–99
	1970–79	80–89	90–99	
EAST ASIA				
Malaysia	0.7	0.7	0.3	11
Thailand	0.7	0.8	0.6	12
Philippines	1.2	1.5	1.2	12
China	0	0.3	0.3	2
Vietnam	6.3	1.2	2.6	10
Indonesia	3.0	1.2	1.3	8
Myanmar (Burma)	2.8	4.7	1.0	2
Cambodia	19.7	10.0	8.5	23
Laos	24.6	8.1	17.4	47
EUROPE AND CENTRAL ASIA				
Slovenia			0.2	19
Croatia			7.3	11
Serbia and Montenegro				16
Bosnia-Herzegovina			21.0	244
Belarus			0.5	13
Russia			0.4	9
Macedonia			4.4	74
Georgia			7.4	40
Kazakhstan			0.7	7
Ukraine			0.5	7
Turkey	0.7	0.7	1.2	8
Azerbaijan			2.6	11
Armenia			10.8	41
Albania			14.9	75
Kyrgyz Rep.			14.4	35
Turkmenistan			0.7	5

	ODA as % of GNP			Annual ODA per capita in US$ 90–99
	1970–79	80–89	90–99	
Moldova			5.6	15
Uzbekistan			0.5	4
Tajikistan			3.5	11
LATIN AMERICA AND CARIBBEAN				
Argentina	0.1	0.1	0.1	6
Chile	0.4	0.1	0.1	7
Uruguay	0.4	0.2	0.2	14
Costa Rica	1.4	5.0	1.2	25
Trinidad and Tobago	0.3	0.2	0.3	18
Mexico	0.1	0.1	0	2
Cuba		0.3	0.2	5
Belize	11.1	9.0	4.7	113
Panama	1.8	1.1	0.6	20
Venezuela	0.1	0	0.1	2
Suriname	12.3	4.0	7.8	138
Colombia	1.0	0.2	0.2	5
Brazil	0.2	0.1	0	1
Peru	0.8	1.3	0.7	16
Paraguay	2.6	1.5	1.0	15
Jamaica	2.0	7.0	2.3	54
Dominican Republic	1.3	2.4	0.8	16
Ecuador	1.3	1.1	1.0	14
Guyana	4.6	8.9	15.7	113
El Salvador	1.7	7.3	5.0	63
Honduras	3.3	6.7	10.6	88
Bolivia	4.1	7.9	7.0	72
Nicaragua	3.0	7.1	24.6	108
Guatemala	1.2	1.6	1.3	2
Haiti	5.2	8.2	8.9	49
MIDDLE EAST AND NORTH AFRICA				
Israel	3.3	4.5	1.9	340
Lebanon	1.8	3.2	1.4	54
Oman	5.9	1.4	5.1	22
Jordan	26.4	19.5	8.5	132

	ODA as % of GNP			Annual ODA per capita in US$ 90–99
	1970–79	80–89	90–99	
Palestinian admin. areas			8.6	133
Iran	0.1	0	0.1	2
Tunisia	5.4	2.6	0.4	26
Algeria	1.3	0.3	0.5	7
Syria	7.6	5.6	2.8	27
Egypt	10.0	5.4	3.6	54
Morocco	2.7	3.6	2.2	27
Iraq	0.2	0.1	0.3	7
Yemen	19.2	9.9	4.9	18
Djibouti	16.3	28.7	23.5	191
SOUTH ASIA				
Sri Lanka	5.0	8.5	3.5	28
India	1.3	0.9	0.3	2
Pakistan	4.4	2.9	1.6	7
Bhutan		12.2	23.4	91
Nepal	3.8	9.9	7.8	17
Bangladesh	7.2	8.8	4.4	13
Afghanistan	3.7	0.4	2.9	6
SUB-SAHARAN AFRICA				
Mauritius	3.6	3.5	1.3	45
South Africa			0.3	10
Swaziland	4.7	3.2	2.1	46
Namibia		0.3	5.1	94
Botswana	18.2	11.4	1.7	62
Gabon	1.7	2.2	2.8	88
Lesotho	10.8	15.1	8.8	46
Ghana	2.8	6.1	7.9	31
Equatorial Guinea		30.5	6.5	86
Zimbabwe	0.1	4.3	6.6	29
Cameroon	4.7	2.6	5.2	30
Kenya	4.3	7.5	7.2	25
Congo. Rep.	7.4	5.0	8.5	57
Madagascar	4.6	8.6	9.6	23
Sudan	3.9	9.9	5.2	16
Togo	8.1	12.9	6.7	39

	ODA as % of GNP			Annual ODA per capita in US$ 90–99
	1970–79	80–89	90–99	
Mauritania	21.8	29.9	24.2	86
Nigeria	0.5	0.2	0.5	2
Congo Dem. Rep. (Zaire)	3.1	4.9	2.1	9
Côte d'Ivoire	2.8	2.5	6.4	52
Zambia	3.5	13.3	33.0	99
Senegal	7.7	14.1	14.0	72
Tanzania	8.2	14.9	11.3	30
Benin	8.3	9.3	10.5	41
Uganda	1.3	6.0	10.9	32
Eritrea			18.8	37
Angola	0.5	1.1	7.7	29
Somalia	27.7	48.9	23.6	29
Gambia	10.8	39.6	14.5	50
Guinea	1.9	8.2	8.7	42
Malawi	10.0	16.8	26.2	43
Rwanda	14.1	11.0	22.9	54
Liberia	3.7	9.8	7.6	36
Mali	12.9	21.9	16.8	41
Central African Rep.	10.9	15.9	17.0	50
Chad	11.5	17.8	15.9	33
Mozambique	2.2	22.5	26.0	59
Guinea-Bissau	15.6	50.5	47.3	83
Burundi	10.7	14.2	29.9	31
Ethiopia	3.6	9.6	13.0	13
Burkina Faso	13.1	13.3	15.1	36
Niger	9.4	13.7	14.1	27
Sierra Leone	3.2	7.3	16.7	22

Notes: (a) Within each region, countries are listed in order of their Human Development Index as of 1998; where data are unavailable, country placement has been estimated. (b) Basis of middle columns is the *recorded* GNP, thus for countries with large unregistered economic sectors must be treated with great caution.

Sources: OECD database: http://www.oecd.org/scripts/cde/; O'Donnell, S. and C. Soludo (1998) *Aid Intensity in Africa*, WPS 99-3, Oxford: Centre for the Study of African Economies. Web address: www. economics.ox.ac.uk/ CSAEadmin/workingpapers/main-wps. html.; UNDP (2000) *Human Development Report*, web address: http://www.undp.org/hdr2000/.

Appendix D: The debt

Composition of debt stocks in billions of US dollars

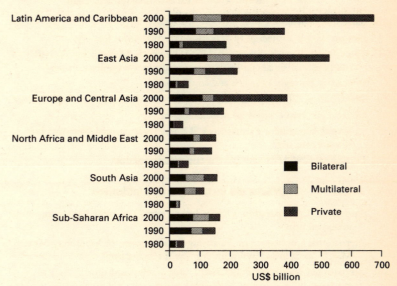

Source: World Bank (2001) *Global Development Finance 2001*.

Appendix E: Sources of information and debate

On international financial institutions and debt

Bank Information Center: http://www.bicusa.org/

Bretton Woods Project: http://www.brettonwoodsproject.org/

Central and Eastern European NGO Network Monitoring Activities of International Financial Institutions: http://www.bankwatch.org/

50 Years is Enough: http://www.50years.org/

Globalization Challenge Initiative: http://www.challengeglobalization.org/

Jubilee Plus: http://www.jubilee2000uk.org/

Structural Adjustment Participatory Review International Network: http://www.saprin.org/

TRASPARENCIA: http://www.trasparencia.org.mx/

Official aid institutions and initiatives

EuropeAid Co-Operation Office: http://europa.eu.int/comm/europeaid/index_en.htm

International Conference on Financing for Development Monterrey, Mexico, March 2002: http://www.un.org/esa/ffd/index.html

International Monetary Fund (IMF): http://www.imf.org/

World Bank: http://www.worldbank.org/

OECD Development Assistance Committee (DAC): http://www.oecd.org/dac/htm/

United Nations Development Programme (UNDP): http://www.undp.org/

Research on poverty, development, aid policy and management

Centre for Development Research (Denmark): http://www.cdr.dk/

European Centre for Development Policy Management (Netherlands): http://www.oneworld.org/ecdpm

Global Development Network (UK): http://www.ids.ac.uk/gdn/

id21 Development Research (UK): http://www.id21.org/

One World [Aid Policy] (UK): http://www.oneworld.org/thinktank/aidman/index.html

Overseas Development Institute (UK): http://www.odi.org.uk/

World Institute for Development Economics Research (Finland): http://www.wider.unu.edu/

World Bank Institute (USA): http://www.worldbank.org/wbi/home.html

Development, North–South relations and aid: other sites

AID/WATCH (Australia): http://www.aidwatch.org.au/

Alternative Information and Development Centre (South Africa): http://www.aidc.org.za

Focus on the Global South (Thailand): http://www.focusweb.org

Foreign Policy in Focus (USA): http://www.foreignpolicy-infocus.org/

Global Issues: http://www.globalissues.org/

glossary of aid industry and debt terms: http://www.jubilee2000uk.org/databank/glossary.htm

International Centre for Trade and Sustainable Development (ICTSD): http://www.ictsd.org/

South-North Network Cultures and Development (Belgium): http://www.networkcultures.net/

Reality of Aid Homepage: http://www.devinit.org/realityofaid/

Social Watch (Uruguay): http://www.socwatch.org.uy/

Third World Network (Malaysia): http://www.twnside.org.sg

Suggested Reading

Anderson, Mary (1999) *Do No Harm: How Aid Can Support Peace – Or War*, Boulder, CO: Lynne Rienner.

Caufield, Catherine (1996) *Masters of Illusion: The World Bank and the Poverty of Nations*, New York: Henry Holt.

Edwards, Michael (1999) *Future Positive: International Co-operation in the 21st Century*, London: Earthscan.

George, Susan and Fabrizio Sabelli (1994) *Faith and Credit: The World Bank's Secular Empire*, London: Penguin.

Hill, Polly (1986) *Development Economics on Trial*, Cambridge: Cambridge University Press.

Mkandawire, Thandika and Charles Soludo (1999) *Our Continent, Our Future: African Perspectives on Structural Adjustment*, Trenton, NJ: Africa World Press, CODESRIA and IDRC.

Tarp, Finn (ed.) (2000) *Foreign Aid and Development: Lessons Learnt and Directions for the Future*, London: Routledge.

Uvin, Peter (1998) *Aiding Violence: The Development Enterprise in Rwanda*, West Hartford, CT: Kumarian Press.

Waal, Alex de (1997) *Famine Crimes: Politics and the Disaster Relief Industry in Africa*, Oxford: James Currey.

Wedel, Janine (1998) *Collision and Collusion: The Strange Case of Western Aid to Eastern Europe 1989–1998*, New York: St Martin's Press.

Wuyts, Marc and others (eds) (1992) *Development Policy and Public Action*, Oxford: Oxford University Press in association with the Open University.

Index

Participating Organizations

Both ENDS: A service and advocacy organization that collaborates with environment and indigenous organizations, both in the South and in the North, with the aim of helping to create and sustain a vigilant and effective environmental movement.

Damrak 28-30, 1012 LJ Amsterdam, The Netherlands
Tel: +31 20 623 0823   Fax: +31 20 620 8049
E-mail: info@bothends.org
Website: www.bothends.org

Catholic Institute for International Relations (CIIR): CIIR aims to contribute to the eradication of poverty through a programme that combines advocacy at national and international level with community-based development.

Unit 3 Canonbury Yard, 190a New North Road,
    London N1 7BJ, UK
Tel: +44 (0)20 7354 0883   Fax: +44 (0)20 7359 0017
E-mail: ciir@ciir.org
Website: www.ciir.org

Corner House: The Corner House is a UK-based research and solidarity group working on social and environmental justice issues in North and South.

PO Box 3137, Station Road, Sturminster Newton,
    Dorset DT10 1YJ, UK
Tel: +44 (0)1258 473795   Fax: +44 (0)1258 473748
E-mail: cornerhouse@gn.apc.org
Website: www.cornerhouse.icaap.org

Council on International and Public Affairs (CIPA): CIPA is a human rights research, education and advocacy group, with a particular focus on economic and social rights in the USA and elsewhere around the world. Emphasis in recent years has been given to resistance to corporate domination.

777 United Nations Plaza, Suite 3C, New York, NY 10017, USA
Tel: +1 212 972 9877   Fax: +1 212 972 9878
E-mail: cipany@igc.org
Website: www.cipa-apex.org

Dag Hammarskjold Foundation: The Dag Hammarskjöld Foundation, established in 1962, organizes seminars and workshops on social, economic and cultural issues facing developing countries, with a particular focus on alternative and innovative solutions. Results are published in its journal *Develpment Dialogue*.

Övre Slottsgatan 2, 753 10 Uppsala, Sweden.
Tel: +46 18 102772 Fax: +46 18 122072
E-mail: secretariat@dhf.uu.se
Website: www.dhf.uu.se

Development GAP: The Development Group for Alternative Policies is a non-profit development resource organization working with popular organizations in the South and their Northern partners in support of a development that is truly sustainable and that advances social justice.

927 15th Street, NW, 4th Floor, Washington, DC 20005, USA
Tel: +1 202 898 1566 Fax: +1 202 898 1612
E-mail: dgap@igc.org
Website: www.developmentgap.org

Focus on the Global South: Focus is dedicated to regional and global policy analysis and advocacy work. It works to strengthen the capacity of organizations of the poor and marginalized people of the South and to better analyse and understand the impacts of the globalization process on their daily lives.

c/o CUSRI, Chulalongkorn University, Bangkok 10330, Thailand
Tel: +66 2 218 7363 Fax: +66 2 255 9976
E-mail: Admin@focusweb.org
Website: www.focusweb.org

Inter Pares: Inter Pares, a Canadian social justice organization, has been active since 1975 in building relationships with Third World development groups and providing support for community-based development programmes. Inter Pares is also involved in education and advocacy in Canada, promoting understanding about the causes and effects of, and solutions to, poverty.

58 rue Arthur Street, Ottawa, Ontario, K1R 7B9 Canada
Tel: + 1 613 563 4801 Fax: + 1 613 594 4704

Public Interest Research Centre: PIRC is a research and campaigning group based in Delhi that seeks to serve the information needs of activists and organizations working on macro-economic issues concerning finance, trade and development.

142, Maitri Apartments, Plot No. 28, Patparganj, Delhi: 110092, India
Tel: + 91 11 2221081, 2432054   Fax: + 91 11 2224233
E-mail: kaval@nde.vsnl.net.in

Third World Network: TWN is an international network of groups and individuals involved in efforts to bring about a greater articulation of the needs and rights of peoples in the Third World; a fair distribution of the world's resources; and forms of development that are ecologically sustainable and fulfil human needs. Its international secretariat is based in Penang, Malaysia.

228 Macalister Road, 10400 Penang, Malaysia
Tel: +60 4 226 6159   Fax: +60 4 226 4505
E-mail: twnet@po.jaring.my
Website: www.twnside.org.sg

Third World Network–Africa: TWN–Africa is engaged in research and advocacy on economic, environmental and gender issues. In relation to its current particular interest in globalization and Africa, its work focuses on trade and investment, the extractive sectors and gender and economic reform.

2 Ollenu Street, East Legon, PO Box AN19452, Accra-North, Ghana.
Tel: +233 21 511189/503669/500419   Fax: +233 21 511188
E-mail: twnafrica@ghana.com

World Development Movement (WDM): The World Development Movement campaigns to tackle the causes of poverty and injustice. It is a democratic membership movement that works with partners in the South to cancel unpayable debt and break the ties of IMF conditionality, for fairer trade and investment rules, and for strong international rules on multinationals.

25 Beehive Place, London SW9 7QR, UK
Tel: +44 (0)20 7737 6215   Fax: +44 (0)20 7274 8232
E-mail: wdm@wdm.org.uk
Website: www.wdm.org.uk

The Global Issues Series

Calestous Juma, *The New Genetic Divide: Biotechnology in the Age of Globalization*

Roger Moody, *Digging the Dirt: The Modern World of Global Mining*

Jeremy Seabrook, *The Future of Culture: Can Human Diversity Survive in a Globalized World?*

Keith Suter, *Curbing Corporate Power: How Can We Control Transnational Corporations?*

Nedd Willard, *The War on Drugs: Is This the Solution?*

For full details of this list and Zed's other subject and general catalogues, please write to: The Marketing Department, Zed Books, 7 Cynthia Street, London N1 9JF, UK or e-mail:

sales@zedbooks.demon.co.uk

Visit our website at: http://www.zedbooks.demon.co.uk

This book is also available in the following countries:

EGYPT

MERIC (The Middle East Readers' Information Center)
2 Bahgat Ali Street, Tower D/Apt. 24 Zamalek, Cairo
Tel: 20 2 735 3818/736 3824   Fax: 20 2 736 9355

FIJI

University Book Centre, University of South Pacific, Suva
Tel: 679 313 900   Fax: 679 303 265

GHANA

EPP Book Services, PO Box TF 490, Trade Fair, Accra
Tel: 233 21 773087   Fax: 233 21 779099

MOZAMBIQUE

Sul Sensacoes, PO Box 2242, Maputo
Tel: 258 1 421974   Fax: 258 1 423414

NAMIBIA

Book Den, PO Box 3469, Shop 4, Frans Indongo Gardens,
Windhoek
Tel: 264 61 239976   Fax: 264 61 234248

NEPAL

Everest Media Services, GPO Box 5443, Dillibazar, Putalisadak
Chowk, Kathmandu
Tel: 977 1 416026   Fax: 977 1 250176

Papua New Guinea
Unisearch PNG Pty Ltd, Box 320, University, National Capital District
Tel: 675 326 0130   Fax: 675 326 0127

Rwanda
Librairie Ikirezi, PO Box 443, Kigali
Tel/Fax: 250 71314

Sudan
The Nile Bookshop, New Extension Street 41, PO Box 8036, Khartoum
Tel: 249 11 463 749

Tanzania
TEMA Publishing Co Ltd, PO Box 63115, Dar Es Salaam
Tel: 255 51 113608   Fax: 255 51 110472

Uganda
Aristoc Booklex Ltd, PO Box 5130, Kampala Road, Diamond Trust Building, Kampala
Tel/Fax: 256 41 254867

Zambia
UNZA Press, PO Box 32379, Lusaka
Tel: 260 1 290409   Fax: 260 1 253952